UNITED STATES DEPARTMENT OF LABOR
Frances Perkins, *Secretary*

BUREAU OF LABOR STATISTICS
Isador Lubin, *Commissioner*

Strikes in the United States

1880–1936

+

By

FLORENCE PETERSON
of the
Bureau of Labor Statistics

Bulletin No. 651

August 1937

UNITED STATES
GOVERNMENT PRINTING OFFICE
WASHINGTON : 1938

Republished 1971
Scholarly Press, Inc., 22929 Industrial Drive East
St. Clair Shores, Michigan 48080

Library of Congress Catalog Card Number: 70-145232
ISBN 0-403-01148-5

CONTENTS

Tables

Charts

PREFACE

A strike or lock-out is an evidence of discontent and an expression of protest. While some strikes arise over minor internal shop matters, most of them have broader application and are directed toward a change in basic working conditions or employer-employee relationship. The number of strikes and their magnitude is, therefore, one indication of the degree of industrial unrest existing at any particular time or in any particular situation.

Although an important indicator, strike statistics can never exactly measure industrial unrest. Discontent may be greatest precisely when and because workers exist so precariously that they have no hope of bettering their immediate position through the use of economic weapons. Other political and social statistics must be used to measure the extent of unrest when it is coupled with despair.

In general, strike statistics measure such unrest as prevails under circumstances that lead workers to hope that they may better their conditions or mitigate a worsening of conditions through strike action. For example, they tend to be used more sparingly when large numbers of unemployed stand in the streets as competitors for existing jobs. A public opinion or government hostile or indifferent to the claims of labor may decrease the number of strikes while actually increasing the basic unrest.

The strike is a cultural development, a conventionalized expression of discontent. It involves mass action and presupposes a belief in the efficacy of mass action. It aims at a temporary and complete interruption of the process of production, with the expectation that work will be resumed when a settlement is effected. In this respect it differs sharply from the anarchic and continuous expression of discontent that manifests itself in sabotage.

The strike is also a more or less definite overt act, growing out of discontent but not measuring with any precision the intensity of that discontent. Statistics of the number of strikes or of their magnitude cannot reflect the obviously differing degrees of discontent felt by the workers in sweated plants, driven almost to the stage of revolt, and by a group of relatively well-paid craftsmen who seize a strategic opportunity to drive a better bargain with an employer.

Finally, the frequency and duration of strikes reflect the temper of employers as well as of workers, the extent to which they are unwilling to recognize the union as the representative of the employees, and the extent to which they feel they must resist or are able to resist the demands of a union which they have recognized. Employer resistance, like workers' overt expressions of protest, varies with the conditions prevailing at the time. The condition of the industry and labor market, the attitude of the public and government, the strength of the union, all influence the employer's willingness to allow unrest to reach the state of strike action.

In view of the factors mentioned above, it is evident that any series of strike statistics extending over a period of years and into a variety of circumstances is not a complete measurement of the extent of industrial unrest. Strike statistics are of interest chiefly as showing the changing frequency with which recourse is had to one method of settling problems that arise in the employer-employee relationship.

The interest, in other words, is largely confined to the strike per se. But such an interest cannot be satisfied merely by knowing how many strikes have occurred or how many workers have been involved. It becomes necessary to set such facts in their social, economic, and political background to arrive at significant interpretations. Why do strikes occur at one time rather than another? Under what conditions are strikes most likely to succeed? As an aid to the study of such questions strike statistics should record and classify not only the gross number of strikes, but also their causes and results, the characteristics of the parties involved in their beginning and settlement, and any other information which contributes toward a better understanding of the group interests involved and the methods used to advance these interests.

ISADOR LUBIN,
Commissioner of Labor Statistics.

AUGUST 1, 1937.

Bulletin No. 651 of the

United States Bureau of Labor Statistics

Strikes in the United States, 1880–1936

Introduction

In all the realm of industrial statistics, employer-employee disputes present some of the most baffling problems. In addition to the factor of judgment which enters into all statistical procedure, strikes and lock-outs, by their very nature, lead to differences of viewpoint and approach in their measurement and classification. Since they are controversies in which the interests of employer, workers, and the public are at stake, each group naturally interprets and evaluates the situation in the way the dispute affects it. This divergency of viewpoint persists throughout every phase of the statistical treatment of strikes and lock-outs—definition, unit of measurement, magnitude, causes, and results. Furthermore, the facts with reference to strikes and lock-outs very often are too involved or indeterminate to be accurately and simply classified from whatever approach they are viewed. Causes leading up to any one dispute may be many and varied and the basic causes may never be actually voiced by either party. So also with the results, especially when the dispute ends with no written contract or definite oral agreement. Even the date of the ending is not always clear-cut; some strikes begun years ago have never been officially called off by their initiators, despite the fact that the employer concerned is carrying on his business in a normal manner.

In view of these divergencies of approach as well as of the impossibility of always getting sufficiently detailed information, a portion of the statistics on strikes is necessarily based on arbitrary estimates and rule-of-thumb procedure. Nevertheless, through the use of specific definitions and the adoption of some broad general policies, a certain degree of comparability and uniformity of treatment can be obtained.[1]

[1] See appendixes II and III for methods used in analyzing and collecting strike data.

The history of statistics on strikes and lock-outs in the United States can be divided into six periods: (1) the years previous to 1880, for which no statistics are available, but for which some summarized accounts of individual strikes have been compiled; (2) the year 1880, when data on strikes and lock-outs were gathered at the time the Tenth Census was taken; (3) 1881–1905, during which time four periodic surveys providing a continuous count of the strikes and lock-outs were made by the Commissioner of Labor; (4) 1906–13, when no studies were made and for which no information is available; (5) 1914–26, when the Bureau of Labor Statistics maintained a fairly adequate reporting service on the number of strikes; in only a limited number of cases, however, were data obtained on number of persons involved, man-days idle, and other items; (6) 1927 to the present, during which time the Bureau of Labor Statistics has collected and published monthly data on the number of strikes, workers involved, man-days idle, and other pertinent information.

This bulletin contains the major statistical data that are available on strikes and lock-outs from the earliest recorded date through the year 1936. Since original schedules and other source material have been destroyed, dependence has necessarily been placed upon previously published material for early periods. Some readjustments and combinations have been made in previously published tables in order to make them readily comparable with data for later periods. For example, strikes and lock-outs were treated separately in earlier reports. These are combined in this bulletin since no such separation was made in later years.

The major portion of this bulletin deals with strikes and lock-outs since 1927. During this period changes of a more or less important nature were made in methods of collecting and interpreting the source material. In 1934 the statistical work was reorganized. The number of possible sources or "leads" was materially increased, the industry classification was revised, and other classifications were added. Some changes were made in the definitions and inclusiveness of terms used. In order to provide continuous series in as many classifications as possible, all available data on strikes occurring since 1927 were reviewed and necessary revision made so that figures for this period might be comparable. Appendixes II and III contain an explanation of the methods used in obtaining and analyzing data on strikes, and some of the difficulties and anomalies existing in strike statistics.

Definition of Strike and Lock-out

A strike is a temporary stoppage of work by a group of employees in order to express a grievance or to enforce a demand; a lock-out is a temporary withholding of work from a group of employees by an employer (or a group of employers) in order to coerce them into accepting the employer's terms.

Previous to 1922, the Bureau presented separate tables for strikes and for lock-outs. Because of the inherent confusion existing in any industrial dispute, the difficulty of separating a strike situation from a lock-out was early recognized.[2] In later years no effort was made to distinguish the two, and all labor disputes involving stoppages of work were grouped together as "strikes and lock-outs."[3] This phrase was abandoned in 1935, the term "strike" being used in the generic sense to include all stoppages of work due to labor disputes, whether initiated by employer (lock-out) or by the workers.

Technically, the distinction between a strike and a lock-out turns on the party which actually initiates the stoppage. Even though it were possible to make a literal interpretation, the notion of responsibility or moral obligation would be implied—concepts which are impossible to define for statistical purposes. Furthermore, a strike might develop into a lock-out or vice versa, as is indicated by the following illustrations:

An employer says he cannot operate a plant unless wages are reduced. The workers refuse to accept the reduction. The plant shuts down and reopens a month later at the old wage. Here the employer sought to enforce terms upon the workers who refused to accept them. While the workers would call this a lock-out, the employer would be likely to call it a strike because his employees refused to work at the wages which he considered reasonable.

A group of workers go out on strike for a wage increase. After a few weeks they express a willingness to return to work without the increase. In the meantime, general business conditions or the employer's strategic position have so altered that the employer refuses to take them back unless they accept a wage reduction. The strike thereupon becomes a lock-out.

Sometimes one party anticipates the action of the other. Employees are dissatisfied and strike talk is prevalent, although no date is set. The employer decides to act first and closes the plant or lays off the dissatisfied group for a specific time "to teach them a lesson." If there had been no lock-out, there would have been a strike.

---

[2] See p. 29.

[3] It is an interesting fact that in its first reports Great Britain also distinguished between strikes and lock-outs but abandoned the attempt in 1893. Most foreign statistics on industrial disputes are grouped together as "strikes and lock-outs." (Methods of Compiling Statistics of Industrial Disputes, International Labour Office, Geneva, 1926.)

Were strikes and lock-outs of approximately like frequency, the theoretical distinction between them might necessitate an attempt to distinguish them in tabulation despite all the difficulties involved. But because of the relatively strong position which the employer usually has in the bargaining relationship, he very seldom needs to resort to a lock-out. Probably not more than 1 or 2 percent of the total disputes at the present time can be called lock-outs. In earlier years the proportion was slightly greater (see p. 29). Since their industrial causes and effects are practically the same, and because of the relative insignificance in the number of lock-outs, it seems reasonable to use the term "strike" to cover all industrial disputes involving stoppages of work.

Though the distinction between a strike and a lock-out need not be maintained, the precise phrasing of the definition adopted for either will affect the resulting statistical series. It is therefore necessary to analyze carefully the exact interpretation of each of the phrases in the definitions given.

A strike is a *temporary* stoppage. So far as the intention and attitude of the strikers is concerned, they look upon themselves as continuing to retain the status of employees of the company against which they are striking, with vested interests in their individual jobs. If the dispute develops into a permanent severance of relations between the employer and this group of workers, the situation ceases to be a strike.

A *stoppage* of work is effected either by walking out, not reporting for work at the usual or expected time, or reporting for duty but refusing to perform any work ("sit-down"). A walk-out is a fairly clear-cut situation, but the other two forms of stoppage are sometimes difficult to interpret. For instance, workers in seasonal or intermittent trades—fruit pickers, seamen or longshoremen, building workers, etc.—may refuse to go to work on terms offered by an employer. There is no actual walk-out, since work has never started on the season's fruit picking, loading or unloading the boat, or constructing the building. To the employer who needs to have the work done, refusal to work means a serious stoppage. Such situations are considered to be strikes, since the Bureau interprets a strike to exist when an employer offers jobs to a specific group of workers who refuse to accept until certain terms or conditions are adjusted. Restriction of output or sabotage sometimes approximates a "sit-down" strike. The Bureau interprets the situation as a strike only when the participants publicly state the fact of a stoppage for certain specific causes. It is the practice with some unions to call a stoppage while new agreements or wage rates are being negotiated. Although the union distinguishes such a stoppage from a strike, the Bureau classifies it as a strike if the situation has the characteristics included in the above-mentioned definition.

A strike or lock-out implies stoppage of work by a *group*. An individual stoppage is a "quit" or "lay-off." For purposes of convenience, the Bureau includes in its statistical analysis only those disputes which involve six or more persons and last 1 day or longer. This arbitrary limitation presents some anomalies. For example, a strike of 5 bakers in a small bakery shop may represent the entire working force and mean a closing of the shop, while a strike of 500 employees in a large plant may not tie up the plant's operations. Nevertheless, because of the difficulty of securing reports on small disputes and the necessity for adopting some limitation, the Bureau excludes all disputes involving fewer than six persons and lasting less than 1 day.

The strike must involve a group of *employees;* that is, there must be a recognized employer-employee relationship between the parties involved in the dispute. Statistics on labor disputes, therefore, exclude so-called buyers' strikes, farmers' strikes—except in the case of farm labor—student strikes, etc. There are certain border-line situations in which it is difficult to determine whether the strikers have the status of employee or entrepreneur, as, for example, the small dealer who is producing or distributing goods or services for another person or company. The Bureau considers an employer-employee relationship to exist when one of the parties maintains direction and control over the work of the other; that is, the right to approve or disapprove employment, and control over working conditions. Thus the term "employee" covers gasoline-station attendants, even though on a lease and contract sales arrangement, fishermen who must sell their catch to one certain wholesaler who determines the price, and persons who work at home at piece rates for a manufacturer or wholesaler.

The purpose of a strike or lock-out is *to express a grievance* or *to enforce a demand.* It is a fairly simple matter to interpret a stoppage of work as a strike or lock-out when either the worker group or the employer makes definite demands upon the other. Some situations, however, are not so easy to define, such as jurisdictional disputes, quarrels between rival unions, sympathetic protests, organization drives by outside unions where employees within the plant seemingly take no active part. In the usual jurisdictional dispute it would appear that the employer is passive—that it is a quarrel solely between worker groups who have no grievance against their employer. In some cases the employer very obviously has an interest as to which union does a particular piece of work, because of differences in wage rates. In all cases, each group is demanding from the employer that it get the assignment for certain work, and thus jurisdictional disputes can justifiably be called strikes.

Disputes between rival unions present a somewhat different picture. In these cases a second group with similar trade jurisdiction seeks to displace a union which has already been recognized by the employer. (Since the American Federation of Labor does not permit dual unionism within its ranks, at least one of the two groups fighting for control is a union not affiliated with the American Federation of Labor. Sometimes neither organization is affiliated.) While the immediate issue causing the stoppage of work appears to be the rivalry of two factions of workers, the employer is, nevertheless, an integral factor in the situation. The very fact that there are two rival unions fighting for control generally signifies discontent by one group of workers with the terms which the other union has obtained from the employer and the hope that the second union can obtain better terms.

The employer-employee relationship need not necessarily be direct and proximate to permit a strike situation. In a so-called sympathetic strike, an individual employer may not be responsible for any of the dissatisfactions which bring about the strike. These are strikes, nevertheless, since they are called for the purpose of demonstrating the solidarity of workers and broadening the group pressure upon the employer against whom there is a strike for specific cause.[4] Similarly, a local union in an organization drive may picket a plant where none of the employees belong to the union, nor apparently have expressed a desire to join. The picketing leads to the closing of the plant. Although his employees have made no demands upon this particular employer, such a situation is interpreted to be a strike, since it is a means by which organized labor seeks to increase its area of control and set up an effective instrument through which these employees can, in the future, make demands upon the employer.

General strikes.—The term "general strike" is used by the Bureau to refer to stoppages of work by all or a large majority of workers in different industries and crafts within a certain community. Such strikes are usually called in sympathy for a particular group of strikers or in protest against some action taken by public authorities during a strike of a particular group.

The term "general strike" is differentiated from "general industry" strike. The latter refers to a widespread strike in a particular in-

---

[4] U. S. C., Title 29, section 13 (c) (Norris-LaGuardia Anti-injunction Act) defines a labor dispute to include "Any controversy concerning terms or conditions of employment, or concerning the association or representation of persons in negotiating, fixing, maintaining, changing, or seeking to arrange terms or conditions of employment, regardless of whether or not the disputants stand in the proximate relation of employer and employee." Thus, if a dispute arises between members of a union and an employer, other workers in the same trade or industry elsewhere in the country may not be enjoined from acting against their own employer to further the cause of those members who are directly engaged in the labor dispute.

dustry. When called by the office of an international union for the entire industry, the strike becomes interstate. On the other hand, all the locals of a union in a particular city may unite in calling a strike; for instance, a strike against all the barber shops, laundries, or cleaning and dyeing establishments within a city. Both of these situations are termed "general industry" strikes.

Measurement of Strikes

The three basic measures now used by the Bureau in strike statistics are the number of strikes, the number of workers involved, and the man-days idle. For a particular purpose one of these measures may be more useful than the others. The number of strikes, for instance, is an approximation of the number of times group action has been taken on the calling of strikes. The number of workers involved is useful in terms of the incidence of strikes on the working population.[5] The total number of man-days idle gives a rough estimate of the amount of time lost by persons while involved in strikes.[6]

As the following paragraphs indicate, each of these units of measurement has many variable characteristics and the unit is more or less arbitrarily determined in many instances. For that reason, as well as the fact that the size of the strike must necessarily be given consideration, no one unit of measurement should be used as the sole indicator of the severity or extent of strikes—the number of strikes, the workers involved, and the man-days idle during strikes must all be taken into account.

In a large number of cases there is a question as to what should be counted as one strike. For instance, shall a general strike called by an international union, extending into several States and hundreds of establishments, be called one strike or as many as there are employers, States, or cities affected? Shall strikes in several branches of one corporation, located thousands of miles apart, be considered one strike or as many as the number of communities affected or the number of local unions which agreed to the stoppage?

The *initiating force* or *cause* of the strike is the chief determining factor now used by the Bureau in deciding what shall be the unit of measurement. In other words, the number of different organizations

[5] It must be noted that this figure cannot be used to obtain the proportion of all workers who have been involved in strikes during any year, since some of the same persons may have been involved in more than one strike.

[6] Such an estimate is likely to be misleading, however. See discussion on cost of strikes, p. 10.

initiating the strike and the reason for calling the strike take precedence over the number of establishments or localities affected.[7]

An industrial dispute is an expression of conflicting wills or interests of employers and employees, and is brought about by a determination of one group to force the other to correct certain grievances. The will of the workers may be expressed through the executive office of their international union which calls a general strike throughout the entire industry; or workers in various trades in a city may express their will through the city trades assembly, which calls a city-wide strike of all trades. Such instances are considered as single strikes since the workers are operating through a common agency. If, however, several local unions in the same city or different cities call strikes, even though for a common cause, these are counted separately. The unit of measurement, however, cannot always be determined by the scope of jurisdiction of the union or unions, since some strikes are not officially authorized by the union. In such cases, the unit of measurement is based upon evidence of a common cause and the area of concerted action.

In addition to the more or less arbitrary unit of measurement which is used in counting the number of strikes is the obvious fact that a strike of 10 workers is counted equally with a strike of half a million workers. These inherent variable characteristics in the unit used in counting industrial disputes make it evident that the number of strikes should not be used as the sole indicator. The number of workers involved and man-days idle are of at least equal value in measuring the importance and extent of industrial disputes.

There is a difference of opinion among those concerned with strike statistics as to how inclusive the term "number of workers involved" should be. Sometimes two classifications are made, viz, "directly" and "indirectly" involved. Those "directly involved" are generally defined to include those employees who initiated or voted the strike,

---

7 This does not mean that there would not be a good deal of value in knowing the total number of establishments involved in strikes—another matter from counting strikes on the basis of establishments affected. Unfortunately, it is not always possible to obtain the number of establishments involved in large general strikes, so that this fourth means of measuring the extent of strikes is impossible (see appendix II, p. 164).

It may be noted that during the period 1881–86 the business establishment was the unit used. This was later changed, although the establishment was retained as the unit for measuring the results of strikes until 1905. The Third Annual Report of the Commissioner of Labor, 1887 (pp. 11–12) has this statement:

"It has been found absolutely necessary to make the establishment the unit in the tabular presentation, and not the strike. * * * With the isolated strikes occurring in single establishments there is no difficulty; oftentimes with general strikes where many establishments are involved there is none; but there are other cases where it may be called 1 strike or 10 or 50, by different individuals. Disagreement may arise in a certain industry in a certain city and a strike in 10 establishments be precipitated. Here a single cause is at work within a limited area, and it may be designated as 1 strike; but this is a simple general strike. In the case of one that is complex many localities may be involved, though not all, necessarily, for the same period of time; one general cause may have its influence, but special ones will have more here and there; beginning with those of a certain trade it may extend to cognate industries; and lastly, its area does not take account of political divisions, so that when it is determined how it shall be counted in the industrial section at one end of a State, and whether it should be again counted in a similarly affected section at the other end, there still remains the point to be decided whether it shall be counted again in adjoining or maybe quite distant States."

or those covered by the terms of settlement; those "indirectly involved" are defined as the remaining employees who were forced to stop work when the shop closed because of the strike. By others the term "indirectly involved" is used to include persons not employed in the establishment where the strike took place but who, nevertheless, were affected by the strike; for example, an automobile assembly plant closed down because the transmission plant was on strike. Under these various concepts, the number involved could vary greatly.

For reasons of practicability, the Bureau arbitrarily confines tne number involved to include only employees in the plant or establishment where the strike takes place. No attempt is made to separate within the establishment those directly and those indirectly involved in starting the strike or in the terms of settlement. In some cases such a distinction can be made comparatively easily. For instance, the exact number initiating, and the number indirectly affected, can be determined in cases where a craft union, such as machinists or shoe cutters, calls a strike which necessitates the closing of the entire plant. In the majority of cases, however, the dissatisfaction which gives rise to the strike is not confined to a particular department or occupation. A greater or lesser number of employees throughout the plant decide to strike; some others are more or less secretly favorable to the strike but would not have initiated it themselves; some employees are secretly or openly opposed to the strike. In other words, certain employees initiate a strike and the others are willingly or unwillingly drawn into it. It would be necessary for a psychologist to have a personal interview with each employee in such situations in order to determine the number who were responsible for or who actually favored the strike. Also, as attitudes change as the strike progresses, this number would vary from day to day.

The same kind of intangible factors enter into any attempt to include in the number involved only those affected by the terms of settlement, or those belonging to the labor organization which called the strike. Many strikes terminate with no formal settlement. In others, resulting in compromise settlements, certain individuals or groups may gain some or all their demands while the remainder return to work with no change in their status. It is equally difficult to decide in each case what is the constituency of the union calling the strike. Some strikes are called in order to demonstrate dramatically the strength of, or arouse interest in, a newly organized union. Not even the union's officers know the exact number who are sympathetic with the organization. As the strike progresses, interest and membership in the union may wane or increase.

For statistical purposes, the only practical procedure seems to be to include in the number involved all employees within the establishment who stop work or are thrown out of work because of an industrial dispute. Even this figure can be only an estimate in some instances. The reports obtained are frequently biased, the employer having a tendency to minimize and the union to magnify the number. In large general industry strikes involving many companies and many communities, nobody knows the exact number. Furthermore, the number may change from day to day as the strike grows in size or gradually wanes. In such cases, the Bureau makes as accurate an estimate as is possible from the data obtainable.[8]

The number of man-days idle affords one of the best criteria of the magnitude of a strike, since it incorporates the two elements of number of workers involved and the number of work days these persons lost during the strike.

The man-days idle during a strike are determined by figuring the calendar days idle minus holidays and any other days these employees would not have worked had there been no strike. For instance, if the plant had been operating on a 3- or 4-day week, the number of man-days idle is based on a 3- or 4-day week. If the plant was operating on more than one shift per day, the man-days idle figure includes the number of workers engaged in each shift. Proper allowance is made in cases where the number engaged in the strike fluctuates as the strike progresses.

Cost of Strikes

In former years, the figure now classified under "man-days idle" appeared under the heading "man-days lost." This term has been discarded because its connotation may be inaccurate. While certain workers are idle during a strike, it does not necessarily follow that the days' work or wages have been lost. Anticipating a strike, there may have been overtime and building up for stock before the strike began. There may be overtime after the strike closes to fill delayed orders, or there may exist such a chronic oversupply that a prolonged strike does not materially affect the year's output. In other words, at times neither the employer nor workers suffer any net annual loss due to cessation of work during the strike. Furthermore, a prolonged strike in one area may mean a shift in production to another area

[8] It should be noted that the number of workers given in the tables is the maximum or total involved in the strike throughout its progress, since it is impracticable to show the different number of workers participating at different times. This leads to certain unavoidable anomalies in the statistical presentation, especially in the monthly tables. For instance, a strike which involved a certain number of persons is listed as beginning in a certain month; the actual number of persons engaged in that strike that particular month may be much less than the total given, since the strike did not attain its maximum or total strength until the following month.

with no lessening of the total national output.[9] Even though certain employers and groups of workers suffer disastrous loss, other employers and workers may gain. Such gains of others attributable to the strike cannot be measured as a rule, but from a national point of view this must be taken into account.

If it is impossible to estimate accurately the total man-days' work lost or wages lost due to strikes, any figure on the total cost of strikes would be even more fictitious. This vague concept, "cost of strikes", necessarily includes theoretical estimates of cost to employers, workers, and the public. Practically, these three elements cannot be grouped together. The employer might consider a wage increase gained through a strike as a loss to him; the workers obviously consider it a gain which, in time, will more than offset the lack of pay envelopes during the strike. Similarly, local merchants may profit through the increased wages although their business suffered during the strike. Because of these conflicting factors, an estimate of the cost of individual strikes or the cost of all strikes in a given period is misleading as well as inaccurate.

The cost of such matters as extra policing, property damage, etc., which accompany some strikes could be fairly accurately determined. The Bureau, however, has never had the resources which would be necessary to get data of this kind. There is available, therefore, no information as to the cost of policing, loss through property and personal damage, etc., occasioned by strikes.

---

[9] Example: In spite of extended strikes in the coal industry during 1927–29, there was no great change in the annual tonnage produced. There were, however, shifts in production from strike areas to mines where there were few or no strikes. There was a drastic decrease in production in Illinois, Indiana, Ohio, and Pennsylvania, but Kentucky, West Virginia, and Alabama produced more coal than they ever had up to that time.

Chapter I

Early History of Strikes

Industrial disputes in the United States coincide with the beginning of our national history. In 1776, while New York City was occupied by British troops, the printers demanded a wage increase from their employers and were refused. They thereupon ordered a "turn-out" and forced their employers to grant the increased wage.[1]

The second authenticated strike was a successful "turn-out" of 26 Philadelphia printers in 1786, in protest against a reduction of wages to $5.83½ a week. The strike call indicates that benefits were paid to strikers. "We will support such of our brethren as shall be thrown out of employment on account of their refusing to work for less than $6 per week."[2]

The first recorded strike for a 10-hour day was called by some carpenters in Philadelphia in 1791. The carpenters lost the strike and in retaliation organized a cooperative and contracted for jobs "25 percent below the current rate established by master carpenters."[3]

In March 1800 occurred the sailors' strike in New York which for many years was thought to be the first strike in the United States.[4] A number of sailors, demanding an increase from $10 to $14 a month, marched around the city compelling other seamen to join the strike until their leader was arrested and lodged in jail, when the strike unsuccessfully terminated.

---

[1] The Third Annual Report of the Commissioner of Labor, 1887, gives a summary, in chronological order, of all the strikes and lock-outs recorded up to that time. Most of his information was obtained from published reports of various State bureaus of labor statistics, particularly Massachusetts and Pennsylvania, and later Ohio. This listing of early strikes and lock-outs is far from complete. In 1908–10, Dr. John R. Commons and associates, under the auspices of the American Bureau of Industrial Research, carried on an exhaustive search of all early newspapers, legal documents, and court records for source material having a bearing on American industrial society. This material was published in 10 volumes under the title "A Documentary History of American Industrial Society." References and interpretations of this source material were later made by Dr. Commons and associates in the History of Labour in the United States, published in 1918. These publications provide valuable material on early disputes.

Little is known about strikes in colonial times. The Third Annual Report (p. 1030) cites the strike of journeymen bakers in 1741, who refused "to bake bread but on certain terms." This action was not a strike of wage earners against employers. The price of bread was regulated by public authorities and these bakers, since they sold their own goods directly to the consumer, were acting more in the capacity of merchants protesting against imposed prices.

[2] U. S. Department of Commerce and Labor. Bureau of Labor. Bull. No. 61, pp. 861–863, A Documentary History of the Early Organizations of Printers, by Ethelbert Stewart. Washington, 1905.

[3] Commons, John R., and associates: History of Labour in the United States. The Macmillan Co., New York, 1918, vol. I, p. 110.

[4] History of the People of the United States, McMaster. Appleton & Co., New York, 1885, vol. II, p. 618, gives the date of this strike as October 1802. The Third Annual Report of the Commissioner of Labor (p. 1031), taken from the report of the Bureau of Statistics of New Jersey, 1885, p. 272, gives the date as November 1803. Mention, however, was made of this strike in the Federal Gazette, Apr. 11, 1800, which gives the date as Mar. 26, 1800.

The most notable strikes of this period were those conducted by journeyman shoemakers of New York and Philadelphia, which resulted in several criminal conspiracy cases. The court records of these cases give a colorful picture of the causes and conduct of the strikes and reveal surprising similarities to strike situations today.[5]

The Federal Society of Journeymen Cordwainers, which had been organized in Philadelphia in 1794, called a strike in 1796 and again in 1798. Both resulted in wage increases. A strike in 1799, called by this same society of over 100 shoemakers, introduced the paid walking delegate. Previously an unpaid "tramping committee" visited various places to detect and deal with "scabs." Strikers took turns in serving on this committee. Since such frequent changes in personnel proved to be inefficient, the cordwainers chose one of the committee and paid him to do the visiting.[6] In order to completely tie up the employers, the society insisted that those who worked on custom-made shoes go on strike with the bootmakers, although the strike demand was for an increase in wages on boots only. This strike, which lasted about 10 weeks and which was not without violence, was only partially successful.

A strike called in 1805 by the Philadelphia Society of Cordwainers resulted in the first attempt by employers of this country to invoke the aid of the courts and law to prohibit strikes and organization of workers. Leaders of the strike were prosecuted, under the English common-law doctrine, for criminal conspiracy. In spite of vigorous defense and appeal to public opinion,[7] the jury found them "guilty of a combination to raise their wages."

The Journeymen Cordwainers' Society of Baltimore ordered a general industry strike in January 1809. The county court indicted 39 members, charging them with compelling an employer to discharge certain employees and preventing them from obtaining employment elsewhere. This indictment indicates that the Baltimore shoe workers were seeking closed-shop conditions during the strike. The records do not indicate that the judge ever imposed a sentence on the defendants in this trial.[8]

In November 1809, about 200 journeyman cordwainers of New York City engaged in a "general turn-out." The strike was originally called by the cordwainers' association against one company. Suspecting that this company was secretly getting work done at other shops, a general strike was called. The leaders of this strike were

[5] Reports of these trials are printed verbatim in A Documentary History of American Industrial Society, by Commons and Gilmore. The Arthur H. Clark Co., Cleveland, 1910, vols. III and IV.

[6] The testimony at the trial (A Documentary History of American Industrial Society, vol. III, p. 74) reveals a member of such committee "scabbing" on days he did not serve on the committee. This is the first strike in which we have record of the term "scab."

[7] Commons, John R., and Gilmore, Eugene A.: A Documentary History of American Industrial Society. The Arthur H. Clark Co., Cleveland, 1910, vol. III, p. 236.

[8] Idem, p. 249.

immediately indicted for employing unlawful means to gain increased wages. Although the defendants were convicted for conspiracy, they were fined only $1 each and costs.[9]

The first known strike in which women participated was among contract workers in Pawtucket, R. I., in 1824, when "female weavers" struck with the men in an attempt to resist a reduction in wages and increase in hours. In 1825 a strike of women alone occurred for higher wages—the tailoresses of New York.

During these years of the twenties many strikes occurred, most of them for higher wages but some for the 10-hour day. The first great strike for the 10-hour day was called by 600 carpenters in Boston in 1825. Newspapers of the time indicate that tailors, carpenters, house painters, stonecutters, riggers, stevedores, common laborers, hand-loom weavers, and cabinetmakers in Buffalo, Philadelphia, New York, and Baltimore went out on frequent strikes.[10]

The first recorded strike of factory operatives was called by textile workers in Paterson, N. J., in 1828. This was also the first known instance of the calling out of militia to quell a labor disturbance. The strikers demanded a 10-hour day but went back to work without gaining their demand. Later, during the same year, strikes were called in cotton mills in Philadelphia and Baltimore.[11]

The period from 1776 to 1830 not only witnessed a considerable number of industrial disputes in comparison with the relatively few persons working for wages at that time, but the causes of these strikes and the tactics pursued by the strikers and the employers bear close similarity to those existing today. These years saw the introduction by the workers of the walking delegate, strike benefits, the use of the general strike when an individual strike proved ineffective, picketing, social ostracism and sometimes physical violence toward "scabs", and the use of militia and the courts by the employers and public authorities.

In general, there were at least two differences between the strikes in this early period and those of later date. First, practically all the early strikes occurred among hand craftsmen. This, of course,

[9] These conspiracy cases, in addition to setting legal precedent for organizations of workers and their ability to strike, were a test between the Jeffersonian Democrats and the Federalists over the introduction of English common law in this country. One of the leading Jeffersonian newspapers, the Philadelphia *Aurora*, attacked the court and the law under which these convictions were made. In its Nov. 28, 1805, issue appeared this editorial: "Hitherto the people had travelled the level road to equal justice * * *. Of all the barbarous principles of feudalism entailed on us by England, none was left but slavery, and even this would be generally restricted in 1808. Yet, would it be believed, at the very time when the state of the Negro was about to be improved attempts were being made to reduce the whites to slavery. Was there anything in the Constitution of the United States or in the Constitution of Pennsylvania which gave one man a right to say to another what should be the price of labor? There was not. It was by the English common law that such things became possible." (Commons, John R., and associates: History of Labour in the United States, vol. I, p. 142.)

[10] Commons, John R., and associates: History of Labour in the United States. New York, 1918, vol. I, pp. 156–159.

[11] Idem, pp. 418–419.

merely reflected the nature of industrial processes at that time, since factory production, even in textiles, was just getting a foothold. Second, with the exception of the shoe workers and printers, the strikes were spasmodic walk-outs of unorganized workers, or workers who organized expressly for the strike, the organization disbanding after the strike. Permanent, stable labor organizations existed only among the printers and shoe workers in the larger cities.

Strikes in the 1830's.—There were a few isolated strikes during the first years of the thirties. Due to the depression of 1837, the number decreased toward the end of the decade. But during the 3 years from 1834 to 1836, there were 152 strikes mentioned in the Philadelphia newspapers and trade papers of the time, an unprecedented number which caused no little alarm among the employers and the public. "The times," said the Philadelphia *Gazette* of June 8, 1835,[12] "are completely out of joint * * *. Our streets and squares are crowded with an idle population. Some manifestations of violence have already taken place; * * *. Our buildings are at a stand, and business generally is considerably impeded." The New York *Daily Advertiser*, issue of June 6, 1835,[13] observed that "strikes are all the fashion" and that "it is an excellent time for the journeymen to come from the country to the city."

Two chief causes of the strikes of this period were the growing insistence on the part of the workers for the 10-hour day, and the rise in cost of living due to the inflation and speculation which took place in 1835–36. Among the notable strikes of this period were:[14]

The first strike in Lowell, Mass., occurred in February 1834, in protest against a 15-percent reduction in wages. Some 800 to 2,000 went on strike but in a few days all except the ringleaders returned to work at the reduced rates.[15]

In March 1834 the Schuylkill Factory Co. at Manayunk, Pa., announced they would continue operation only on condition their employees would accept a 25-percent reduction. All the employees immediately quit work and organized a picket force. The company then offered a 15-percent reduction, which was rejected. Thereupon the company brought in families from outside, gave them police protection, and broke the strike.[16]

In April 1835 the carpenters, masons, and stonecutters of Boston joined in a strike for a 10-hour day. This strike won sympathy among workers throughout the country. Trade-unions from various cities sent them money and passed resolutions to stand by the "Boston House Wrights who, in imitation of the noble and decided stand taken

---

[12] Quoted in History of Labour in the United States, vol. I, p. 390.
[13] Quoted in the Third Annual Report of the Commissioner of Labor, Washington, 1888, p. 1029.
[14] These cases are described in History of Labour in the United States, vol. I, pt. 3, ch. 3 and appendix 2.
[15] Idem, p. 425.
[16] Idem, p. 420.

by their Revolutionary Fathers, have determined to throw off the shackles of more mercenary tyrants than theirs." [17] In spite of the wide support given this strike, it was finally lost.

During the same summer the building-trades mechanics and factory operators in Philadelphia joined in the mass movement for the 10-hour day. Groups of different crafts quit work, organized processions, and marched through the streets with fife and drum and flags. These demonstrations definitely turned the tide in favor of shorter hours. Several cities established the 10-hour day for public servants, from 6 a. m. to 6 p. m., with 1 hour for breakfast and 1 hour for dinner. A number of private employers in Philadelphia were forced to follow.

In July 1835 the textile workers in Paterson, N. J., demanded that their hours be reduced from 13½ to 10 hours a day. Upon the refusal of the employers to grant a hearing to their committee, a strike was called which involved 20 mills and 2,000 persons. Financial aid was extended the strikers by workingmen in Newark and New York City. After 2 months the employers conceded a reduction of 1½ hours per day and the strike ended.

Due to the rapid rise in the cost of living in 1836, the Philadelphia cordwainers asked for wage increases. Upon refusal they went on a strike which lasted 3 months. The employers won this strike by combining with shoe merchants and leather dealers in an agreement not to deal with any employer who paid the wages the workingmen asked.

In February 1836 the bookbinders in Philadelphia went out on strike in protest against a wage reduction. The employers issued a list of the strikers for publication throughout the country, advertised for bookbinders in other cities, and agreed with booksellers that they should give no work to any master binder who employed members of trade-unions. With the help of financial contributions from unions in New York, Washington, Albany, Newark, and Boston, the strikers were enabled to hold out for 3 months, when they obtained a satisfactory settlement.

Strikes during the 1840's.—The prolonged depression lasting from 1837 until the gold discoveries of 1849 practically destroyed aggressive trade-unionism and discouraged the calling of strikes. State labor bureaus reported a few strikes, some of them attended with a good deal of violence.[18] Most of the strikes, whether for the 10-hour day or in protest against wage reduction, proved to be unsuccessful. Boilers in Pittsburgh rolling mills were unsuccessful in their strike of 1842, called in protest against a wage reduction. Three years later a successful strike brought them a wage increase. Twelve hundred journey-

---

[17] Quoted in History of Labour in the United States, vol. I, p. 389, from *Pennsylvanian*, Philadelphia. July 31, 1835.

[18] Third Annual Report of the Commissioner of Labor. Washington, 1888, pp. 1037–1040.

man tailors of Pennsylvania won advances in prices in 1847, after a 4-months' strike. In 1848 Pennsylvania passed a 10-hour law for textile and paper mills and bagging factories. Numerous strikes seemed necessary to put this law in operation— in some cases with accompanying reduction of wages.

Strikes during the 1850's.—Numerous strikes occurred between 1850 and 1852 among building workers, shoemakers, and printers in New York, Philadelphia, and Boston. Many of these strikes were unsuccessful. In the absence of trade agreements with fixed wages, workers frequently struck in the spring for higher wages and again in the fall to prevent the lowering of wages.[19]

During the 2 years 1853 and 1854, there was a great increase in the number of strikes. It is estimated that this number totaled 400. Strikes were called for wage increases, closed shop, shorter hours, abolition of night work, greater frequency and regularity of wage payment, substitution of cash pay for store scrip, and restriction of apprentices. Because labor was organized somewhat better, and also due to the prevailing prosperity, more of these strikes were successful than during the previous 2 years.[20]

There were relatively few strikes during the last half of the decade, due to two depression periods—the one in 1854–55 and the more serious one of 1857. During the preceding prosperous years, unions had neglected to build up strike funds and were, therefore, unable to conduct strikes against the wage decreases which accompanied the depression. Indeed, unemployment became so severe that the unions practically disappeared.

There were a few strikes in Massachusetts textile mills but most of them failed. In 1858 the shoe workers' union at Randolph, Mass., made an unsuccessful attempt to regain predepression wages. A strike in the same trade at Natick, Mass., in 1859 gained a slight wage advance. The same year, 1,700 shoe workers in Philadelphia went on strike for uniform rates in all shops. About 1,000 obtained work at the prices asked and many who failed to obtain work moved West.

Coal miners in Monongahela Valley in Pennsylvania struck against the irregular sizes of cars and for scales at each pit for weighing each miner's coal. The strike lasted from July to November with women participating in the picketing. The strike not only failed but 27 men and women were convicted of riotous conduct. Glass blowers at Millville, Pa., and Glassboro, N. J., struck against the employment of an excessive number of apprentices. The manufacturers united, imported nonunion men from Pittsburgh, and had 14 strikers arrested for conspiracy. The strike failed and the union collapsed.[21]

19 Commons, John R., and associates: History of Labour in the United States, vol. I, p. 576.
20 Idem, pp. 607–614.
21 Third Annual Report of the Commissioner of Labor. Washington, 1888, pp. 1044–1046.

Strikes during the 1860's.—Two significant strikes took place in 1860. The Lynn shoe workers called a strike for increased wages, which spread throughout the shoe area of Massachusetts, and brought about the largest labor demonstrations which Massachusetts had experienced up to that time. The strike failed in a few weeks and employers filled the strikers' places with workmen from Maine and New Hampshire. In the same year the machinists and blacksmiths' union called a strike in the Baldwin Locomotive Works in Philadelphia against a proposed reduction in wages. The strike ended in defeat within 4 months.[22]

In spite of rapidly rising prices, there were comparatively few strikes during the Civil War years. Leading papers mentioned 38 in 1863, 108 the next year, and 85 in 1865.[23] Coal miners engaged in a number of strikes, most of which were successful because of the rise in prices of coal. The majority of strikes in other industries were not successful in bringing about increased wages or shorter hours.

The Iron Moulders' International, the strongest labor organization of that time, called a strike in Cincinnati in 1867, against a 60-percent wage reduction announced by the National Stove Manufacturers' and Iron Founders' Association, the first national employers' association in this country. The strike lasted 9 months and strike benefits almost broke the union's treasury. The failure of this strike, and a strike in Pittsburgh a few months later, led the union to discourage strikes and turn its attention to cooperatives.[24]

In 1865 the iron manufacturers of Pittsburgh locked out the puddlers when they demanded a wage increase. This dispute was settled by arbitration, the earliest recorded wage arbitration case in the United States.[25]

The recently organized Order of St. Crispin (shoe workers) called a number of strikes during the latter part of the sixties and the early years of the seventies. Many of these were successful. During one of these strikes, New England shoe workers received their first threat of competition with low-wage orientals when Chinese coolies from California were imported into Massachusetts as strikebreakers.[22]

A strike of miners in 1868, demanding enforcement of the 8-hour law which the Pennsylvania State Legislature had passed that year, caused almost general suspension of work throughout the anthracite fields. Strikes among cigar makers in New York City and Cincinnati in 1869 resulted in employers introducing the mold machine, thereby displacing skilled hand workers.[22]

[22] Third Annual Report of the Commissioner of Labor. Washington, 1888, p. 1046 ff.

[23] Commons, John R., and associates: History of Labour in the United States, vol. II, p. 23.

[24] Idem, pp. 48–53; and Third Annual Report of the Commissioner of Labor. Washington, 1888, p. 1051.

[25] Monthly Labor Review, November 1929, p. 16.

Strikes during the 1870's.—This decade witnessed a strong revival of national trade-unions. During the first 2 years these unions demanded, and frequently obtained, increased wages and reductions in hours. The latter part of the decade was characterized by defensive strikes—a desperate effort to stave off wage reductions which followed in the wake of the business depressions of 1873 and 1877.

A strike of 100,000 workers in New York City in 1872, the largest labor dispute up to that time, resulted in the 8-hour day for practically all the building trades as well as for a few other trades. Strikes against the numerous wage reductions which were introduced in 1873 were particularly prevalent among shoe workers, cigar makers, and textile and iron workers. The numerous strikes of textile workers in Fall River against periodic wage cuts were uniformly unsuccessful. Employers filled vacancies with French-Canadian immigrants and strikers were forced to sign agreements to join no labor organization as the price of reemployment.[26]

A strike of New York cigar makers in 1873, against a large concern, stimulated employers throughout the city to scatter their work among small tenement-house shops. Four years later the cigar workers' union called a strike against this system. Although it attracted wide public attention to the evils of the sweat-house system, the strike was lost. There were many bitter strikes in the bituminous-coal mines, particularly in Ohio. Very few met with any degree of success. A 7-months' strike of anthracite miners against wage reductions in 1874 resulted in the breaking up of the trade-agreement system which had existed since 1869, the dissolution of the once powerful Workingmen's Benevolent Association, and the revival of the "Molly Maguires." The latter were finally crushed in 1876.[27]

The year 1877 is generally referred to as the year of "the great railroad strikes." Starting on the Baltimore & Ohio at Martinsburg, W. Va., they quickly spread to most of the lines operating from St. Louis to the Atlantic Seaboard, confined largely to freight trains. While the basic general cause was the successive reductions in wages which had been made during preceding years, other reasons for discontent were the irregularity of employment, delay in payment of wages, and introduction of the double-header freight trains of 34 cars instead of the customary 17 and its displacement of engineers. These railroad strikes were marked by much violence and property damage. For the first time in this country Federal troops were called out in time of peace to quell strikes. All of these railroad strikes failed in bringing any immediate gains to the workers.[28]

[26] Third Annual Report of the Commissioner of Labor. Washington, 1888, p. 1058 ff.
[27] Commons, John R., and associates: History of Labour in the United States, 1918, vol. II, pp. 178–191.
[28] Third Annual Report of the Commissioner of Labor. Washington, 1888, pp. 1071–1079. Also, Dacus, J. A.: Annals of the Great Strikes. L. T. Palmer & Co., Chicago, 1877.

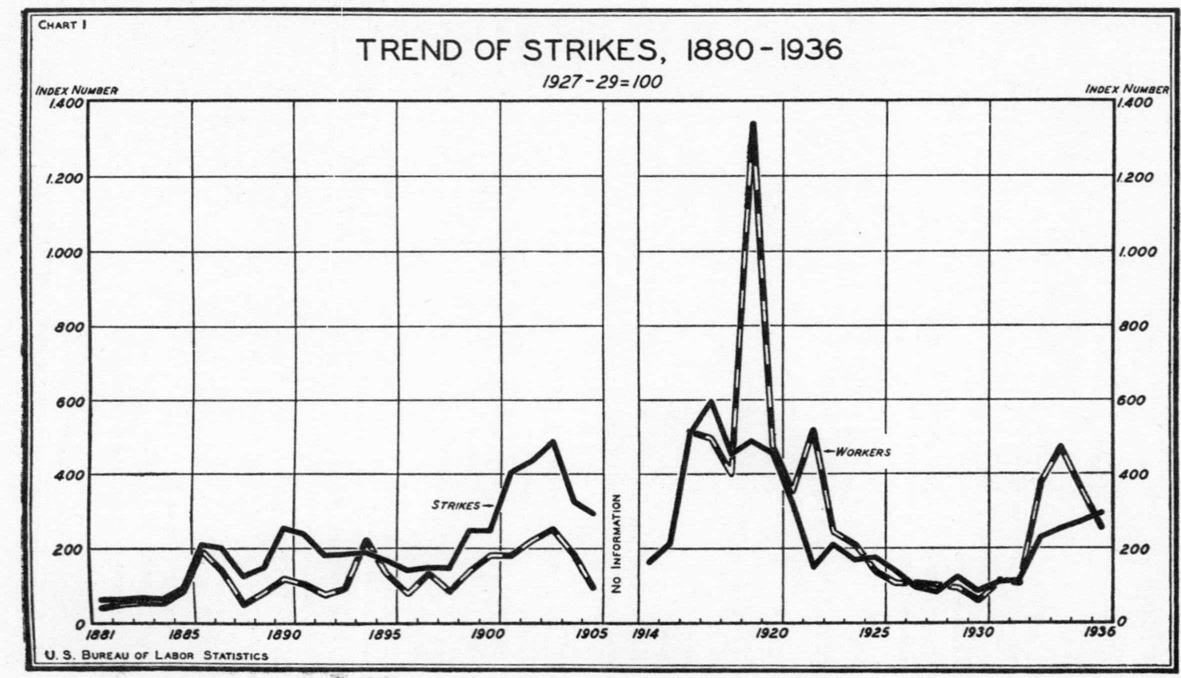
CHART I
TREND OF STRIKES, 1880-1936
1927-29=100
INDEX NUMBER
1,400
1,200
1,000
800
600
400
200
0
1881
1885
1890
1895
1900
1905
1914
1920
1925
1930
1936
STRIKES
WORKERS
NO INFORMATION
U. S. BUREAU OF LABOR STATISTICS

Chapter II

General Trend of Strikes from 1881 to 1936

The trend of strikes since 1881 indicates a general tendency to follow the business cycle. In the main, strikes tend to diminish when business activity declines and job opportunities disappear. Business recovery is generally accompanied by revival of trade-union activity and industrial disputes. However, this relationship does not occur with year-to-year regularity. There has been less strike activity in some years of business prosperity than in depression years. For instance, in 1894 there were more persons involved in strikes than in the relatively prosperous years preceding the depression of the 1890's. During the 1927–29 period there were fewer strikes than during the depression of 1920–21, or even the prolonged depression of 1893–98. It would appear that other conditions such as the political situation, the state of mind of the workers, and the type of labor leadership have as much to do with the amount of strike activity as the purely economic factors of prices and business conditions. (See chart 1.)

Table 1.—*Number of strikes and workers involved, 1881–1936*

[1906–13 omitted][1]

Year	Number of—		Index (1927–29=100)		Year	Number of—		Index (1927–29=100)	
	Strikes	Workers involved	Strikes	Workers		Strikes	Workers involved	Strikes	Workers
1881	477	130, 176	64	42	1914	1, 204	(1)	162	(1)
1882	476	158, 802	64	51	1915	1, 593	(1)	214	(1)
1883	506	170, 275	68	55	1916 [2]	3, 789	1, 599, 917	509	514
1884	485	165, 175	65	53	1917	4, 450	1, 227, 254	598	495
1885	695	258, 129	93	83	1918	3, 353	1, 239, 989	451	399
1886	1, 572	610, 024	211	196	1919	3, 630	4, 160, 348	488	1, 337
1887	1, 503	439, 306	202	141	1920	3, 411	1, 463, 054	458	470
1888	946	162, 880	127	52	1921	2, 385	1, 099, 247	321	353
1889	1, 111	260, 290	149	84	1922	1, 112	1, 612, 562	149	517
1890	1, 897	373, 499	255	120	1923	1, 553	756, 584	209	243
1891	1, 786	329, 953	240	106	1924	1, 249	654, 641	168	210
1892	1, 359	238, 685	183	77	1925	1, 301	428, 416	175	138
1893	1, 375	287, 756	185	93	1926	1, 035	329, 592	139	106
1894	1, 404	690, 044	189	222	1927	707	329, 939	95	106
1895	1, 255	407, 188	169	131	1928	604	314, 210	81	101
1896	1, 066	248, 838	143	80	1929	921	288, 572	124	93
1897	1, 110	416, 154	149	134	1930	637	182, 975	86	59
1898	1, 098	263, 219	148	85	1931	810	341, 817	109	110
1899	1, 838	431, 889	247	139	1932	841	324, 210	113	104
1900	1, 839	567, 719	247	182	1933	1, 695	1, 168, 272	228	376
1901	3, 012	563, 843	405	181	1934	1, 856	1, 466, 695	250	472
1902	3, 240	691, 507	435	222	1935	2, 014	1, 117, 213	271	359
1903	3, 648	787, 834	490	253	1936	2, 172	788, 648	292	254
1904	2, 419	573, 815	325	184					
1905	2, 186	302, 434	294	97					

[1] No information available. See p. 2.

[2] The number of workers involved in strikes between 1916–26 is known for only a portion of the total. However, the missing information is for the smaller disputes and it is believed that the total here given is fairly accurate. See p. 36 and table 16, p. 39.

During the first 5 years for which strike statistics are available, 1881–85, strikes were comparatively infrequent in the United States. At this time the Knights of Labor [1] were competing with rapidly growing trade-unions composed mostly of skilled workers. Both groups engaged in some strikes, the Knights of Labor being particularly active in the railroad [2] and telegraph [3] industries. The depression of 1884–85 is reflected in the relatively large proportion of strikes in protest against wage decreases and hour increases. (See table 8, p. 33.)

Following the depression of 1884–85, there was a Nation-wide wave of strikes. Many of these were sympathetic strikes, the Knights of Labor at that time being prone to call out workers in various trades to aid strikers in other plants. A number were the result of the great mass movement for the 8-hour day, which was inaugurated by the trade-unions in 1886. That year is remembered for the Haymarket riot;[4] the railroad strikes,[2] which were serious enough to bring about a congressional investigation; and the strikes and lock-outs in the packing industry in Chicago, which were chiefly over the issue of the 8-hour day.

The number of strikes declined in 1888–89. Many of those which took place were of a defensive character. Trades which had been successful in their strikes for the 8-hour day were now forced to strike against a return of the longer day. There were almost as many strikes against hour increases and wage decreases as there were for a reduction in hours and increases in wages. (See tables 8 and 9, pp. 33–34.)

The 8-hour-day campaign was renewed in 1890–91, especially in the building trades, and strikes multiplied. There were a number of strikes in the steel industry in 1892, including the well-known Homestead strike.[5] Most of these were lost and were followed by a gradual elimination of the union in practically all the large steel concerns in the country.

On the whole, there was a decrease in strike activity during the depression of 1893–98. However, there were more persons involved in strikes in 1894 than there had been in any previous year. A large portion of these were in coal mining and in shops of the Pullman

[1] The Noble Order of the Knights of Labor, which was founded in 1869, first became important in the labor movement after 1878, when it abolished secrecy and adopted a program calling for the organization of all toilers "to check the power of wealth."

[2] The 1885 and 1886 railroad strikes were confined very largely to the shopmen of railroads in the Southwest, the Missouri Pacific (Gould) system.

[3] The telegraphers' strike of 1883 involved the majority of the commercial telegraphers of the country.

[4] At a mass meeting of strikers in Haymarket Square, an unknown person threw a bomb, killing and wounding a number of policemen. Eight labor leaders were convicted on the charge of being accessories before the fact. Four were hanged, one committed suicide while in jail, and three received prison sentences. The latter were pardoned by Governor Altgeld in 1893.

[5] A pitched battle at Homestead, Pa., between strikers and Pinkerton detectives hired by the Carnegie Steel Co. resulted in a number of deaths and serious injuries.

Palace Car Co.[6] in protest against wage reductions. In 1897 the United Mine Workers won a general bituminous-coal strike which brought wage increases and an 8-hour day in most of the central competitive fields.

Strikes increased with the return of industrial prosperity and the expansion of labor organizations in 1899 and the first years of the twentieth century. Many of these, as was to be expected after a long period of wage reductions, were for wage increases, although union recognition became an increasingly important issue. About as many workers were involved in union-recognition strikes between 1901 and 1905 as were involved in wage disputes. (See table 8, p. 33.) One of the major issues in the anthracite strike in 1900 was the recognition of the union. Although wage increases and other concessions were granted, formal recognition was not given to the United Mine Workers of America and this, together with demands for a wage increase and hour decrease, brought on the anthracite strike of 1902.[7] An important strike in 1903–4 was that called by the Western Federation of Miners [8] in the Colorado Cripple Creek region for the 8-hour day.

Since there are no strike statistics for the period 1905–14, it is not known how many strikes took place. The depression of 1907–8 no doubt discouraged strike activity during those years. Following this depression there were a great many industrial disputes in the textile, iron, and mining industries. In 1910 the clothing workers of Chicago engaged in a city-wide strike. The invasion by the I. W. W. into the eastern textile and clothing centers led to numerous strikes, the most important being those in wool textiles at Lawrence, Mass., in 1912, and in the silk mills in Paterson, N. J., in 1912–13. Wage increases were won at Lawrence but the Paterson strike for the most part brought no gains to the workers. At about the same time the New York and Philadelphia clothing workers struck for an 8-hour day and union recognition. A majority of the shops signed union agreements.

---

[6] The Pullman strike was called by the American Railway Union, an industrial union, organized by Eugene Debs. Many railroad workers went on strike in sympathy with the Pullman employees, although the railroad brotherhoods were opposed to the strike. The strike is significant in labor history because of the numerous injunctions issued by the Federal courts upon the initiative of the Department of Justice and because President Cleveland sent United States troops to Chicago in spite of the protest of the Governor of the State.

[7] This 5-months' strike was terminated when the operators agreed to arbitration by the Anthracite Coal Strike Commission, appointed by President Theodore Roosevelt. This strike "was doubtless the most important single event in the history of American trade unionism until that time * * * for the first time a labor organization tied up for months a strategic industry and caused wide suffering and discomfort to the public without being condemned as a revolutionary menace to the existing social order calling for suppression by the Government; it was, on the contrary, adjudged a force within the preserves of orderly society and entitled to public sympathy." Perlman, Selig: History of Trade Unionism in the United States. The Macmillan Co., New York, 1923, p. 177.

[8] The Western Federation of Miners, headed by William D. Haywood, was then a part of the Industrial Workers of the World. There had been a bitter strike in this same area for an 8-hour day in 1893.

In 1911 there were numerous strikes among railroad shopmen in Chicago and on roads west and south of Illinois. The Structural Iron Workers, in their efforts to get recognition, engaged in numerous strikes. During one of these the Los Angeles Times Building was dynamited.[9] In 1912-13 there were continuous strikes in the West Virginia coal fields for union recognition and the same working conditions as the United Mine Workers had obtained in the central competitive field. The depression of 1914 discouraged much strike activity, although one of the widely known strikes occurred that year, the strike of the Colorado Fuel and Iron Company.[10]

It was not until late in 1915 that American business generally began to feel the effects of the war in Europe. With the rising prices and the increasing need for labor, industrial disputes more than doubled in 1916 and reached their all-time high of 4,450 in 1917. A large proportion of the wartime strikes occurred in the building and metal trades, in the shipyards, and in the lumber, coal, copper, and transportation industries. Textile and clothing strikes also were more numerous than usual. (See table 15, p. 38.)

The most serious strikes, so far as the conduct of the war was concerned, were those which took place at Bridgeport, Conn., and in the Northwest lumber industry. The latter, which tied up the entire Northwest lumber industry during the greater part of 1917, were primarily for the 8-hour day, although wages and working conditions were important factors.[11] The machinists' strikes in the munition factories at Bridgeport were for wage increases and against union discrimination.[12]

As numerous as the wartime strikes were, they were of comparatively short duration and did not involve, on the average, a large number of workers.[13] The largest number of persons, over 4 million, were involved in the strikes of 1919. The chief causes of these widespread disputes were the ever rising cost of living [14] and the determination

[9] The dynamiting of the Times Building was the climax of numerous disturbances in this area in which that paper had vigorously taken sides with the employers. The MacNamara brothers, officers of the Structural Iron Workers' Union, were indicted and confessed to this dynamiting when brought to trial.

[10] This strike was called by the local union of the United Mine Workers for union recognition, wage increases, and changes in working and living conditions. The strikers, ejected from company houses, settled in tent colonies on adjacent land. On Apr. 20, 1914, militia set fire to one of these colonies, the Ludlow Camp. This became known as the "Ludlow massacre."

[11] In spite of appeals from the Secretary of War and the President's Mediation Commission, the Lumbermen's Protective Association refused the hour reduction, even going so far as to pledge themselves to discriminate against any member who would grant the 8-hour day. Finally, in the spring of 1918, the basic 8-hour day was granted. It was at this time that the Loyal Legion of Loggers and Lumbermen was organized.

[12] A number of Government agencies intervened to settle these strikes but dissatisfaction continued throughout the war, although some wage increases were granted. In lieu of trade-union recognition, an elaborate employee-representation plan was established by the War Labor Board.

[13] This, no doubt, was due to the numerous Government labor boards which were established to maintain industrial peace for the duration of the war.

[14] Cost of living rose steadily until, in 1920, it was twice as high as in 1914. See Monthly Labor Review, September 1935, p. 832.

of trade-unions to extend further the influence of union organization in areas in which they had obtained a foothold during the war.

Some of the outstanding strikes which took place during 1919 were the general strike in Seattle,[15] the strike of Boston policemen,[16] and the New England telephone strike.[17] The largest strikes were in steel and bituminous-coal mining. The steel strike, in which 367,000 workers were involved, was primarily over the question of union recognition.[18] While this controversy was still in progress, a strike was called in the bituminous-coal industry. Approximately 425,000 miners were involved, tying up 75 percent of the industry. The chief cause of this strike was a failure to get a new agreement with wage advances in line with the increased cost of living.[19]

Although there were no such large disputes in 1920 as there had been during the preceding year, the total number of strikes remained at a high level. A large proportion were for wage increases. The wage issue was sharply reversed in 1921 [20] when there were almost 1,000 strikes in protest against wage decreases. (See table 18, p. 39.) The largest strike during this year was that of 140,000 marine workers in all the principal ports. The printing unions engaged in an unprecedented number of strikes in their drive for a 44-hour week.[21]

There were less than half as many strikes in 1922 as in 1921, although the number of workers involved in strikes was 50 percent greater. The latter was largely due to the strike of 400,000 railroad-shop craftsmen against wage reductions ordered by the Railroad Labor Board,[22] and strikes in anthracite and bituminous coal which involved

---

15 This was probably the first general or city-wide strike of any size which had ever occurred in the United States. It was estimated that 60,000 workers engaged in this strike (Feb. 6-11), which was called in sympathy with the metal-trades workers in the local shipyards.

16 The policemen of Boston, dissatisfied over wages and working conditions, formed a policemen's union and affiliated with the American Federation of Labor. When a number of them were discharged for joining the union, the entire police force went on strike.

17 The New England telephone strike for wage increases practically cut off all telephone communication throughout New England for 6 days. The wage increases were granted. There were a number of telephone strikes during the summer of 1919, most of which resulted in wage increases.

18 This strike was lost, the men gradually returning to work within a few months. See Monthly Labor Review, December 1919, pp. 79-94. Also see Monthly Labor Review, May 1937, p. 1237, for a later account of collective bargaining in the steel industry.

19 This strike lasted from October to December 1919. The men returned to work after accepting the compromise proposal offered by President Wilson. See Monthly Labor Review, December 1919, pp. 61-78, for account of this strike.

20 Cost of living dropped about 17 percent from its high point in 1920. See Monthly Labor Review, September 1935, p. 832.

21 Accounts of some of these strikes are given in the Monthly Labor Review, May 1922, p. 183. An evidence that many of these strikes were successful is the fact that the index of union hours in book and job printing dropped 8 percent in 1921. See U. S. Bureau of Labor Statistics, Bull. No. 631: Union Scales of Wages and Hours in the Printing Trades, May 15, 1936, Washington, 1937.

22 See Monthly Labor Review, December 1922, pp. 1-21. During the progress of this strike, other matters than the wage question assumed importance. A sweeping injunction was issued which practically forbade every traditional strike activity carried on by unions. The loss of prestige which the Railroad Labor Board suffered during this strike contributed to its abandonment soon afterward. Many company unions were established in the railroad shops during the course of this dispute.

a total of about 600,000 miners,[23] and a New England textile strike involving over 60,000 workers.[24] The decrease in strikes was most marked in the building trades, where they dropped from 583 to 113.[25]

Although the number of strikes increased in 1923, there were less than half as many workers involved as in 1922. Most of this increase was due to strikes for higher wages, indicating an effort to regain some of the wage losses of the 1921–22 depression. Beginning in 1924 there was an almost steady decline in the number of strikes each year until, in 1928, there were fewer strikes than there had been in any year since 1884.[26] The total number of workers involved in strikes during these years was also small in spite of the fact that there were several large strikes. The largest was the 1927 strike of 165,000 bituminous-coal miners.[27] During 1929, a peak year in business activity, there was some increase in the number of strikes but they were all small disputes, the total number of workers involved being less than in preceding years.

Beginning with the depression in 1930, the number of strikes declined and remained low during the following 3 years. Practically half of the strikes in 1931 and 1932 were in protest against wage reductions. (See table 28, p. 61.)

With the passage of the National Industrial Recovery Act and the beginning of business recovery, industrial disputes became more numerous. In spite of the steady increase in number each year from 1933 to 1936, these strikes did not equal those of the war and post-war period.

---

23 See Monthly Labor Review, November 1922, pp. 1–22. The question of the continuation of the existing collective-bargaining machinery was a vital issue in these strikes.

24 Monthly Labor Review, May 1923, pp. 13–36.

25 The depression did not affect wages in the building trades until agreements were being negotiated in the spring of 1922. Average wage rates then dropped about 6 percent but were largely restored in 1923. See U. S. Bureau of Labor Statistics, Bull. No. 626: Union Scales of Wages and Hours in the Building Trades, May 15, 1936, Washington, 1937, p. 5.

26 This, of course, ignores the period 1906–13 for which no figures are available.

27 A list of all strikes from 1927–36 involving 10,000 or more workers is given in appendix I, p. 161.

Chapter III

Strike Statistics, 1880 to 1905

Strikes During 1880

The first attempt by any Federal agency to procure statistics on strikes and lock-outs was that made by the Bureau of the Census in 1880.[1] Schedules were sent to employers and workers involved in all disputes occurring during 1880 of which notice appeared in the press. No doubt a number of disputes, especially such small local strikes as occur in the building trades, were never mentioned in the public press and, therefore, were not included in this report.

The total number of establishments involved in strikes and lock-outs, concerning which some information was received, amounted to 762. States in which 10 or more disputes occurred are shown below.

	Number of strikes		Number of strikes
Pennsylvania	304	Massachusetts	25
New York	104	West Virginia	22
Ohio	93	Maryland	18
Illinois	35	Indiana	15
New Jersey	32	Iowa	14
Missouri	30	Kentucky	11

The distribution of the strikes reported for 1880, by causes and results, is shown in tables 2 and 3.

TABLE 2.—*Causes of strikes in 1880* [1]

Industry	Total [2]	Wage increase	Wage decrease	Reduction of hours	Unionism	Miscellaneous and unknown
Total	813	503	79	7	22	202
Agriculture	1	1				
Construction	41	29	1			11
Mining	187	104	34		1	45
Professional and personal	5	4				1
Trade and transportation	53	40		2	2	9
Manufacturing	526	325	44	5	19	133
Iron and steel	259	163	24	1	5	66
Boot and shoe	13	3	1		1	8
Cigar	42	18	4		8	12
Glass	31	19			1	11
Printing	38	22	1			15
Textiles	50	32	6	1	1	10
Other	93	68	8	3	3	11

[1] Adapted from table II, pp. 18–21, Tenth Census, vol. XX.
[2] Greater number of causes than of strikes is due to the fact that some involve more than 1 cause. This table is a distribution of causes rather than of strikes by major causes as is shown in later tables.

[1] Tenth Census, vol. XX, pt. 4. This census count was made by establishments or plants affected by strikes. These figures cannot, therefore, be compared with those given for later years where one strike might include a number of plants.

TABLE 3.—*Results of strikes in 1880* [1]

Causes	Total causes [2]	Successful	Compromise	Unsuccessful	Unknown
Total	813	169	85	227	332
Wage increase	503	127	62	118	196
Against wage decrease	79	3	8	34	34
Hour reduction	7			5	2
Unionism	22	7		7	8
Miscellaneous and unknown	202	32	15	63	92

[1] Adapted from table IV, p. 25, Tenth Census, vol. XX.
[2] See footnote 2, table 2.

Strikes From 1881 to 1905

In 1887 the Bureau of Labor (then in the Department of Interior) examined the files of the leading daily papers, trade magazines, and commercial periodicals in the United States for all years from 1881 through 1886. Members of the staff then visited the areas in which strikes had occurred and obtained detailed information from everybody who might have some knowledge of the strike or lock-out. It was believed that in this way the Bureau "secured information relating to nearly every strike, if not every strike, which occurred in the United States during the period covered." [2]

A similar study was made in 1894, which included the years 1887 to July 1894.[3] Another study was made in 1901, which included the last 6 months of 1894 and through the year 1900.[4] In 1906 the Bureau of Labor continued the study, using the same procedure for the next 5 years. In the report on these strikes and lock-outs was included a summary covering the entire 25-year period from 1881 to 1905.[5] Tables 4 to 10, covering the period 1881 to 1905, are based on data published in this last-mentioned report of the Commissioner of Labor dealing with strikes and lock-outs.

The definitions used in this early period were very similar to those used today, thereby permitting comparisons with recent reports. A strike was "a concerted withdrawal from work by a part or all of the employees of an establishment, or several establishments, to enforce a demand." [6] Disputes lasting less than 1 day were omitted and duration was measured in calendar days, including holidays and Sundays, similar to the current procedure. Only continental United States was covered. A strike or lock-out was considered ended when employees went back to work or "when a sufficient number of new employees had been taken on to put the establishment in practically good running order." [7] This is the same measure as is used at the

[2] Third Annual Report of the Commissioner of Labor. Washington, 1888, p. 10.
[3] Tenth Annual Report of the Commissioner of Labor. Washington, 1896, vol. 1.
[4] Sixteenth Annual Report of the Commissioner of Labor. Washington, 1901.
[5] Twenty-first Annual Report of the Commissioner of Labor. Washington, 1907.
[6] Idem, p. 11.
[7] Idem, p. 109.

present time in dealing with strikes of long duration which have no definite time of settlement.

An effort was made, not without difficulty,[8] to distinguish strikes from lock-outs and separate tables were compiled for each. During the 25-year period there were 4.2 lock-outs for each 100 strikes. As small as this number is, the proportion is higher than in later years, for, as nearly as it can be determined, lock-outs amount to less than 1 percent of the labor disturbances at the present time. In order to make the earlier data comparable with current reports, strikes and lock-outs have been combined in the following tables.[9]

TABLE 4.—*Number of strikes, workers, and establishments involved, 1881–1905* [1]

Year	Number of—			Average per strike or lock-out	
	Strikes and lock-outs	Workers involved	Establishments involved	Workers	Establishments
1881	477	130,176	2,937	273	6
1882	476	158,802	2,147	334	5
1883	506	170,275	2,876	336	6
1884	485	165,175	2,721	341	6
1885	695	258,129	2,467	371	4
1886	1,572	610,024	11,562	388	7
1887	1,503	439,306	7,870	292	5
1888	946	162,880	3,686	172	4
1889	1,111	260,290	3,918	234	4
1890	1,897	373,499	9,748	197	5
1891	1,786	329,953	8,662	185	5
1892	1,359	238,685	6,256	176	5
1893	1,375	287,756	4,860	209	4
1894	1,404	690,044	9,071	492	7
1895	1,255	407,188	7,343	325	6
1896	1,066	248,838	5,513	233	5
1897	1,110	416,154	8,663	375	8
1898	1,098	263,219	3,973	340	4
1899	1,838	431,889	11,640	235	6
1900	1,839	567,719	11,529	309	6
1901	3,012	563,843	11,359	187	4
1902	3,240	691,507	15,552	213	5
1903	3,648	787,834	23,536	216	7
1904	2,419	573,815	12,518	237	5
1905	2,186	302,434	9,547	138	4
Total and average	38,303	9,529,434	199,954	249	5

[1] Adapted from tables in the Twenty-first Annual Report of the Commissioner of Labor. Washington, 1907, pp. 15, 20, 487, and 736.

During the 25-year period, about 10 million workers were involved in 38,303 strikes. During the first half of the 1880's the number was small. From 1886 to 1900 the average number each year almost

[8] "It was sometimes hard to determine whether a difficulty was a strike or a lock-out. Such a case occur when the employes have determined to order a strike and have so ordered it, but not actively entered upon it, and prior to the date on which the strike was to be carried out the management ordered a lock-out. As a rule, however, popular opinion as to whether the difficulty was a strike or a lock-out was observed, and the Bureau has, therefore, made a positive classification of strikes and lock-outs, leaving no difficulties to be classed as mixed strikes and lock-outs." Third Annual Report of the Commissioner of Labor. Washington, 1888, pp. 10–11.

[9] See Introduction, p. 3, for discussion of strikes vs. lock-outs.

tripled, and from 1901 to 1905 the average number each year was twice that of the preceding 15 years. The peak year during the entire period was in 1903, when the 3,648 strikes which occurred involved almost 788,000 workers in 23,536 establishments. For a more detailed year-to-year account of these strikes, see chapter II.

The industry classifications used in the early strike statistics do not follow those used currently. Except in a few industries, therefore, the data are not comparable with the later statistics.

TABLE 5.—*Strikes for 25-year period 1881–1905, by industry* [1]

Industry	Number of strikes and lock-outs	Number of workers involved
Agricultural implements	96	24,181
Agriculture	35	13,227
Automobiles and bicycles	83	9,225
Awnings, tents, and sails	10	374
Bakery	450	35,265
Blacksmithing and horseshoeing	94	8,717
Boots and shoes	1,168	201,707
Brass and brass goods	123	13,975
Brewing	185	25,740
Brick and tile	339	92,801
Brooms and brushes	43	2,140
Building trades	9,819	1,329,461
Canning and preserving	48	9,164
Car building	452	92,729
Carpets	179	69,826
Carriages and wagons	132	26,897
Clothing, men's	1,222	510,165
Clothing, women's	664	239,986
Coal and coke	3,403	2,531,192
Coffins and undertakers' goods	17	936
Confectionery	17	2,820
Cooperage	338	28,677
Cotton and woolen goods	112	65,031
Cotton goods	691	297,480
Cutlery and edge tools	102	11,324
Domestic service	349	33,278
Electric and gas apparatus and supplies	72	9,468
Electric light and power	85	4,421
Flour mill products	44	4,805
Foundry and machine shop	1,751	299,363
Freight handling and teaming	941	291,260
Furnishing goods, men's	213	45,244
Furniture and upholstering	577	73,282
Gas	48	5,618
Glass	595	162,937
Gloves and mittens	53	34,921
Hardware	297	40,963
Harness and saddlery	157	8,903
Hats and caps	398	62,849
Hosiery and knit goods	216	42,954
Iron and steel	880	454,652
Ironwork, ornamental	35	4,603
Jewelry and silverware	82	10,257
Laundry work	74	12,820
Leather	222	37,255
Leather goods	21	1,334
Lime and cement	50	9,248
Lithographing	68	12,100
Lumber and timber products	275	73,626
Metallic goods	215	17,054
Millinery goods	16	3,190
Mining, ore	233	97,918
Musical instruments	133	23,082
Paper	92	21,112
Paper goods	64	5,996
Planing mill products	403	68,303
Pottery	90	28,523
Printing and publishing	1,116	63,675
Public works	147	23,194
Railroad and road building	378	91,604
Railroad transportation	509	218,393
Rope, twine, and bagging	49	10,516
Rubber goods	81	19,480
Shipbuilding	277	66,331
Silk goods	407	101,997
Slaughtering and meat packing	166	152,544
Smelting and refining	75	20,977
Stone quarrying and cutting	1,111	166,969
Stoves and furnaces	368	47,117
Street railway transportation	306	125,253
Streets and sewers	447	70,742
Telegraph and telephone	330	22,697
Tin and sheet metal goods	252	28,672
Tobacco: Chewing and smoking	31	17,383
Tobacco: Cigars and cigarettes	1,931	329,506
Trunks and valises	53	4,589
Typewriters, cash registers, and sewing machines	41	10,725
Watches and clocks	40	4,765
Water transportation	133	51,997
Wooden goods	83	14,271
Woolen goods	410	92,403
Miscellaneous	991	129,255
Total	38,303	9,529,434

[1] Adapted from tables in the Twenty-first Annual Report of the Commissioner of Labor. Washington, 1907, pp. 16 and 20.

There seemed to be a tendency to break down a strike or lock-out which spread across State lines into as many strikes or lock-outs as there were States involved. No strikes or lock-outs were classified as interstate. Because of this, the number of strikes and lock-outs given for this period would tend to be slightly exaggerated in comparison with recent figures. Strikes and lock-outs involving two or more States where "it was impossible to make such division of the facts as would allow of their tabulation in proper proportion under each of the States involved", were tabulated under the State most affected.[10] This tended to concentrate the full force of the strike or lock-out in one State, although only a majority of the entire number of workers involved might have worked in that State. This situation, however, probably did not occur very frequently.

TABLE 6.—*Strikes for 25-year period, 1881–1905, by States* [1]

State	Number of strikes and lock-outs	Number of workers involved	State	Number of strikes and lock-outs	Number of workers involved
Alabama	303	81, 038	Nebraska	116	31, 854
Arizona	16	4, 339	Nevada	4	242
Arkansas	74	11, 425	New Hampshire	195	33, 455
California	679	110, 919	New Jersey	1, 562	279, 581
Colorado	401	97, 499	New Mexico	30	4, 964
Connecticut	998	122, 466	New York	10, 525	1, 943, 705
Delaware	78	10, 020	North Carolina	31	6, 679
District of Columbia	124	11, 819	North Dakota	29	2, 099
Florida	431	110, 538	Ohio	2, 680	609, 853
Georgia	277	47, 039	Oklahoma	29	9, 590
Idaho	22	7, 085	Oregon	81	20, 045
Illinois	3, 765	1, 425, 285	Pennsylvania	4, 323	2, 327, 308
Indiana	1, 179	227, 126	Rhode Island	377	78, 563
Iowa	469	82, 843	South Carolina	41	5, 010
Kansas	180	42, 094	South Dakota	24	1, 502
Kentucky	425	71, 980	Tennessee	477	74, 541
Louisiana	214	89, 497	Texas	341	36, 993
Maine	249	49, 375	Utah	66	6, 975
Maryland	401	78, 568	Vermont	73	20, 129
Massachusetts	2, 902	563, 125	Virginia	237	50, 306
Michigan	681	144, 327	Washington	230	26, 593
Minnesota	568	92, 787	West Virginia	304	131, 367
Mississippi	32	2, 984	Wisconsin	834	132, 214
Missouri	1, 044	182, 606	Wyoming	43	8, 229
Montana	139	20, 853			
			United States	38, 303	9, 529, 434

[1] Adapted from tables in the Twenty-first Annual Report of the Commissioner of Labor. Washington, 1907, pp. 18 and 23.

The data having to do with relation of labor organizations to strikes and lock-outs are not strictly comparable to similar data for recent years. In the earlier period the distinction was made between strikes ordered by labor organizations and those not so ordered. This excluded so-called "illegal" strikes, or those not authorized by the central office of the union or business agent acting under power conferred by the central office. At the present time no such distinction is attempted.[11] Strikes and lock-outs are classified according to whether

[10] Twenty-first Annual Report of the Commissioner of Labor. Washington, 1907, p. 109.

[11] See appendix II, p. 166.

or not most of the strikers belong to a union and act as an organized group when the strike is declared and settled. Just how much this difference in method of classification affects the comparability of the figures for the two periods it is difficult to determine. In recent years there has been a tendency on the part of the national or central office of the union to make a strike "official" after it actually takes place, even though the proper sanction was not given or even asked for when the strike was first called. It is not clear whether this policy was adhered to by the officers of the unions during this earlier period.

TABLE 7.—*Strikes ordered by labor organizations, 1881–1905*[1]

Year	Percentage ordered by labor organizations		Percentage not ordered by labor organizations	
	Strikes	Workers involved	Strikes	Workers involved
	Percent	*Percent*	*Percent*	*Percent*
1881	47.3	56.2	52.7	43.8
1882	48.5	65.0	51.5	35.0
1883	56.7	66.5	43.3	33.5
1884	54.2	60.5	45.8	39.5
1885	55.3	67.1	44.7	33.9
1886	53.3	75.0	46.7	25.0
1887	66.3	73.7	33.7	26.3
1888	68.1	73.3	31.9	26.7
1889	67.3	77.2	32.7	22.8
1890	71.3	75.1	28.7	24.9
1891	74.8	77.6	25.2	22.4
1892	70.7	77.1	29.3	22.9
1893	69.4	75.5	30.6	24.5
1894	62.8	85.4	37.2	14.6
1895	54.2	69.2	45.8	30.8
1896	64.6	72.3	35.4	27.7
1897	55.3	73.9	44.7	26.1
1898	60.4	69.1	39.6	30.9
1899	62.0	71.1	37.9	28.9
1900	65.4	80.4	34.6	19.6
1901	75.9	82.9	24.1	17.1
1902	78.2	88.0	21.8	12.0
1903	78.8	83.7	21.2	16.3
1904	82.1	90.6	17.9	9.4
1905	74.7	73.4	25.3	26.6
Total	69.0	77.5	31.0	22.5

[1] Adapted from tables in the Twenty-first Annual Report of the Commissioner of Labor. Washington, 1907, pp. 32 and 42.

In the original tables as many as 60 to 65 different causes or groups of causes were listed. These have been combined in tables 8 and 9 and all strikes are classified under 9 major causes or groups of causes.

TABLE 8.—*Major causes of strikes, 1881–1905* [1]

Year	Wage increase	Wage increase and hour decrease	Hour decrease	Wage decrease and hour increase	Recognition, wages, hours	Recognition, union rules, and other	Sympathy	Miscellaneous [2]	Total
1881	302	9	17	54	4	28	2	61	477
1882	258	4	15	76	4	34	3	82	476
1883	226	3	5	138	10	45	2	77	506
1884	138	5	7	191	13	37	6	88	485
1885	275	6	15	190	5	62	20	122	695
1886	667	80	163	163	32	178	37	252	1,572
1887	502	37	113	184	35	264	71	297	1,503
1888	254	18	52	216	19	144	34	209	946
1889	342	13	54	253	23	150	67	209	1,111
1890	607	51	173	208	49	269	188	352	1,897
1891	489	62	93	223	49	285	204	381	1,786
1892	398	27	79	189	37	224	117	288	1,359
1893	337	16	58	372	36	221	62	273	1,375
1894	432	19	24	390	23	183	120	213	1,404
1895	533	25	15	237	41	176	7	221	1,255
1896	294	27	14	212	49	248	7	215	1,066
1897	411	24	21	224	33	160	9	228	1,110
1898	404	35	29	177	46	190	9	208	1,098
1899	743	92	61	118	85	386	29	324	1,838
1900	633	144	96	118	91	323	29	465	1,839
1901	912	123	231	147	139	877	71	512	3,012
1902	1,118	158	189	139	200	851	87	498	3,240
1903	1,198	184	248	148	284	916	88	582	3,648
1904	576	68	89	211	130	834	93	418	2,419
1905	642	56	118	126	90	710	61	383	2,186
Total	12,691	1,286	1,979	4,704	1,527	7,795	1,423	6,898	38,303
Percent of total	33.1	3.4	5.2	12.3	4.0	20.3	3.7	18.0	100.0

[1] Adapted from tables X and XIX in the Twenty-first Annual Report of the Commissioner of Labor. Washington, 1907, pp. 580 and 763.

[2] Many of these strikes were listed in the original tables as "Concerning the employment of certain persons." The explanation given for this term is "demands for or against discharge of certain employees or foremen, objections against working with Negroes and foreigners, etc., in which disputes the question of union rules is not involved" (Twenty-first Annual Report of the Commissioner of Labor, p. 113). A considerable number of these miscellaneous strikes were originally classified under "Saturday part holiday" and "method and time of payment." The latter probably referred not so much to piece and bonus systems as to payment in scrip or kind. Also, the absence of State laws and union agreements requiring wages to be paid at specified dates, e. g., weekly, semimonthly, created situations where workers went on strike for more frequent or convenient pay days. Other causes included in this miscellaneous group are back wages due, overtime work and pay, docks and fines, and general working conditions.

About the same criteria as those now employed were used to measure the results of strikes and lock-outs: "A strike was reported as successful when the employees succeeded in enforcing full compliance with all of their demands; partly successful, when they succeeded in enforcing compliance with a part of their demands, or partial compliance with some or all of their demands; and failed, when they did not succeed in enforcing even partial compliance with any of their demands." [12]

It should be noted that in table 10 the results are in terms of establishments affected by strikes. In later tables the results are given in terms of number of strikes and workers involved in strikes.

[12] Twenty-first Annual Report of the Commissioner of Labor. Washington, 1907, p. 79.

TABLE **9.**—*Workers involved in strikes due to various causes, 1881–1905* [1]

Year	Wage increase	Wage increase and hour decrease	Hour decrease	Wage decrease and hour increase	Recognition, wages, hours	Recognition, union rules, and other	Sympathy	Miscellaneous [2]	Total
1881	86, 678	4, 138	8, 658	18, 868	1, 296	3, 377	532	6, 629	130, 176
1882	94, 981	228	4, 060	33, 364	73	12, 203	154	13, 739	158, 802
1883	66, 891	14, 866	263	49, 086	3, 877	23, 789	250	11, 253	170, 275
1884	52, 557	8, 866	8, 640	75, 332	1, 983	1, 553	510	15, 734	165, 175
1885	113, 638	12, 476	11, 904	76, 250	5, 227	8, 419	6, 519	23, 696	258, 129
1886	186, 073	83, 745	100, 506	74, 386	21, 188	57, 394	35, 161	51, 571	610, 024
1887	120, 706	20, 295	20, 256	87, 625	7, 278	84, 150	25, 483	73, 513	439, 306
1888	61, 189	2, 008	6, 110	30, 212	5, 145	17, 306	12, 466	28, 444	162, 880
1889	105, 032	988	5, 699	95, 760	10, 770	17, 838	3, 569	20, 634	260, 290
1890	171, 898	24, 734	44, 450	34, 507	9, 286	22, 304	15, 662	50, 658	373, 499
1891	142, 220	21, 374	27, 812	29, 789	16, 820	38, 053	10, 604	43, 281	329, 953
1892	50, 364	6, 131	29, 535	36, 096	6, 989	52, 279	14, 159	43, 132	238, 685
1893	74, 418	6, 080	9, 666	72, 149	18, 529	40, 750	10, 174	55, 990	287, 756
1894	272, 541	11, 008	16, 761	168, 769	5, 593	19, 494	154, 256	41, 622	690, 044
1895	191, 879	27, 314	7, 785	78, 438	32, 037	18, 751	1, 228	49, 756	407, 188
1896	69, 867	12, 158	4, 255	73, 834	22, 790	29, 965	761	35, 208	248, 838
1897	226, 403	36, 033	2, 826	69, 702	18, 746	17, 680	2, 468	42, 296	416, 154
1898	98, 626	22, 221	5, 049	58, 336	8, 795	20, 768	3, 172	46, 252	263, 219
1899	199, 104	50, 147	19, 898	18, 584	30, 416	35, 109	14, 678	63, 953	431, 889
1900	125, 893	43, 403	15, 988	24, 360	190, 675	91, 237	13, 035	63, 128	567, 719
1901	136, 215	26, 727	106, 134	18, 457	37, 768	123, 489	28, 214	86, 839	563, 843
1902	169, 575	56, 065	32, 660	20, 953	206, 451	72, 203	28, 313	105, 287	691, 507
1903	228, 020	61, 222	63, 332	43, 594	103, 923	131, 356	30, 867	125, 520	787, 834
1904	143, 530	9, 033	9, 005	110, 763	77, 050	132, 547	23, 934	67, 953	573, 815
1905	88, 436	19, 318	16, 204	67, 417	11, 839	45, 161	13, 385	40, 674	302, 434
Total	3, 276, 734	580, 578	577, 456	1, 466, 631	854, 544	1, 117, 175	449, 554	1, 206, 762	9, 529, 434
Percent of total	34. 4	6. 1	6. 1	15. 4	9. 0	11. 7	4. 7	12. 7	100. 0

[1] Adapted from tables X and XIX in the Twenty-first Annual Report of the Commissioner of Labor. Washington, 1907, pp. 580 and 763.
[2] See footnote 2, table 8.

TABLE **10.**—*Results of strikes, 1881–1905* [1]

Year	Percent of establishments in which strike or lock-out was—			Year	Percent of establishments in which strike or lock-out was—		
	Favorable to workers	Unfavorable to workers	Compromise		Favorable to workers	Unfavorable to workers	Compromise
1881	61. 2	31. 8	7. 0	1894	42. 8	44. 8	12. 4
1882	53. 2	38. 8	8. 0	1895	56. 8	33. 7	9. 5
1883	57. 6	27. 0	15. 4				
1884	54. 1	42. 5	3. 4	1896	58. 8	33. 8	7. 4
1885	53. 2	37. 7	9. 1	1897	56. 9	15. 5	27. 6
				1898	63. 0	30. 8	6. 2
				1899	73. 5	12. 6	13. 9
1886	38. 3	43. 5	18. 2	1900	38. 3	45. 1	16. 0
1887	48. 7	45. 1	6. 2				
1888	50. 7	43. 9	5. 4	1901	47. 7	34. 2	18. 1
1889	46. 1	34. 8	19. 1	1902	44. 8	33. 9	21. 3
1890	51. 8	38. 3	9. 9	1903	37. 0	42. 1	20. 9
				1904	32. 7	50. 6	16. 7
1891	36. 8	54. 5	8. 7	1905	39. 5	46. 1	14. 4
1892	35. 5	53. 9	10. 6				
1893	50. 2	39. 0	10. 8	All	46. 5	38. 7	14. 8

[1] Adapted from tables IV and XVI in the Twenty-first Annual Report of the Commissioner of Labor. Washington, 1907, pp. 479 and 737.

Chapter IV

Strikes From 1914 to 1926

In 1914, for the first time since 1905, the Bureau of Labor Statistics made an attempt to get a record of all the strikes and lock-outs throughout the United States. The compilation was made from material gathered from printed sources only—newspapers, labor journals, trade journals, etc. In appraising its work for this year the Bureau stated: "It would be manifestly incorrect to compare the incomplete data collected in this manner with the more comprehensive reports secured by the investigations of trained field agents. In spite of the incompleteness of the data for 1914, however, the figures give considerable information of value in regard to the labor disturbances which occurred in that year."[1]

TABLE 11.—*Strikes, by months, 1914–26* [1]

Year	January	February	March	April	May	June	July	August	September	October	November	December	Month not stated	Total
1914 [2]														1,204
1915 [3]	73	60	97	112	140	72	126	172	189	114	123	84	231	1,593
1916 [4]	188	206	294	434	617	354	313	326	252	261	197	149	198	3,789
1917	288	211	318	445	463	323	448	360	349	322	257	197	469	4,450
1918	191	223	312	321	392	296	288	278	212	145	208	250	237	3,353
1919	199	198	192	270	431	322	381	417	425	334	165	140	156	3,630
1920	280	214	288	427	422	317	298	264	231	192	106	108	264	3,411
1921	238	172	194	292	575	152	167	143	124	90	92	76	70	2,385
1922	131	96	75	109	104	64	101	95	85	64	64	43	81	1,112
1923	69	72	123	212	246	133	146	106	93	117	66	59	111	1,553
1924	102	70	118	144	155	98	89	81	71	74	61	40	146	1,249
1925	94	89	83	161	161	108	103	123	104	77	63	45	90	1,301
1926	62	74	84	127	141	73	84	98	85	60	48	33	66	1,035

[1] This and subsequent tables include a few strikes and lock-outs involving fewer than 6 persons and lasting less than 1 day; also some occurring outside continental United States (see table 12).
[2] Adapted from Monthly Review, July 1915 and April 1916. Monthly data not available.
[3] Idem, April 1917.
[4] Idem, July 1929.

In 1915 the Bureau inaugurated a method for the collection of strike and lock-out material which has been followed, in general, since that time. Leads or announcements of strikes and lock-outs were obtained through clipping services, newspapers, and labor and trade journals. Schedules were then mailed to the interested parties, asking

[1] Monthly Review, U. S. Bureau of Labor Statistics, July 1915, p. 20.

for verification and additional details.[2] Since that time, however, there have been changes in the number of papers read, the type of questions asked on the schedules, and the amount of persistence used in getting replies. All these factors necessarily affect the exhaustiveness with which knowledge of disputes becomes known, as well as the accuracy of details concerning the disputes.

In two specific respects the statistical data shown for the period 1914–26 are not comparable with the statistics for earlier or later periods. First, they include strikes and lock-outs involving fewer than six persons and lasting less than 1 day as contrasted with the earlier and later data which exclude these classifications and, second, they include strikes and lock-outs in Alaska, and American territory outside continental United States (Hawaii, Puerto Rico, Canal Zone, and Virgin Islands). It is not known how many of the small disputes are included in the tables for this period, although the number is probably not large due to the inherent difficulty in learning about small, brief disputes in such a large country as the United States. The number of disputes recorded for Alaska and the insular areas is shown in table 12. The year in which most of them occurred (1920) they amounted to 3½ percent of the total for that year.

The industries in which the strikes and lock-outs took place are not known in a large number of cases. Of the total number of disputes recorded for the period, only 72 percent can be assigned to specific industries (see table 15). Labor-union affiliation is not known for a large portion of these disputes, especially during the war and post-war period (see table 17). Data on causes and results are somewhat more complete (see tables 18 and 19).

The most serious discrepancy in the statistics for these years is the lack of complete coverage on the number of workers involved in the disputes and the number of man-days idle. Because of the various interpretations which can be applied to the counting of strikes, the number of workers involved and man-days idle afford a more accurate index of labor disturbances than the number of strikes and lock-outs. Unfortunately, there is no available information regarding the number of man-days' work lost by employees involved in the strikes and lock-outs from 1914 through 1926, and the number of workers involved is recorded for only about two-thirds of the disputes (see table 16).

[2] "During these 5 years this information has been obtained from agents of the Bureau in the field, reports of Commissioners of Conciliation of the Department of Labor, and other similar boards, reports of the various State labor boards, lists of strikes issued by labor, trade, and other organizations, and from clipping bureaus, supplemented by an examination of 25 daily papers printed in the more important industrial cities of the country, 100 labor papers, as many trade-union periodicals, and 20 leading trade papers. During the year 1918, 3,997 circulars of inquiry asking information in regard to about 3,500 reputed strikes and lock-outs were sent to employers reported to have had strikes in their establishments and to officials of unions whose members had been concerned in or were believed to have knowledge of labor troubles. Of this number, 1,392 were returned answered in whole or in part, 420 were returned undelivered for various reasons, and the remainder were unanswered." Monthly Labor Review, June 1919, p. 307.

The following tables include all the statistical data which are available for the strikes which took place between 1914 and 1926.

TABLE 12.—*Strikes, by States, 1914–26* [1]

State	1914 [2]	1915 [3]	1916	1917	1918	1919	1920	1921	1922	1923	1924	1925	1926
Total	1,204	1,593	3,789	4,450	3,353	3,630	3,411	2,385	1,112	1,553	1,249	1,301	1,035
Alabama	7	4	15	20	13	18	25	15	4	6	------	3	5
Arizona	3	5	7	20	4	7	9	4	1	1	------	------	1
Arkansas	8	3	20	36	11	7	15	7	2	2	3	4	------
California	53	27	55	112	94	102	120	99	37	47	29	40	34
Colorado	10	6	17	48	32	31	22	27	7	3	5	10	5
Connecticut	21	153	326	178	92	135	128	61	30	52	26	46	29
Delaware	4	14	12	17	14	11	10	4	1	1	------	4	8
District of Columbia	2	1	8	14	13	10	14	5	4	6	5	11	6
Florida	3	------	9	16	20	30	9	19	5	4	2	10	16
Georgia	13	11	8	28	40	39	29	21	3	4	4	5	9
Idaho	1	------	5	32	10	10	5	3	------	1	------	------	------
Illinois	95	74	159	282	248	267	254	164	63	72	80	84	72
Indiana	45	30	75	73	76	106	99	61	15	35	28	45	32
Iowa	16	13	26	65	41	57	47	42	15	14	15	12	14
Kansas	5	7	15	53	41	45	14	21	4	5	6	12	2
Kentucky	16	15	13	38	19	26	22	17	10	11	12	2	12
Louisiana	10	4	8	39	23	51	37	29	8	16	7	3	5
Maine	11	6	30	40	36	40	22	24	11	7	6	10	1
Maryland	19	13	48	59	72	41	57	27	12	19	25	17	7
Massachusetts	99	160	383	353	347	396	377	201	139	217	97	162	113
Michigan	36	33	71	64	60	84	63	71	18	19	10	14	12
Minnesota	24	15	30	53	40	49	50	45	9	14	4	5	9
Mississippi	1	1	4	13	5	2	4	9	------	1	------	------	------
Missouri	33	43	97	122	105	69	63	54	26	27	35	11	9
Montana	10	3	15	77	33	23	16	21	2	7	1	1	4
Nebraska	3	4	21	28	11	17	12	11	3	1	2	2	1
Nevada	2	------	------	2	7	5	4	1	3	1	1	------	------
New Hampshire	7	5	20	20	17	34	32	6	30	6	8	5	8
New Jersey	74	200	417	227	138	183	145	125	71	78	92	92	84
New Mexico	------	------	------	4	2	4	1	2	------	------	------	------	------
New York	156	222	592	711	689	536	600	384	202	403	281	301	216
North Carolina	3	------	8	7	14	22	21	26	6	6	4	7	2
North Dakota	1	------	------	2	3	------	4	8	2	1	1	------	------
Ohio	91	137	290	279	197	237	206	167	73	65	68	73	68
Oklahoma	6	6	24	35	19	32	24	29	9	2	6	10	2
Oregon	8	7	23	58	18	38	22	23	8	15	13	5	8
Pennsylvania	107	164	574	494	311	280	250	222	101	234	261	184	162
Rhode Island	14	40	77	105	53	78	89	42	37	25	5	25	28
South Carolina	3	4	5	7	3	11	5	12	2	1	1	------	1
South Dakota	1	------	------	3	3	3	5	3	------	------	1	------	------
Tennessee	15	7	26	42	26	40	27	28	8	7	10	3	7
Texas	35	39	28	56	41	50	73	64	10	15	16	11	4
Utah	9	9	3	21	14	22	14	5	1	1	2	2	------
Vermont	2	2	10	8	9	13	12	2	13	------	------	4	1
Virginia	5	6	16	35	37	28	31	14	5	3	4	1	3
Washington	53	37	58	294	130	113	69	63	22	36	15	15	5
West Virginia	14	27	40	64	50	63	49	28	8	28	23	20	11
Wisconsin	43	20	63	57	54	77	68	41	21	10	15	14	8
Wyoming	------	1	------	2	5	4	6	4	------	1	1	1	------
Interstate	4	1	4	25	4	21	10	19	27	23	10	12	8
Alaska and islands	3	14	34	12	9	63	121	5	24	------	9	3	3

[1] Monthly Labor Review, July 1929, table 3, p. 134.
[2] Idem, April 1916, p. 19.
[3] Idem, April 1917, p. 603.

Table 13.—*Sex of workers involved in strikes, 1916–26* [1]

Sex of persons involved	Number of strikes beginning in—										
	1916	1917	1918	1919	1920	1921	1922	1923	1924	1925	1926
Males only	3,121	3,611	2,467	2,818	2,347	1,750	676	983	877	891	831
Females only	122	158	90	88	78	30	22	31	23	31	33
Both sexes	269	190	278	521	343	558	357	445	280	338	150
Not reported	277	491	518	203	643	47	57	94	69	41	21
Total	3,789	4,450	3,353	3,630	3,411	2,385	1,112	1,553	1,249	1,301	1,035

[1] Monthly Labor Review, July 1929, p. 135. No information available for 1914–15.

Table 14.—*Number of establishments involved in strikes, 1917–26* [1]

Establishments involved	Number of strikes beginning in—									
	1917	1918	1919	1920	1921	1922	1923	1924	1925	1926
1	3,078	2,541	2,136	1,989	1,071	745	1,133	820	898	649
2	143	70	142	86	113	28	56	34	60	26
3	73	42	99	59	94	17	35	23	25	23
4	41	23	59	40	62	17	15	16	24	10
5	18	90	52	35	43	9	10	17	12	14
Over 5	403	327	910	426	584	104	103	84	98	94
Not reported	694	260	232	776	418	192	201	255	184	219
Total	4,450	3,353	3,630	3,411	2,385	1,112	1,553	1,249	1,301	1,035

[1] Monthly Labor Review, July 1929, p. 138. No information available for 1914–16.

Table 15.—*Number of strikes in specified industries, 1914–26* [1]

Industry	1914 [2]	1915 [3]	1916	1917	1918	1919	1920	1921	1922	1923	1924	1925	1926
Total strikes and lock-outs	1,204	1,593	3,789	4,450	3,353	3,630	3,411	2,385	1,112	1,553	1,249	1,301	1,035
Total for industries listed	731	983	2,579	3,233	2,476	2,572	2,341	2,007	860	1,181	955	998	828
Building trades	275	259	394	468	434	473	521	583	113	208	270	349	272
Clothing	78	131	227	495	436	322	336	240	240	395	238	231	194
Furniture	18	16	50	43	26	35	26	17	4	12	35	56	46
Iron and steel	14	33	72	56	74	76	25	25	10	10	7	7	2
Leather	-----	5	34	19	16	27	32	26	17	17	5	5	11
Lumber	40	13	44	299	76	46	38	25	10	19	6	9	3
Metal trades	129	289	547	515	441	581	452	194	83	113	58	48	75
Mining, coal	51	69	373	355	162	148	161	87	44	158	177	100	78
Mining, other	-----	-----	43	94	46	28	22	8	5	1	1	4	-----
Paper manufacturing	-----	14	54	41	40	47	39	42	12	16	6	6	10
Printing and publishing	20	5	27	41	40	71	83	506	56	19	12	14	9
Shipbuilding	-----	-----	31	106	140	109	45	20	4	6	1	-----	-----
Slaughtering, meat cutting, and packing	-----	7	70	38	42	74	42	30	6	11	14	2	5
Stone	-----	21	61	26	14	13	29	34	61	15	15	17	11
Textiles	54	93	261	247	212	273	211	114	115	134	80	139	90
Tobacco	-----	8	63	47	50	58	38	19	13	16	12	4	14
Transportation, steam and electric	52	20	228	343	227	191	241	37	67	31	18	7	8

[1] Monthly Labor Review, July 1929, p. 139.
[2] Idem, April 1916, p. 18.
[3] Idem, April 1917, p. 604.

Table 16.—*Number of workers involved in strikes, 1916–26* [1]

Year	Total number of strikes beginning each year	Number of strikes in which number of workers is reported: Strikes	Workers involved	Year	Total number of strikes beginning each year	Number of strikes in which number of workers is reported: Strikes	Workers involved
1916	3,789	2,667	1,599,917	1922	1,112	899	1,612,562
1917	4,450	2,325	1,227,254	1923	1,553	1,199	756,584
1918	3,353	2,151	1,239,989	1924	1,249	898	654,641
1919	3,630	2,665	4,160,348	1925	1,301	1,012	428,416
1920	3,411	2,226	1,463,054	1926	1,035	783	329,592
1921	2,385	1,785	1,099,247				

[1] Adapted from Monthly Labor Review, July 1929, table 9, p. 138. Although the number of workers involved was obtained on only about ⅔ of the total number of strikes, the missing information is for the smaller disputes. The unknown number for the smaller strikes is probably offset by the "generous" figure used in large strikes. Information on the latter was usually taken from newspaper reports, which are likely to give slightly exaggerated figures.

Table 17.—*Relation of workers to labor unions* [1]

Relation of workers to union	Number of strikes: 1916	1917	1918	1919	1920	1921	1922	1923	1924	1925	1926
Connected with unions	2,458	2,392	1,903	2,033	2,506	2,038	844	1,265	1,063	1,018	823
Not connected with unions	446	209	362	143	137	62	37	77	69	142	93
Organized after strike began	71	55	26	30	8	5	5	18	14	16	19
Union and nonunion workers							12	29	31	38	15
Not reported	814	1,794	1,062	1,424	760	280	214	164	72	87	85
Total	3,789	4,450	3,353	3,630	3,411	2,385	1,112	1,553	1,249	1,301	1,035

[1] Adapted from Monthly Labor Review, July 1929, p. 136. No information available for 1914 and 1915.

Table 18.—*Major causes of strikes, 1914–26* [1]

Cause of strikes	1914 [2]	1915 [3]	1916	1917	1918	1919	1920	1921	1922	1923	1924	1925	1926
Total strikes	1,204	1,593	3,789	4,450	3,353	3,630	3,411	2,385	1,112	1,553	1,249	1,301	1,035
Wages and hours	403	770	2,036	2,268	1,869	2,036	2,038	1,501	583	721	537	537	478
Wage increase	192	367	1,301	1,571	1,397	1,115	1,429	120	156	445	255	277	260
Wage decrease	92	107	35	36	36	86	147	973	301	49	132	121	53
Wage increase—hour decrease	36	159	481	378	256	578	269	34	16	58	30	29	39
Hour decrease	48	80	113	132	79	117	62	294	22	16	18	7	19
Hour increase	-----	8	7	18	6	25	8	18	12	5	5	6	4
Wages, hours, and other	35	49	99	133	95	115	123	62	76	148	97	97	103
Organization	253	312	721	799	584	869	622	373	208	308	244	219	206
Recognition	94	95	408	346	248	536	314	197	143	161	161	110	121
Recognition, wages, and hours	67	57	169	207	144	170	138	131	21	68	29	35	24
Discrimination in employment and discharge	92	160	144	246	192	163	170	45	44	79	54	74	61
Miscellaneous	152	234	401	591	439	475	446	348	258	441	360	445	303
General conditions	72	41	68	116	93	123	116	83	72	80	79	89	66
Jurisdiction	16	28	19	21	16	16	20	10	10	13	23	59	17
Sympathy	25	17	33	71	35	108	67	36	33	31	22	39	29
Other	39	148	281	383	295	228	243	219	143	317	236	258	191
Unknown	396	277	631	792	461	250	305	163	63	83	108	100	48

[1] Adapted from Monthly Labor Review, July 1929, table 7, p. 136.
[2] Adapted from table in Monthly Review, July 1915, p. 21.
[3] Idem, April 1917, p. 605.

TABLE **19.**—*Results of strikes, 1916–26* [1]

Result	Number of strikes ending in—										
	1916	1917	1918	1919	1920	1921	1922	1923	1924	1925	1926
In favor of employers	748	395	465	687	677	701	248	368	283	253	226
In favor of employees	749	631	627	627	472	256	259	403	354	349	288
Compromise	777	720	691	797	448	291	105	168	138	138	147
Employees returned pending arbitration	73	137	204	50	61	80	16	46	45	51	36
Not reported	101	191	211	59	214	198	113	160	139	198	83
Total [2]	2,448	2,074	2,198	2,220	1,872	1,526	741	1,145	959	989	780

[1] Adapted from Monthly Labor Review, July 1929, p. 140. No information available for 1914 and 1915.

[2] It should be noted that there is considerable difference between the number of strikes ending each year, in the above table, and the number of strikes beginning each year, in previous tables. This is probably due to the fact that no information was obtained on a large number of disputes as to ending date and results. The above table should, therefore, be considered as incomplete.

Chapter V

Analysis of Strikes, 1927-36[1]

Strikes by Years

There were fewer strikes during each of the years 1927 to 1932 than there were in any year since 1885.[2] These 6 years included 1 year of business recession, 2 years of prosperity, and 3 years of extreme business depression. During 1927, however, there were more man-days of idleness because of strikes than for any of the succeeding 9 years. (See chart 2.)[3] This was due to the general coal strike which started in April and continued through the rest of the year. In 1928 there was another protracted strike in the bituminous-coal industry although this did not involve as many workers as the 1927 strike.

TABLE 20.—*Strikes from 1927 to 1936, by years*

Year	Number of strikes			Number of workers involved in strikes			Man-days idle during year
	Beginning in year	In progress during year	Ending in year	Beginning in year	In progress during year	Ending in year	
1927	707	(1)	666	329, 939	(1)	319, 442	26, 218, 628
1928	604	645	620	314, 210	324, 707	322, 866	12, 631, 863
1929	921	946	924	288, 572	290, 413	286, 163	5, 351, 540
1930	637	659	651	182, 975	187, 225	181, 901	3, 316. 808
1931	810	818	796	341, 817	347, 141	345, 669	6, 893, 244
1932	841	863	852	324, 210	325, 682	324, 960	10, 502, 033
1933	1, 695	1, 706	1, 672	1, 168, 272	1, 168, 994	1, 143, 910	16, 872, 128
1934	1, 856	1, 890	1, 817	1, 466, 695	1, 491, 779	1, 480, 343	19, 591, 949
1935	2, 014	2, 087	2, 003	1, 117, 213	1, 128, 646	1, 101, 902	15, 456, 337
1936	2, 172	2, 256	2, 156	788, 648	815, 395	709, 748	13, 901, 956

1 Information not available.

Strike activity was at its minimum in 1930, the first year of the depression. The rapid recession of business activity discouraged strikes for wage increases. At the same time comparatively few wage cuts were put into effect that year. By 1931 and 1932 wage reductions became general and protest strikes became more numerous. The relatively large number of man-days lost because of strikes in 1932 is largely due to the prolonged strikes in the southern Illinois coal fields.

1 Tables prepared by Don Q. Crowther, of the Bureau of Labor Statistics.

2 The years 1906-13 are ignored in this analysis, since no strike data are available for that period.

3 No figures for man-days idle are available previous to 1927.

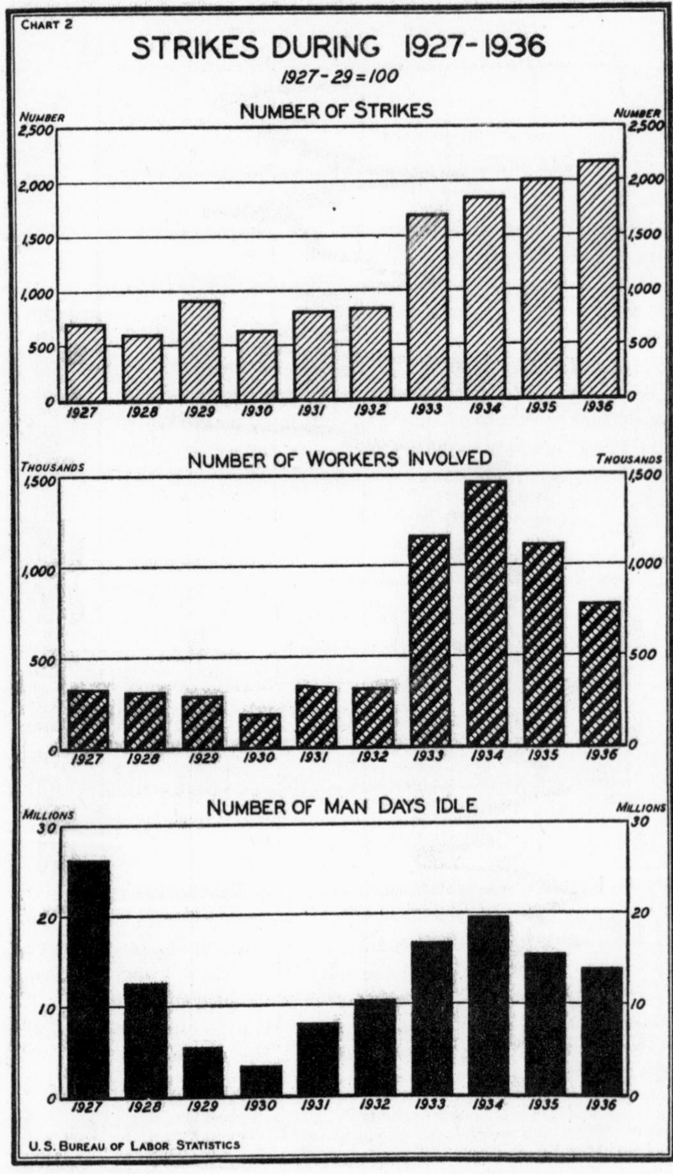
CHART 2
STRIKES DURING 1927-1936
1927-29=100
NUMBER OF STRIKES
NUMBER
2,500
2,000
1,500
1,000
500
0
1927 1928 1929 1930 1931 1932 1933 1934 1935 1936
NUMBER OF WORKERS INVOLVED
THOUSANDS
1,500
1,000
500
0
NUMBER OF MAN DAYS IDLE
MILLIONS
30
20
10
0
U.S. BUREAU OF LABOR STATISTICS

The first year of recovery and the impetus for increased labor activity ensuing from the National Industrial Recovery Act doubled the number of strikes in 1933. Rising prices and union-organization drives brought on a slightly increased number of strikes from that time through 1936. While there were more strikes in 1936 than in the preceding years, there were not as many workers involved nor man-days lost. There were no extremely large strikes in 1936, such as the textile strike in 1934 and the bituminous-coal strike in 1935, nor as many fairly large strikes of prolonged duration as there were in 1933. (See appendix I.)

Seasonal Trend

In general, the smallest number of strikes occur during the winter months from November through February. In each of the 10 years fewer strikes occurred in December than in either of the next 2 months. In all but one of the years there were fewer strikes in November than in the succeeding January, but only in 1927 were there fewer than in December. (See chart 3.)

Strikes begin to increase in the spring, especially in May, and remain at a relatively high level all summer. In 5 of the 10 years the largest number of strikes took place in May, and in a sixth year the highest number was shared between April and May. In 1930 there were more strikes in July than in any other month of that year. In 1933 and 1935 the greatest number occurred during August. There was a seasonal increase in strikes during May 1936, but the maximum for the year did not occur until September.

About the same seasonal characteristics pertain to the number of workers involved in strikes. In 6 years out of the 10, December witnessed the smallest number of workers involved in strikes begun that month. November, January, and February had the smallest number in the other 4 years. The peak month for number of workers idle because of strikes begun during the month was not as consistent as that for number of strikes, due to the influence of one or two large strikes on the total number of workers. Thus, in 1 year (1930) the largest number of workers involved in strikes was in February; in 4 years April had the greatest number; July had the greatest number in 1931; September in 3 years (1933, 1934, and 1935); and October in 1936.

The number of workers involved in strikes in progress during any month indicates the full impact of strikes which began in preceding months and remained unsettled, as well as those involved in strikes beginning in the month. Due to this cumulative effect, there may be a large number of workers involved in strikes in progress during a certain month even though the number involved in new strikes is on

13894°—38——4

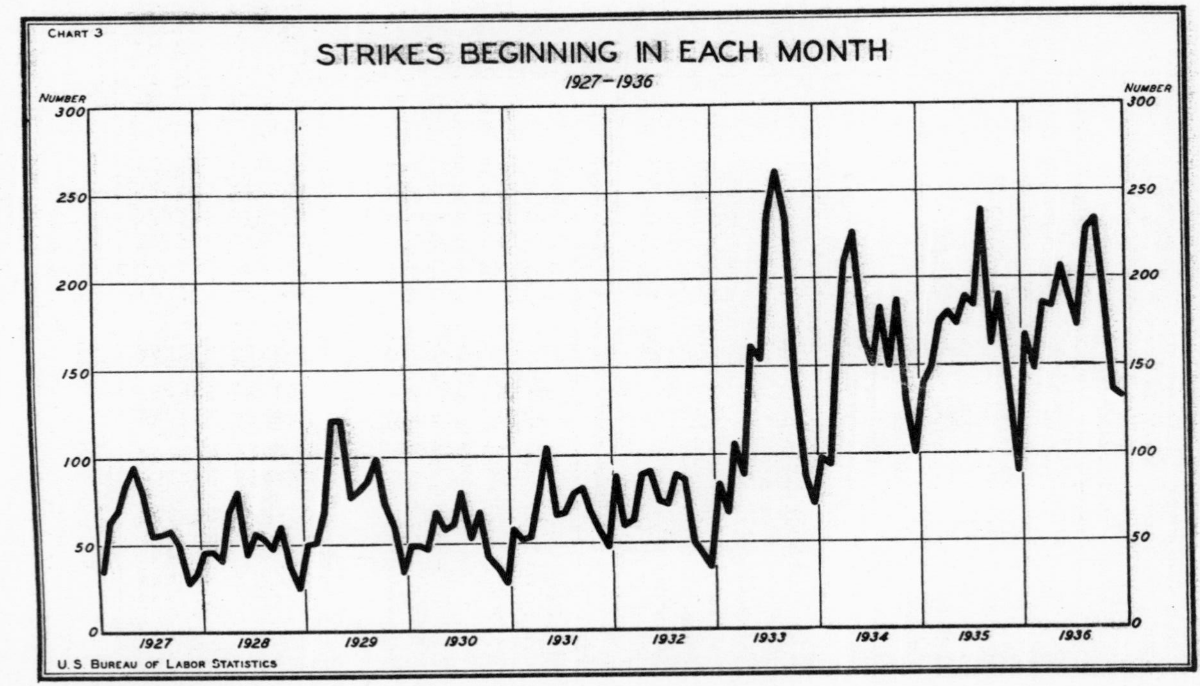
CHART 3
STRIKES BEGINNING IN EACH MONTH
1927–1936
NUMBER
300
250
200
150
100
50
0
1927
1928
1929
1930
1931
1932
1933
1934
1935
1936
U. S. BUREAU OF LABOR STATISTICS

the decline. For instance, because of the prolonged bituminous-coal strike in 1927, the number of workers involved in strikes in progress during May and the succeeding months was very high although the number of workers in strikes beginning in those months was unusually small. Another prolonged general coal strike and clothing and textile strikes in Massachusetts and New York City caused the largest number of workers to be out in June 1928. A large strike in the New York clothing industry occurred in July 1929. The large number of workers in February 1930 was primarily due to a dressmakers' strike in New York City. During August 1931, a coal strike in Pennsylvania and a strike in the men's clothing industry of New York contributed substantially to the total number of workers involved in strikes. Large strikes in progress in the construction industry in New York City, and in the bituminous-coal regions of Illinois, accounted for the large number of workers in May 1932. In September 1933 strikes in anthracite and bituminous coal, as well as several strikes in New York clothing plants, caused a large number of persons to be out. A general textile strike took place in September 1934, and a general bituminous-coal strike in September 1935. Maritime strikes on all three coasts and strikes in the glass and automobile industries contributed toward the large number involved in strikes in December 1936.

In general, the number of man-days idle because of strikes increases each spring and summer and is lowest during December and January. During 2 years in the 10-year period the number of man-days remained relatively high in December. In 1927 this was due to the coal strike; in 1936, to the maritime strikes and strikes in the glass and automobile industries.

Table 21.—*Strikes from 1927 to 1936, by months*

Month	1927	1928	1929	1930	1931	1932	1933	1934	1935	1936
	Number of strikes beginning in month									
January	35	45	50	49	58	88	83	98	140	167
February	63	46	51	49	52	60	67	94	149	148
March	70	41	68	47	53	63	106	161	175	185
April	84	69	121	68	78	89	89	210	180	183
May	95	80	121	58	104	91	161	226	174	206
June	80	44	77	61	66	74	154	165	189	188
July	55	56	81	79	67	72	237	151	184	173
August	56	53	86	53	78	89	261	183	239	228
September	58	48	99	68	81	86	233	150	162	234
October	50	60	73	42	68	50	145	187	190	192
November	28	37	60	36	57	43	87	130	142	136
December	33	25	34	27	48	36	72	101	90	132

Table 21.—*Strikes from 1927 to 1936, by months*—Continued

Month	1927	1928	1929	1930	1931	1932	1933	1934	1935	1936
	Number of strikes in progress during month									
January	----------	86	75	71	66	110	94	132	213	251
February	79	96	84	74	73	97	101	143	232	250
March	108	88	103	88	87	103	141	222	277	304
April	138	104	158	103	106	117	133	283	294	313
May	163	120	179	97	146	137	217	329	307	340
June	164	92	156	91	113	125	219	276	319	309
July	134	96	143	113	105	119	297	277	317	324
August	111	89	144	86	125	134	348	297	377	355
September	102	85	146	104	118	131	347	259	311	379
October	94	94	124	81	112	85	267	297	332	335
November	80	75	93	64	98	66	178	229	274	252
December	72	59	67	48	86	58	136	201	210	258
	Number of workers involved in the strikes beginning in month									
January	5, 140	17, 081	15, 045	11, 180	11, 159	13, 417	23, 676	81, 650	81, 194	32, 406
February	9, 725	35, 995	27, 254	38, 266	31, 488	44, 621	13, 626	89, 562	64, 238	63, 056
March	16, 280	8, 414	18, 747	17, 639	32, 214	36, 025	45, 183	91, 559	53, 089	75, 191
April	189, 943	89, 347	41, 277	11, 918	39, 034	52, 998	37, 807	185, 282	67, 857	65, 379
May	21, 031	17, 078	37, 389	11, 213	36, 758	49, 971	68, 310	145, 830	102, 491	72, 824
June	19, 602	33, 225	24, 986	18, 566	31, 968	18, 520	96, 187	56, 244	48, 917	63, 429
July	19, 416	18, 318	37, 148	18, 716	50, 105	30, 095	175, 177	180, 268	70, 046	38, 017
August	8, 419	11, 366	28, 741	20, 487	13, 849	38, 916	224, 696	80, 071	74, 313	68, 752
September	13, 731	9, 110	22, 356	14, 840	39, 273	19, 615	290, 408	423, 915	453, 820	65, 994
October	14, 140	28, 301	19, 389	10, 175	35, 388	11, 251	81, 447	69, 441	48, 223	100, 845
November	7, 187	40, 459	12, 715	4, 660	16, 036	4, 898	74, 231	37, 869	38, 279	70, 116
December	5, 325	5, 516	3, 525	5, 315	4, 545	3, 883	37, 524	25, 004	14, 746	72, 639
	Number of workers involved in the strikes in progress during month									
January	----------	27, 578	16, 886	15, 430	16, 483	14, 889	24, 398	106, 734	92, 630	59, 153
February	11, 932	48, 153	32, 707	45, 582	34, 585	49, 902	23, 738	160, 713	96, 533	89, 735
March	21, 749	41, 865	29, 126	26, 672	47, 572	79, 229	54, 193	128, 886	98, 457	122, 162
April	198, 306	95, 047	49, 005	19, 019	70, 493	65, 747	53, 061	229, 552	124, 174	95, 526
May	206, 070	91, 741	60, 303	18, 893	70, 105	103, 641	101, 295	234, 364	151, 163	123, 030
June	202, 561	113, 189	60, 762	25, 327	58, 061	103, 108	128, 207	119, 509	129, 784	133, 531
July	202, 541	106, 196	65, 244	30, 748	91, 194	88, 972	251, 723	250, 328	141, 829	125, 281
August	180, 553	89, 138	45, 418	28, 928	94, 273	102, 977	312, 539	162, 980	150, 835	118, 268
September	184, 981	83, 183	30, 366	26, 109	62, 809	63, 441	382, 213	480, 318	514, 427	130, 875
October	184, 136	103, 759	28, 026	25, 979	76, 746	21, 713	296, 110	104, 207	133, 742	148, 570
November	181, 890	92, 728	19, 548	22, 422	48, 968	10, 551	241, 316	94, 494	100, 732	157, 007
December	182, 293	55, 105	12, 103	15, 396	19, 246	6, 232	69, 397	73, 279	61, 782	184, 859
	Number of man-days idle during month									
January	54, 209	315, 293	66, 658	236, 927	181, 466	131, 895	278, 257	822, 400	720, 778	635, 519
February	118, 346	445, 273	156, 047	503, 189	320, 736	467, 159	136, 862	867, 912	836, 498	748, 491
March	249, 905	400, 707	300, 387	342, 187	317, 185	544, 687	521, 289	1, 237, 055	966, 980	1, 331, 162
April	3, 570, 181	1, 447, 876	653, 585	425, 908	935, 418	1, 390, 337	730, 320	2, 333, 230	1, 178, 851	699, 900
May	3, 712, 396	1, 704, 045	950, 097	225, 925	569, 806	2, 078, 812	1, 066, 664	1, 956, 868	1, 697, 848	1, 019, 171
June	3, 635, 099	1, 905, 190	931, 488	189, 823	807, 554	1, 822, 979	1, 083, 537	1, 565, 601	1, 311, 278	1, 327, 678
July	3, 618, 813	1, 694, 794	900, 680	203, 733	700, 501	1, 618, 441	1, 775, 301	2, 221, 663	1, 297, 730	1, 105, 480
August	3, 330, 092	1, 730, 937	395, 219	165, 405	883, 605	1, 416, 504	2, 060, 855	2, 188, 239	1, 191, 663	911, 216
September	3, 294, 922	1, 115, 323	273, 891	206, 141	548, 952	630, 449	3, 594, 401	4, 136, 108	3, 027, 040	1, 063, 100
October	1, 522, 635	726, 118	307, 312	345, 701	1, 044, 383	238, 292	3, 508, 918	909, 459	1, 562, 908	1, 053, 878
November	1, 544, 661	717, 280	260, 169	269, 389	420, 299	114, 782	1, 620, 415	969, 061	1, 003, 852	1, 940, 628
December	1, 567, 369	429, 027	156, 007	202, 480	163, 339	47, 696	495, 309	384, 353	660, 911	2, 065, 733

Number of Workers[4]

The number of workers involved in a strike includes those workers within the plant or establishment who stop work or are thrown out of work because of the strike. Thus the number shown in the tables is not limited to the employees of the plant who actually took part in the strike. On the other hand, it does not include workers in other plants who may have been affected by the strike.[5]

More than half of the strikes (54 percent) involved fewer than 100 workers each. About 30 percent involved between 100 and 500 workers. During the 10 years, strikes involving 500 and more workers comprised only 16 percent of the total. In 1933 as many as 22 percent and in 1934 as many as 19 percent involved 500 and more workers. These years also had the greatest proportion of very large strikes—2½ percent of the total in each year involving 5,000 and more workers.

During the 10-year period 1927–36, there was an average of about 515 workers involved in each strike. The average number of workers per strike each year is a measure of the relative severity of all the strikes which occur during the year. Since the average, however, is materially affected by a few extremely large strikes, the median figure gives a more accurate picture of the sizes of strikes each year. Since 1933 a larger proportion of the strikes included more workers than in the preceding years. Thus about half of the strikes each year from 1927 to 1932 involved fewer than 56 workers, with the exception of 1929 when the median was 70. More large strikes in 1933 and 1934 increased the median number of workers to 150 and 114, respectively. There was practically no difference in the characteristic sizes of strikes in 1935 and 1936, half of them in each year involving fewer than 74 or 75 workers.

---

[4] For information on results of strikes in relation to number of workers involved, see table 32. A list of strikes which involved 10,000 workers or over is given in appendix I.

[5] It should be noted that strikes involving fewer than 6 workers are omitted from all these statistical analyses. See pp. 5 and 9.

TABLE 22.—*Strikes by number of workers involved*

Year	Totals	Strikes in which the number of workers involved was—								Average number of workers per strike	Median workers involved in strikes
		6 and under 20	20 and under 100	100 and under 250	250 and under 500	500 and under 1,000	1,000 and under 5,000	5,000 and under 10,000	10,000 and over		
Number of strikes											
1927	707	157	291	104	67	48	36	3	1	467	50
1928	604	117	256	85	55	41	41	4	5	520	52
1929	921	167	354	176	90	63	63	7	1	313	70
1930	637	125	264	118	64	32	31	2	1	287	53
1931	810	177	322	155	59	39	45	7	6	422	56
1932	841	201	334	144	79	34	38	4	7	386	53
1933	1, 695	178	524	367	253	172	158	26	17	689	150
1934	1, 856	259	590	386	262	178	135	28	18	790	114
1935	2, 014	340	755	420	219	143	113	15	9	555	75
1936	2, 172	392	840	414	238	158	102	20	8	363	74
Percent of strikes											
1927	100. 0	22. 2	41. 2	14. 7	9. 5	6. 8	5. 1	0. 4	0. 1		
1928	100. 0	19. 4	42. 3	14. 1	9. 1	6. 8	6. 8	. 7	. 8		
1929	100. 0	18. 1	38. 5	19. 1	9. 8	6. 8	6. 8	. 8	. 1		
1930	100. 0	19. 6	41. 5	18. 5	10. 0	5. 0	4. 9	. 3	. 2		
1931	100. 0	21. 9	39. 7	19. 1	7. 3	4. 8	5. 6	. 9	. 7		
1932	100. 0	23. 9	39. 8	17. 1	9. 4	4. 0	4. 5	. 5	. 8		
1933	100. 0	10. 5	31. 0	21. 7	14. 9	10. 1	9. 3	1. 5	1. 0		
1934	100. 0	14. 0	31. 7	20. 8	14. 1	9. 6	7. 3	1. 5	1. 0		
1935	100. 0	16. 9	37. 5	20. 9	10. 9	7. 1	5. 6	. 7	. 4		
1936	100. 0	18. 0	38. 6	19. 1	11. 0	7. 3	4. 7	. 9	. 4		

Establishments Involved

It is impossible to obtain data on the number of establishments involved in many of the large strikes, especially when these strikes extend into numerous cities and States. For that reason there are no separate classifications of strikes which extend into more than 10 establishments.[6] The establishments involved in a strike may be different plants of the same company or plants of several companies either in the same city or scattered over a more extensive area.

During the 10-year period 1927–36, almost 70 percent of the strikes were confined to single establishments. This percentage was fairly uniform for all years except in 1927 when 61 percent[7] and in 1928 when 65 percent of the strikes were confined to single establishments. In only 1 year, 1929, were there more workers involved in strikes confined to single establishments than in strikes of a more general character. During this year there was only 1 large strike, that of 15,000 cloak and suit workers in New York City.

Less than 12 percent of the strikes during the 10 years extended into more than 10 establishments. While 59 percent of the total

6 See appendix II, p. 164.

7 If information on the 90 "not reported" were known, this proportion might be larger.

TABLE 23.—*Strikes by number of establishments involved, 1927–36*

Number of establishments involved	1927	1928	1929	1930	1931	1932	1933	1934	1935	1936
	Number of strikes ending in year									
Total	666	620	924	651	796	852	1,672	1,817	2,003	2,156
1	405	405	636	454	560	603	1,168	1,262	1,418	1,561
2 to 5	74	93	118	88	117	105	217	245	296	287
6 to 10	18	32	53	25	16	32	65	72	57	85
11 and over	79	90	117	84	93	96	201	225	217	203
Not reported	90	----------	----------	----------	10	16	21	13	15	20
	Number of workers involved in strikes ending in year									
Total	319,442	322,866	286,163	181,901	345,669	324,960	1,143,910	1,480,343	1,101,902	709,748
1	48,203	83,372	112,369	56,367	70,247	68,121	241,736	302,043	235,644	328,511
2 to 5	15,715	22,474	36,440	31,769	63,534	25,221	115,756	152,344	108,588	98,730
6 to 10	4,207	38,110	38,928	2,470	15,480	13,236	41,353	54,331	28,394	42,232
11 and over	230,510	178,910	98,426	91,295	189,078	212,779	735,260	969,530	725,314	234,157
Not reported	20,807	----------	----------	----------	7,330	5,603	9,805	2,095	3,962	6,118
	Number of man-days idle as a result of the strikes ending in year									
Total	25,689,915	13,065,634	5,304,638	3,107,948	7,212,127	10,521,437	16,563,940	19,491,844	14,918,234	11,432,536
1	718,590	1,091,104	1,956,824	952,181	1,023,806	1,238,755	2,571,290	4,562,370	3,926,509	5,046,924
2 to 5	155,402	330,409	578,692	792,353	1,396,993	420,105	1,827,057	2,591,841	2,278,791	1,713,470
6 to 10	75,474	326,197	313,685	64,593	263,010	213,204	730,050	911,916	596,706	1,117,364
11 and over	24,298,278	11,317,924	2,455,437	1,298,821	4,462,308	8,570,566	11,143,384	11,401,568	8,079,506	3,444,678
Not reported	442,171	----------	----------	----------	66,010	78,807	292,159	24,149	36,722	110,100

workers were involved in these strikes, they caused 68 percent of the total man-days idle. This would indicate that the extensive strikes on the average were more prolonged than those involving only a few establishments. There was a good deal of variation from year to year in the proportion of total workers and man-days idle in strikes confined to one or many establishments. In 1927 and 1928, largely due to the coal strikes mentioned previously, 95 and 87 percent of the total man-days of idleness were in strikes occurring in more than 10 establishments. In 1932 a few large strikes in textiles, clothing, mining, and several building trades in New York City accounted largely for the fact that 65 percent of the total workers and 81 percent of the man-days idle during that year were in connection with strikes involving more than 10 establishments. On the other hand, in 1936 only 33 percent of the total workers and 30 percent of the man-days idle were in connection with strikes extending into more than 10 establishments.

Sex of Workers

In 60 percent of the strikes occurring during 1927–36, men alone were involved. In 36 percent of the strikes both men and women were involved. (See table 24.) About 73 percent of the total number of persons involved in strikes during this period were men and 17 percent were women. For 10 percent of the workers the sex was not reported. (See table 25.)

TABLE 24.—*Number of strikes ending 1927–36, by sex of workers involved*

Year	Total	Number of strikes involving—			
		Males only	Females only	Males and females	Sex not reported
1927	666	525	11	130	
1928	620	435	11	174	
1929	924	604	23	297	
1930	651	473	14	164	
1931	796	542	12	237	5
1932	852	575	12	259	6
1933	1,672	775	35	811	51
1934	1,817	1,041	33	689	54
1935	2,003	1,126	55	801	21
1936	2,156	1,254	82	799	21
Total for 10-year period	12,157	7,350	288	4,361	158
Percentage for 10-year period	100.0	60.4	2.4	35.9	1.3

According to the 1930 census, 22 percent of those gainfully employed were women. The lesser proportion of women involved in strikes is probably due to the nature of the occupations in which large numbers of them are engaged. Thus, women predominate in domestic service and public-school teaching. Strikes are rare in these occupations, not necessarily because the employees are women, but because of the nature of the occupation. On the other hand, building construction, coal mining, steel, logging, and water, steam, and motor transportation are essentially male occupations and the type of work in which strikes are likely to occur.

TABLE 25.—*Number of persons involved in strikes ending in 1927–36, by sex*

Year	Total	Males	Females	Sex not reported
1927	319, 442	310, 460	8, 982	
1928	322, 866	255, 289	21, 420	46, 157
1929	286, 163	216, 240	30, 671	39, 252
1930	181, 901	138, 493	36, 058	7, 350
1931	345, 669	268, 635	58, 846	18, 188
1932	324, 960	243, 759	45, 322	35, 879
1933	1, 143, 910	748, 620	284, 553	110, 737
1934	1, 480, 343	920, 200	327, 884	232, 259
1935	1, 101, 902	903, 814	129, 912	68, 176
1936	709, 748	538, 736	105, 101	65, 911
Total for 10-year period	6, 216, 904	4, 544, 246	1, 048, 749	623, 909
Percentage for 10-year period	100. 0	73. 1	16. 9	10. 0

Duration of Strikes [8]

On the average, the 12,157 strikes occurring from 1927 to 1936 lasted 22 days. Chiefly due to the prolonged strikes in the bituminous-coal industry, the average duration in 1927 and 1928 was unusually large. In 1931 and 1933 the greater proportions of strikes lasting less than 1 week and fewer number lasting longer than 3 months caused the average duration of all strikes for these years to be less than the 10-year average. The average duration of strikes in each of the 10 years, in terms of calendar days, was as follows:

Year	*Average duration*	*Year*	*Average duration*
1927	26. 5	1932	19. 6
1928	27. 6	1933	16. 9
1929	22. 6	1934	19. 5
1930	22. 3	1935	23. 8
1931	18. 8	1936	23. 3

Aside from the year 1927 when only 27 percent of the strikes were terminated within a week, and the years 1931 and 1933 referred to above, the proportion of short (less than 1 week) strikes did not greatly vary throughout the period. The low proportion of short strikes in 1927 was offset by a greater than usual number of strikes lasting one-half month to 3 months—45.5 percent of the total. The largest proportion of prolonged strikes was in 1928, when over 8 percent continued for 3 months or more. As mentioned above, the lowest proportion of prolonged strikes occurred in 1931 (2.1 percent) and 1933 (1.4 percent).

[8] For information on duration of strikes in relation to results, see table 31.

TABLE **26.**—*Duration of strikes ending 1927–36*

Year	Total	Strikes with duration of—						Total	Strikes with duration of—					
		Less than 1 week	1 week and less than ½ month	½ month and less than 1 month	1 and less than 2 months	2 and less than 3 months	3 months or over		Less than 1 week	1 week and less than ½ month	½ month and less than 1 month	1 and less than 2 months	2 and less than 3 months	3 months or over
	Number of strikes							Percentage of strikes						
1927	666	181	152	138	118	47	30	100.0	27.2	22.8	20.7	17.7	7.1	4.5
1928	620	235	131	98	75	30	51	100.0	38.0	21.1	15.8	12.1	4.8	8.2
1929	924	360	218	143	127	33	43	100.0	38.9	23.6	15.5	13.7	3.6	4.7
1930	651	238	157	111	80	41	24	100.0	36.5	24.1	17.1	12.3	6.3	3.7
1931	796	319	169	136	116	39	17	100.0	40.1	21.2	17.1	14.6	4.9	2.1
1932	852	334	165	149	146	35	23	100.0	39.2	19.4	17.5	17.1	4.1	2.7
1933	1,672	700	362	307	222	57	24	100.0	41.8	21.7	18.4	13.3	3.4	1.4
1934	1,817	703	360	337	288	88	41	100.0	38.7	19.8	18.5	15.9	4.8	2.3
1935	2,003	709	437	347	284	127	99	100.0	35.5	21.8	17.3	14.2	6.3	4.9
1936	2,156	753	512	382	291	106	112	100.0	35.0	23.7	17.7	13.5	4.9	5.2
	Number of workers involved							Percentage of workers involved						
1927	319,442	47,504	31,891	29,872	34,007	8,497	167,671	100.0	14.9	10.0	9.4	10.6	2.7	52.4
1928	322,866	84,243	46,570	89,797	13,421	6,976	81,859	100.0	26.1	14.4	27.7	4.2	2.2	25.4
1929	286,163	113,845	56,047	48,069	37,027	19,948	11,227	100.0	39.8	19.6	16.8	12.9	7.0	3.9
1930	181,901	43,778	75,717	30,320	15,819	6,279	9,988	100.0	24.1	41.5	16.7	8.7	3.5	5.5
1931	345,669	51,873	77,905	94,710	61,189	38,640	21,352	100.0	15.0	22.5	27.4	17.7	11.2	6.2
1932	324,960	55,166	67,894	75,963	64,656	6,816	54,465	100.0	17.0	20.9	23.3	19.9	2.1	16.8
1933	1,143,910	326,756	241,502	265,792	227,063	64,369	18,428	100.0	28.7	21.1	23.2	19.8	5.6	1.6
1934	1,480,343	414,406	227,957	565,863	208,891	45,642	17,584	100.0	28.0	15.4	38.2	14.1	3.1	1.2
1935	1,101,902	568,581	190,312	103,232	111,913	44,213	83,651	100.0	51.5	17.3	9.4	10.2	4.0	7.6
1936	709,748	224,601	142,788	157,068	86,252	60,173	38,866	100.0	31.6	20.1	22.1	12.2	8.5	5.5

	Number of man-days idle							Percentage of man-days idle						
1927	25, 689, 915	142, 911	260, 759	514, 110	1, 182, 838	550, 096	23, 039, 201	100.0	.6	1.0	2.0	4.6	2.1	89.7
1928	13, 065. 634	246, 203	365, 247	1, 126, 223	365, 148	427, 978	10, 534, 835	100.0	1.9	2.8	8.6	2.8	3.3	80.6
1929	5, 304, 638	297, 279	509, 254	808, 858	1, 253, 350	1, 226, 268	1, 209, 629	100.0	5.6	9.6	15.2	23.7	23.1	22.8
1930	3, 107, 948	146, 331	826, 062	441, 148	542, 487	369, 938	781, 982	100.0	4.7	26.5	14.2	17.5	11.9	25.2
1931	7, 212, 127	140, 648	649, 118	1, 317, 612	1, 651, 861	1, 768, 744	1, 684, 144	100.0	2.0	9.0	18.3	22.9	24.4	23.4
1932	10, 521, 437	140, 879	674, 556	1, 051, 992	2, 123, 744	358, 019	6, 172, 247	100.0	1.3	6.4	10.0	20.3	3.4	58.6
1933	16, 563, 940	1, 071, 264	1, 844, 786	3, 531, 278	5, 709, 938	2, 964, 047	1, 442, 627	100.0	6.5	11.1	21.3	34.5	17.9	8.7
1934	19, 491, 844	1, 151, 515	1, 610, 768	6, 916, 711	6, 060, 913	2, 236, 851	1, 515, 086	100.0	5.9	8.3	35.4	31.1	11.5	7.8
1935	14, 918, 234	2, 320, 904	1, 303, 773	1, 471, 969	3, 499, 122	1, 986, 375	4, 336, 091	100.0	15.6	8.7	9.9	23.5	13.3	29.0
1936	11, 432, 536	545, 159	928, 299	2, 161, 736	2, 598, 424	1, 917, 471	3, 281, 447	100.0	4.8	8.1	18.9	22.7	16.8	28.7

Over 31 percent of the workers involved in all strikes during the 10-year period were in strikes lasting less than 1 week. Over 8 percent of the workers were involved in the 4 percent of the strikes lasting 3 months or longer. The larger proportion of workers was principally due to prolonged coal strikes in 1927, 1928, and 1932. In 4 of the 10 years the greatest percentage of workers were involved in strikes lasting less than 1 week. The extensive but short-lived coal strike in 1935 brought the proportion of workers involved in strikes of less than 1 week to as high as 51.5 percent, and the proportion of man-days idle to 15.6 percent.

Throughout the period less than 5 percent of the total man-days idle were during strikes lasting less than 1 week while 42 percent were during the strikes which lasted 3 months or longer. Again, the widespread and prolonged coal strikes were the major influences in causing the percentages of man-days idle in strikes of 3 months or longer duration to be as high as they were in 1927, 1928, and 1932. Although the number of large strikes in 1933 and 1934 was comparatively great (see table 22), most of them were brief. This accounts for the small percentage of man-days idle in strikes lasting 3 months or longer during these years.

Labor Organizations

The largest proportion of strikes taking place from 1927 to 1936 were under the auspices of unions affiliated with the American Federation of Labor.[9] These strikes included about three-fourths of the total number of workers involved in strikes. Only five strikes, involving 1,458 workers, were called by railroad brotherhoods during the entire 10 years.

A relatively large number of strikes were called by independent unions during the years 1929–33.[10] Some of these independent unions later affiliated with the A. F. of L. as, for example, the Amalgamated Clothing Workers, which so affiliated during the latter part of 1933. Others like the National Textile Workers, the Needle Trades Workers Industrial Union, and the National Miners Union dissolved as separate organizations and merged with A. F. of L. affiliates.

Independent unions were connected with a smaller proportion of the total strikes during 1934–36. About 15 percent of the total number of strikes involving independent unions during these 3 years occurred on work-relief and W. P. A. projects.

The comparatively large number of strikes during 1929–33 in which no union was involved [10] is partially accounted for by the fact that many of these workers had once belonged to trade-unions but the locals had disintegrated during the depression. The workers, however, were

9 See appendix II for methods used in classifying strikes by labor organizations involved.

10 There may have been independent unions connected with some of those classified under "no organization." It is difficult to learn all the particulars about such strikes.

accustomed to collective action and the strike weapon. An evidence of this is that a large number of these strikes occurred in the industries and areas which at a previous time had been unionized, e. g., coal mines and shoe factories. Nearly one-fourth of the "no organization" strikes during the years 1934–36 were on work-relief and W. P. A. projects.

In September 1936 the executive council of the American Federation of Labor suspended 10 of its international unions which were associated with the Committee for Industrial Organization. These, together with independent unions which were never affiliated with the A. F. of L. before they joined the C. I. O., participated in 133 strikes involving 105,814 workers during the months from September through December 1936.

TABLE 27.—*Labor organizations involved in strikes ending 1927–36*

Types of labor organization involved	1927	1928	1929	1930	1931	1932	1933	1934	1935	1936
	Number of strikes ending in year									
Total	666	620	924	651	796	852	1, 672	1, 817	2, 003	2, 156
American Federation of Labor	474	424	574	432	473	486	806	1, 379	1, 551	[2] 1, 780
Railroad brotherhoods		1						1	1	2
Nonaffiliated unions	56	57	163	61	102	136	343	231	258	161
Two rival unions	2	3	5	1	6	6	14	14	11	2
Company unions					1		4	9	15	10
Organization involved but type not reported	38	52	37	59	61	24	31	31	2	7
No organization	61	61	145	92	136	118	317	116	160	183
Not reported as to whether or not any organization was involved	35	22		6	17	82	157	36	5	11
	Percentage of total strikes ending in year									
Total	100. 0	100. 0	100. 0	100. 0	100. 0	100. 0	100. 0	100. 0	100. 0	100. 0
American Federation of Labor	71. 1	68. 4	62. 2	66. 3	59. 4	57. 0	48. 2	75. 9	77. 5	[2] 82. 5
Railroad brotherhoods		. 2						(1)	(1)	. 1
Nonaffiliated unions	8. 4	9. 2	17. 6	9. 4	12. 8	16. 0	20. 5	12. 7	13. 0	7. 5
Two rival unions	. 3	. 5	. 5	. 2	. 8	. 7	. 8	. 8	. 5	. 1
Company unions					. 1		. 2	. 5	. 7	. 5
Organization involved but type not reported	5. 7	8. 4	4. 0	9. 1	7. 7	2. 8	1. 9	1. 7	. 1	. 3
No organization	9. 2	9. 8	15. 7	14. 1	17. 1	13. 9	19. 0	6. 4	8. 0	8. 5
Not reported as to whether or not any organization was involved	5. 3	3. 5		. 9	2. 1	9. 6	9. 4	2. 0	. 2	. 5
	Number of workers involved in strikes ending in year									
Total	319, 442	322, 866	286, 163	181, 901	345, 669	324, 960	1, 143, 910	1, 480, 343	1, 101, 902	709, 748
American Federation of Labor	280, 628	197, 563	191, 409	138, 241	212, 375	238, 038	684, 247	1, 220, 894	972, 171	[2] 590, 419
Railroad brotherhoods		400						470	28	560
Nonaffiliated unions	16, 405	41, 375	48, 369	18, 126	101, 301	42, 499	314, 246	152, 264	86, 271	79, 221
Two rival unions	45	32, 345	280	250	264	383	25, 222	67, 463	8, 026	4, 040
Company unions					229		1, 751	2, 905	2, 440	1, 743
Organization involved but type not reported	6, 659	37 595	8, 651	9, 698	6, 267	4, 860	5, 252	4, 969	64	360
No organization	9 152	9, 237	37, 454	15, 403	23, 436	26, 377	78, 857	26, 762	32, 369	32, 941
Not reported as to whether or not any organization was involved	6, 553	4, 351		183	1, 797	12, 803	34, 335	4, 616	533	464

	Percentage of total workers involved in strikes ending in year									
Total	100.0	100.0	100.0	100.0	100.0	100.0	100.0	100.0	100.0	100.0
American Federation of Labor	87.8	61.3	66.9	76.0	61.4	73.3	59.7	82.5	88.3	[2] 83.1
Railroad brotherhoods		.1						(1)	(1)	.1
Nonaffiliated unions	5.1	12.8	16.9	10.0	29.3	13.1	27.5	10.3	7.9	11.2
Two rival unions	(1)	10.0	.1	.1	.1	.1	2.2	4.6	.7	.6
Company unions					.1		.2	.2	.2	.2
Organization involved but type not reported	2.1	11.6	3.0	5.3	1.8	1.5	.5	.3	(1)	.1
No organization	2.9	2.9	13.1	8.5	6.8	8.1	6.9	1.8	2.9	4.6
Not reported as to whether or not any organization was involved	2.1	1.3		.1	.5	3.9	3.0	.3	(1)	.1
	Number of man-days idle as a result of strikes ending in year									
Total	25,689,915	13,065,634	5,304,638	3,107,948	7,212,127	10,521,437	16,563,940	19,491,844	14,918,234	11,432,536
American Federation of Labor	25,137,490	7,888,325	3,195,808	2,496,391	4,967,181	9,469,034	10,580,767	16,635,880	12,765,908	[2] 10,059,390
Railroad brotherhoods		400						1,880	56	22,180
Nonaffiliated unions	198,143	880,621	1,432,343	281,883	1,893,170	554,561	4,470,333	1,868,279	1,658,942	1,113,054
Two rival unions	360	245,472	4,865	1,500	3,065	2,653	702,121	678,064	202,260	13,480
Company unions					687		25,891	13,135	18,403	17,873
Organization involved but type not reported	140,530	3,850,031	196,084	166,776	69,725	161,491	28,295	91,952	695	3,141
No organization	112,787	159,259	475,538	156,365	256,155	199,332	497,656	131,500	269,610	194,819
Not reported as to whether or not any organization was involved	100,605	41,526		5,033	22,144	134,366	258,877	71,154	2,360	8,599
	Percentage of total man-days idle as a result of strikes ending in year									
Total	100.0	100.0	100.0	100.0	100.0	100.0	100.0	100.0	100.0	100.0
American Federation of Labor	97.9	60.4	60.2	80.3	68.9	90.0	63.8	85.2	85.6	[2] 88.0
Railroad brotherhoods		(1)						(1)	(1)	.2
Nonaffiliated unions	.8	6.7	27.0	9.1	26.2	5.3	27.0	9.6	11.1	9.7
Two rival unions	(1)	1.9	.1	(1)	(1)	(1)	4.2	3.5	1.4	.1
Company unions					(1)		.2	.1	.1	.2
Organization involved but type not reported	.5	29.5	3.7	5.4	1.0	1.5	.2	.5	(1)	(1)
No organization	.4	1.2	9.0	5.0	3.6	1.9	3.0	.7	1.8	1.7
Not reported as to whether or not any organization was involved	.4	.3		.2	.3	1.3	1.6	.4	(1)	.1

[1] Less than 1/10 of 1 percent.
[2] Includes strikes in which were involved the 10 international unions suspended by the A. F. of L. in September 1936. See text above.

Major Issues

In table 28 strikes are assigned to 18 classifications according to their major issues or causes. These classifications are divided into three groups: (1) Wages and hours, (2) union organization, (3) miscellaneous. In actual strike situations the major issues are varied and complex, with overlapping between these groups. Thus, in many strikes where the question of union recognition seems to be the major issue, questions of wages and hours are also important. Wages and hours demands are frequently accompanied by questions of seniority, working rules, and other working conditions.[11]

In the 10-year period 1927–36, 44 percent of the strikes were concerned chiefly with questions of wages and hours, 40 percent with union-organization matters, and 16 percent with other issues, such as jurisdiction, work surroundings, objection to certain foremen or working rules, etc. Hours, as a single issue, was the major cause of comparatively few strikes throughout the period although hours combined with wages were factors in a number of the disputes.

About these same proportions pertain to the total number of workers involved in strikes: 44 percent were connected with strikes caused chiefly over questions of wages and hours, 38 percent over union-organization matters, and 18 percent over other questions. About 56 percent of the man-days idle because of strikes between 1927 and 1936 were due chiefly to wages and hours demands, 36 percent to questions of union organization, and 8 percent to other causes.

There was considerable variation from year to year in the proportion of strikes due to various causes. Demands for wage increases was the greatest single cause of strikes in 1927, this being the major issue in 22 percent of the strikes. In that year strikes in protest against wage decreases involved 54 percent of all the workers involved in strikes. Most of these workers were in the bituminous-coal strike. During the next year 18 percent of the strikes were for wage increases, while 12 percent were called in protest against wage decreases. Wage reductions brought on an increasingly larger proportion of strikes, until in 1932 half of all the strikes were due to this reason.

In 1933, with the beginning of business recovery, a reverse trend set in, about 42 percent of the strikes being for wage increases and hour decreases, with about 13 percent against wage decreases. During the next year, 32 percent of the strikes were for wage increases and hour decreases and only 6 percent were in protest against wage decreases. About this same proportion continued until the first month after the invalidation of the National Industrial Recovery Act[12] when, for the first time since 1932, there were almost twice as

[11] See appendix II, p. 166, for discussion of problems pertaining to classification of strikes by major issues involved.

[12] *Schechter* v. *United States*, 295 U. S. 495, May 27, 1935.

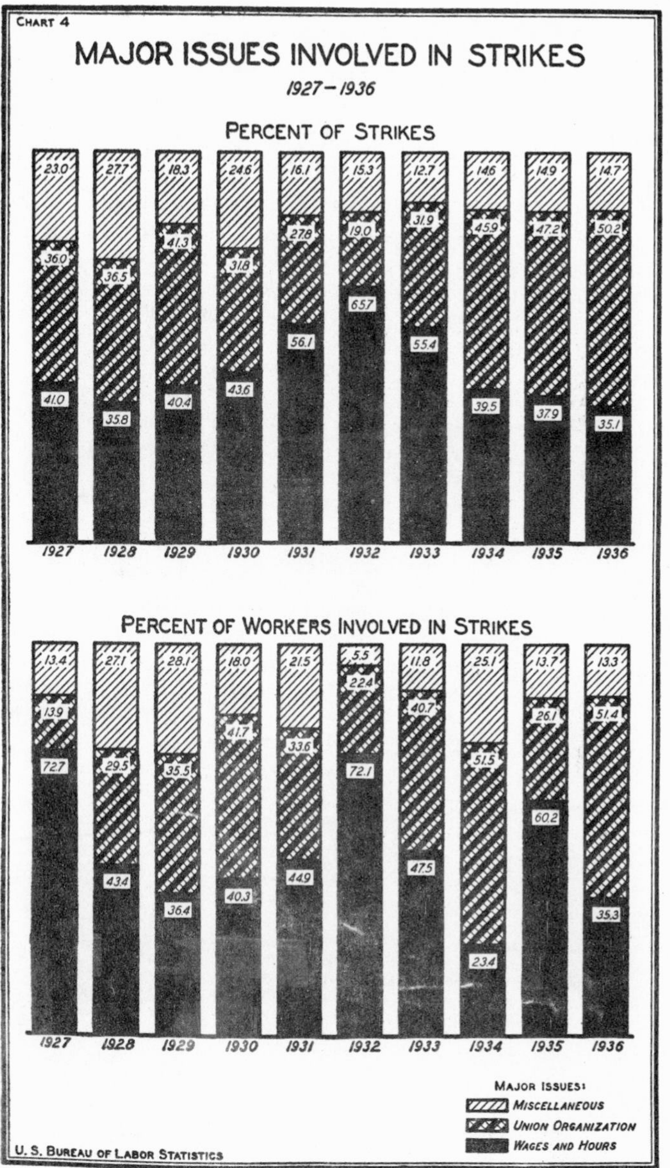
CHART 4
MAJOR ISSUES INVOLVED IN STRIKES
1927–1936
PERCENT OF STRIKES
23.0
36.0
41.0
27.7
36.5
35.8
18.3
41.3
40.4
24.6
31.8
43.6
16.1
27.8
56.1
15.3
19.0
65.7
12.7
31.9
55.4
14.6
45.9
39.5
14.9
47.2
37.9
14.7
50.2
35.1
1927
1928
1929
1930
1931
1932
1933
1934
1935
1936
PERCENT OF WORKERS INVOLVED IN STRIKES
13.4
13.9
72.7
27.1
29.5
43.4
28.1
35.5
36.4
18.0
41.7
40.3
21.5
33.6
44.9
5.5
22.4
72.1
11.8
40.7
47.5
25.1
51.5
23.4
13.7
26.1
60.2
13.3
51.4
35.3
1927
1928
1929
1930
1931
1932
1933
1934
1935
1936
MAJOR ISSUES:
MISCELLANEOUS
UNION ORGANIZATION
WAGES AND HOURS
U. S. BUREAU OF LABOR STATISTICS

13894°—38——5

many strikes in protest against wage decreases as for wage increases. While such protest strikes slightly declined during succeeding months, the proportion for the year (1935) was comparatively high—about 60 percent as many as for wage increases and hour decreases. In 1936 about 9 percent of the strikes were in protest against wage decreases and hour increases and 26 percent for wage increases and hour decreases.[13]

During 1927 and 1928 about one-third of the total number of strikes were due to demands for union recognition, closed shop, and protest against union discrimination and violation of union agreements. In 1929 over 40 percent were chiefly over these issues. The proportion declined during the next 3 years. In 1932 less than one-fifth of all the strikes were due to union-organization matters. Even in the midst of the depression, however, union-organization activity was not entirely absent. In 1930, for instance, almost 42 percent of the workers involved in strikes were in strikes in which union organization matters were the dominant issues. A large proportion of these were in the textile industry.

After the beginning of recovery, the proportion of strikes over union-organization questions increased. In 1935 almost half of the strikes were due to union-organization matters. The comparatively small proportion of workers (26 percent) involved in these strikes is due to the influence of the general bituminous-coal strike for a wage increase. Excluding this mining strike, more workers in 1935 were involved in strikes due to union-organization questions than to wages and hours. In 1936 over half of the total strikes were due to questions of union organization. These strikes involved over half of the workers engaged in industrial disputes during that year.

During the 10-year period less than 3 percent of the strikes, including about an equal proportion of all workers involved in strikes, were due to internal disputes among unions—that is, over matters of jurisdiction or quarrels between rival unions or factions. About 1½ percent of all strikes, including about 5 percent of all workers involved, were sympathetic strikes.

[13] During the latter part of 1935 and in 1936 when strikes in protest against wage decreases and hour increases were declining, strikes for union organization were increasing (see following paragraphs). Any causal relationship between the two is difficult to trace clearly. When wages and hours were secondary factors in organization strikes, many were for wage increases and hour decreases. Since any wage and hour changes which took place between the termination of N. R. A. and the time of the strike are not known, it is impossible to determine whether these strikes were for restoration of wage and hour scales in force during the N. R. A. or for improvements over N. R. A. conditions.

Major issues	1927	1928	1929	1930	1931	1932	1933	1934	1935	1936
	Number of strikes ending in year									
All issues	**666**	**620**	**924**	**651**	**796**	**852**	**1,672**	**1,817**	**2,003**	**2,156**
Wages and hours	**273**	**222**	**373**	**284**	**447**	**560**	**926**	**717**	**760**	**756**
Wage increase	147	113	130	70	90	100	543	487	368	413
Wage decrease	61	75	129	165	329	421	220	112	178	151
Wage increase, hour decrease	47	22	93	39	10	24	152	100	96	146
Wage decrease, hour increase	1	2	----	3	9	10	1	6	73	19
Hour increase	1	3	4	1	4	----	1	2	33	15
Hour decrease	16	7	17	6	5	5	9	10	12	12
Union organization	**240**	**226**	**382**	**207**	**221**	**162**	**533**	**835**	**945**	**1,083**
Recognition	74	86	102	48	66	34	163	226	179	173
Recognition and wages	23	28	62	21	35	29	145	224	194	272
Recognition and hours	5	1	1	3	3	----	1	1	7	7
Recognition, wages, and hours	10	19	32	12	15	21	81	101	168	357
Closed shop	43	63	91	59	52	45	41	109	151	130
Discrimination	45	20	66	44	38	28	95	154	232	120
Other	40	9	28	20	12	5	7	20	14	24
Miscellaneous	**153**	**172**	**169**	**160**	**128**	**130**	**213**	**265**	**298**	**317**
Sympathy	18	7	16	14	6	3	9	45	42	25
Rival unions or factions	2	3	5	1	7	6	15	15	12	2
Jurisdiction	16	21	22	29	22	16	16	22	25	37
Other	117	141	126	116	91	97	150	169	218	251
Not reported	----	----	----	----	2	8	23	14	1	2

TABLE 28.—*Major issues involved in strikes ending 1927–36*—Continued

Major issues	1927	1928	1929	1930	1931	1932	1933	1934	1935	1936
	Percentage of total strikes ending in year									
All issues	100.0	100.0	100.0	100.0	100.0	100.0	100.0	100.0	100.0	100.0
Wages and hours	**41.0**	**35.8**	**40.4**	**43.6**	**56.1**	**65.7**	55.4	**39.5**	**37.9**	**35.1**
Wage increase	22.0	18.3	14.1	10.8	11.3	11.7	32.4	26.8	18.4	19.1
Wage decrease	9.1	12.1	14.0	25.2	41.3	49.4	13.2	6.2	8.9	7.0
Wage increase, hour decrease	7.1	3.5	10.1	6.0	1.3	2.8	9.1	5.5	4.8	6.8
Wage decrease, hour increase	.2	.3	—	.5	1.1	1.2	.1	.3	3.6	.9
Hour increase	.2	.5	.4	.2	.5	—	.1	.1	1.6	.7
Hour decrease	2.4	1.1	1.8	.9	.6	.6	.5	.6	.6	.6
Organization	**36.0**	**36.5**	**41.3**	**31.8**	**27.8**	**19.0**	**31.9**	**45.9**	**47.2**	**50.2**
Recognition	11.0	13.8	11.1	7.4	8.3	4.0	9.7	12.3	8.9	8.0
Recognition and wages	3.5	4.5	6.7	3.2	4.4	3.4	8.7	12.3	9.7	12.6
Recognition and hours	.8	.2	.1	.5	.4	—	.1	.1	.3	.3
Recognition, wages, and hours	1.5	3.1	3.5	1.8	1.9	2.5	4.8	5.6	8.4	16.6
Closed shop	6.5	10.2	9.8	9.0	6.5	5.2	2.5	6.0	7.5	6.0
Discrimination	6.7	3.2	7.1	6.8	4.8	3.3	5.7	8.5	11.7	5.6
Other	6.0	1.5	3.0	3.1	1.5	.6	.4	1.1	.7	1.1
Miscellaneous	**23.0**	27.7	**18.3**	**24.6**	**16.1**	**15.3**	15.7	**14.6**	**14.9**	**14.7**
Sympathy	2.7	1.1	1.7	2.2	.8	.4	.5	2.5	2.1	1.2
Rival unions or factions	.3	.5	.5	.2	.9	.7	.9	.8	.6	.1
Jurisdiction	2.4	3.4	2.4	4.5	2.8	1.9	1.0	1.2	1.2	1.7
Other	17.6	22.7	13.7	17.7	11.3	11.4	8.9	9.3	11.0	11.6
Not reported	—	—	—	—	.3	.9	1.4	.8	(1)	.1
	Number of workers involved in strikes ending in year									
All issues	319,442	322,866	286,163	181,901	345,669	324,960	1,143,910	1,480,343	1,101,902	709,748
Wages and hours	**232,217**	**139,913**	**104,059**	**73,223**	**155,308**	**234,158**	**544,084**	**346,174**	**662,539**	**250,672**
Wage increase	39,159	21,310	30,743	14,886	31,791	19,064	220,162	207,868	561,423	142,663
Wage decrease	172,442	111,619	26,160	38,091	110,141	189,272	61,961	46,529	46,585	45,031
Wage increase, hour decrease	17,878	4,993	35,163	17,091	8,237	23,116	259,144	79,796	31,303	37,178
Wage decrease, hour increase	26	445	—	364	2,378	2,611	70	10,578	16,309	2,665
Hour increase	8	142	225	103	1,930	—	24	760	6,068	17,676
Hour decrease	2,704	1,404	11,768	2,688	831	95	2,723	643	851	5,459

Organization	**44,451**	**95,320**	**101,724**	**75,949**	**115,997**	**72,940**	**465,272**	**762,367**	**287,876**	**365,019**
Recognition	6,785	51,836	19,901	10,133	40,554	2,820	168,784	111,446	34,271	47,347
Recognition and wages	6,827	14,149	16,549	4,575	47,022	32,137	162,717	458,329	68,736	103,521
Recognition and hours	975	250	36	2,642	742		2,000	125	557	325
Recognition, wages, and hours	4,818	14,807	37,360	40,712	12,453	32,708	102,645	131,463	94,879	120,820
Closed shop	7,417	6,282	8,009	7,898	5,784	2,047	6,090	16,586	46,213	42,543
Discrimination	8,051	7,197	16,608	9,309	7,695	2,055	21,118	39,304	34,883	26,019
Other	9,578	799	3,261	680	1,747	1,173	1,918	5,114	8,337	24,444
Miscellaneous	**42,774**	**87,633**	**80,380**	**32,729**	**74,364**	**17,862**	**134,554**	**371,802**	**151,487**	**94,057**
Sympathy	12,634	255	14,268	1,521	1,474	366	1,892	207,897	61,066	4,976
Rival unions or factions	45	32,345	280	250	297	383	65,222	67,665	8,105	4,040
Jurisdiction	7,350	1,645	2,431	1,927	1,689	1,122	1,808	1,935	3,535	4,236
Other	22,745	53,388	63,401	29,031	70,769	15,090	62,130	91,692	78,762	80,647
Not reported					135	901	3,502	2,613	19	158
	Percentage of total workers involved in strikes ending in year									
All issues	100.0	100.0	100.0	100.0	100.0	100.0	100.0	100.0	100.0	100.0
Wages and hours	**72.7**	**43.4**	**36.4**	**40.3**	**44.9**	**72.1**	**47.5**	**23.4**	**60.2**	**35.3**
Wage increase	12.3	6.7	10.7	8.2	9.2	5.9	19.2	14.1	51.0	20.1
Wage decrease	54.0	34.7	9.1	20.9	31.8	58.3	5.4	3.1	4.2	6.3
Wage increase, hour decrease	5.6	1.5	12.4	9.4	2.4	7.1	22.7	5.4	2.3	5.2
Wage decrease, hour increase	(1)	.1		.2	.7	.8	(1)	.7	1.5	.4
Hour increase	(1)	(1)	.1	.1	.6		(1)	.1	.6	2.5
Hour decrease	.8	.4	4.1	1.5	.2	(1)	.2	(1)	.1	.8
Organization	**13.9**	**29.5**	**35.5**	**41.7**	**33.6**	**22.4**	**40.7**	**51.5**	**26.1**	**51.4**
Recognition	2.1	16.1	7.0	5.6	11.7	.9	14.8	7.5	3.1	6.7
Recognition and wages	2.1	4.4	5.8	2.5	13.7	9.9	14.2	31.0	6.2	14.6
Recognition and hours	.3	.1	(1)	1.5	.2		.2	(1)	.1	(1)
Recognition, wages, and hours	1.5	4.6	13.0	22.3	3.6	10.0	9.0	8.9	8.5	17.0
Closed shop	2.3	1.9	2.8	4.3	1.7	.6	.5	1.1	4.2	6.0
Discrimination	2.5	2.2	5.8	5.1	2.2	.6	1.8	2.7	3.2	3.7
Other	3.1	.2	1.1	.4	.5	.4	.2	.3	.8	3.4
Miscellaneous	**13.4**	**27.1**	**28.1**	**18.0**	**21.5**	**5.5**	**11.8**	**25.1**	**13.7**	**13.3**
Sympathy	4.0	.1	5.0	.8	.4	.1	.2	14.0	5.5	.7
Rival unions or factions	(1)	10.0	.1	.1	.1	.1	5.7	4.6	.7	.6
Jurisdiction	2.3	.5	.8	1.1	.5	.3	.2	.1	.3	.6
Other	7.1	16.5	22.2	16.0	20.5	4.7	5.4	6.2	7.2	11.4
Not reported					(1)	.3	.3	.2	(1)	(1)

[1] Less than 1/10 of 1 percent.

TABLE 28.—*Major issues involved in strikes ending 1927–36*—Continued

Major issues	1927	1928	1929	1930	1931	1932	1933	1934	1935	1936
	Number of man-days idle as a result of strikes ending in year									
All issues	**25, 689, 915**	**13, 065, 634**	**5, 304, 638**	**3, 107, 948**	**7, 212, 127**	**10, 521, 437**	**16, 563, 940**	**19, 491, 844**	**14, 918, 234**	**11, 432, 536**
Wages and hours	**24, 049, 622**	**10, 731, 568**	**2, 311, 270**	**1, 309, 636**	**3, 216, 684**	**8, 583, 088**	**6, 309, 415**	**4, 732, 677**	**6, 399, 526**	**3, 685, 852**
Wage increase	836, 312	491, 937	478, 987	218, 527	428, 081	344, 633	2, 581, 084	2, 481, 486	4, 920, 316	1, 820, 000
Wage decrease	22, 883, 857	10, 100, 370	359, 887	835, 821	2, 302, 083	8, 073, 272	1, 156, 214	464, 964	954, 468	879, 170
Wage increase, hour decrease	293, 408	113, 485	1, 122, 055	205, 565	410, 970	108, 089	2, 556, 010	1, 560, 525	273, 308	468, 704
Wage decrease, hour increase	26	10, 410		34, 706	29, 484	54, 759	770	213, 672	196, 391	54, 366
Hour increase	104	5, 780	725	4, 223	16, 035		312	2, 020	48, 297	384, 328
Hour decrease	35. 915	9, 586	349, 616	10, 794	30, 031	2, 335	15, 025	10, 010	6, 746	79, 284
Organization	**843, 535**	**1, 555, 889**	**1, 953, 952**	**1, 467, 228**	**3, 026, 865**	**1, 740, 190**	**8, 664, 221**	**12, 236, 680**	**7, 051, 122**	**6, 882, 037**
Recognition	138, 004	691, 583	385, 161	379, 198	1, 415, 715	38, 357	2, 745, 567	2, 085, 822	746, 253	829, 047
Recognition and wages	195, 001	124, 013	402, 692	228, 926	1, 055, 471	1, 150, 173	2, 558, 618	5, 830, 737	2, 391, 813	2, 273, 459
Recognition and hours	10, 240	14, 250	756	60, 443	10, 070		4, 000	10, 750	4, 122	7, 382
Recognition, wages, and hours	159, 939	411, 540	679, 824	574, 911	365, 823	451, 976	3, 000, 544	3, 538, 547	2, 496, 513	2, 310, 771
Closed shop	104, 913	257, 389	245, 099	126, 951	106, 897	40, 068	69, 602	252, 488	704, 558	667, 983
Discrimination	64, 560	40, 771	199, 182	88, 073	52, 788	35, 378	264, 716	466, 742	623, 241	618, 526
Other	170, 878	16, 343	41, 238	8, 726	20, 101	24, 238	21, 174	51, 594	84, 622	174, 869
Miscellaneous	**796, 758**	**778, 177**	**1, 039, 416**	**331, 084**	**968, 578**	**198, 159**	**1, 590, 304**	**2, 522, 487**	**1, 467, 586**	**864, 647**
Sympathy	339, 716	2, 040	148, 706	11, 686	11, 314	1, 446	7, 994	1, 097, 825	280, 914	29, 599
Rival unions or factions	360	245, 472	4, 865	1, 500	4, 121	2, 653	942, 121	678, 872	203, 603	13, 480
Jurisdiction	103, 798	38, 366	93, 713	22, 957	28, 026	14, 250	40, 509	34, 176	63, 025	62, 236
Other	352, 884	492, 299	792, 132	294, 941	923, 332	171, 081	574, 915	685, 026	919, 626	757, 372
Not reported					1, 785	8, 729	24, 765	26, 588	418	1, 960

	Percentage of total man-days idle as a result of strikes ending in year									
All issues	100.0	100.0	100.0	100.0	100.0	100.0	100.0	100.0	100 0	100.0
Wages and hours	**93.6**	**82.1**	**43.6**	**42.1**	**44.6**	**81.6**	**38.1**	**24.3**	**42.9**	**32.2**
Wage increase	3.3	3.8	9.0	7.0	5.9	3.3	15.6	12.7	33.1	15.8
Wage decrease	89.1	77.2	6.8	27.0	32.0	76.8	7.0	2.4	6.4	7.7
Wage increase, hour decrease	1.1	.9	21.2	6.6	5.7	1.0	15.4	8.0	1.8	4.1
Wage decrease, hour increase	(1)	.1	----	1.1	.4	.5	(1)	1.1	1.3	.5
Hour increase	(1)	(1)	(1)	.1	.2	----	(1)	(1)	.3	3.4
Hour decrease	.1	.1	6.6	.3	.4	(1)	.1	.1	(1)	.7
Organization	**3.3**	**11.9**	**36.8**	**47.2**	**42.0**	**16.5**	**52.3**	**62.8**	**47.3**	**60.2**
Recognition	.5	5.4	7.3	12.2	19.7	.4	16.6	10.7	5.0	7.3
Recognition and wages	.8	.9	7.6	7.4	14.6	10.9	15.4	29.8	16.0	19.9
Recognition and hours	(1)	.1	(1)	1.9	.1	----	(1)	.1	(1)	.1
Recognition, wages, and hours	.6	3.1	12.7	18.5	5.1	4.3	18.2	18.2	16.8	20.2
Closed shop	.4	2.0	4.6	4.1	1.5	.4	.4	1.3	4.7	5.8
Discrimination	.3	.3	3.8	2.8	.7	.3	1.6	2.4	4.2	5.4
Other	.7	.1	.8	.3	.3	.2	.1	.3	.6	1.5
Miscellaneous	**3.1**	**6.0**	**19.6**	**10.7**	**13.4**	**1.9**	**9.6**	**12.9**	**9.8**	**7.6**
Sympathy	1.3	(1)	2.8	.4	.2	(1)	(1)	5.6	1.9	.3
Rival unions or factions	(1)	1.9	.1	(1)	.1	(1)	5.8	3.5	1.4	.1
Jurisdiction	.4	.3	1.8	.7	.4	.1	.2	.2	.4	.5
Other	1.4	3.8	14.9	9.6	12.7	1.7	3.5	3.5	6.1	6.7
Not reported	----	----	----	----	(1)	.1	.1	.1	(1)	(1)

[1] Less than 1/10 of 1 percent.

Results of Strikes to Workers

Any classification of the results of strikes is necessarily a matter of judgment and can be considered only proximate. For this reason, strikes are not categorically classified as successful or unsuccessful but are measured in such relative terms as substantial gains to workers, partial gains or compromises, and little or no gains to workers.[14] Such terminology, however, is likely to be misleading in the case of defensive strikes, that is, strikes against wage decreases or hour increases. Even though such a strike is successful, it merely means a continuation of the status quo and not a betterment of employment conditions, as the term "substantial gains to workers" might imply. During some years, particularly in times of business depression, many of the strikes classified as resulting in substantial gains to workers were really only a successful staving off of less satisfactory conditions. This is revealed in table 30, where the results of strikes in protest against wage decreases and hour increases are shown.

Table 29 indicates the results of all strikes ending during the years 1927–36. During the 10-year period practically the same number of strikes resulted in substantial gains to workers as resulted in little or no gains. About 36 percent brought substantial gains to the workers, 24 percent were compromised, and 35 percent resulted in little or no gains. Results of a few were indeterminate or not reported. More workers were in successful strikes than in strikes bringing no gains. About 30 percent of the total number of workers involved won their strikes, 42 percent compromised, and 22 percent lost. By far the largest proportion of man-days of idleness was spent in strikes resulting in no gains to workers. Strikes which were won included 17 percent of the man-days idle during all strikes, strikes which were compromised included 36 percent of the man-days, and strikes which were lost included 43 percent.

The proportions of successful, compromised, and lost strikes differed from year to year. From 1927 through 1932 about one-fourth of the strikes were successful from the viewpoint of the workers. During 1933 and 1934 more than one-third and in 1935 and 1936 almost half of the strikes brought substantial gains to workers. During the years 1927 to 1932 from 40 to 52 percent of the strikes resulted in no gains to workers. This is in contrast to the next 4 years, when only 27 to 33 percent of the strikes resulted in no gains (see chart 5).

Because of the influence of the prolonged and large strikes [15] the percentages of workers and man-days idle in the three categories varied from the number of strikes. Thus the loss of the general coal strike in 1927 caused 66 percent of the total workers involved and 92 percent of the total man-days idle during strikes of that year to be classified under

[14] See Appendix II, p. 167, for explanation of interpretation of results of strikes.

[15] See appendix I, p. 161.

"Little or no gains." The failure of another prolonged coal strike in 1928 caused the percentage of man-days idle in the lost-strikes category to be relatively high. A dispute between unions in the anthracite fields in the same year caused the highest percentage of workers in any year to be listed under the fourth category of "Jurisdiction or rival unions."

Short but extensive strikes among cloak and suit workers in New York in 1929 and among dressmakers in 1930 resulting in compromises, account partially for the large proportion of workers and man-days idle involved in compromised strikes in 1929 and 1930. During 1931 there were several large strikes in textiles, clothing, and coal which resulted in compromise settlements. A 4-months' strike in the Illinois coal fields in 1932 caused the proportion of man-days idle in the lost-strike category to be as high as it was. In 1933 most of the large strikes resulted in successful and compromise settlements and this accounts for the comparatively low percentages of workers and man-days idle in the "Little or no gains" classification.

The general textile strike enhanced the percentage of compromised strikes in 1934, so far as workers and man-days idle were concerned. The brief but extensive coal strike in 1935 materially helped to raise the proportion of workers in successful strikes to 54 percent.

Since most of the strikes in 1936 involving as many as 10,000 workers resulted in favorable settlements and none were lost, there was greater parity in proportions of number of strikes, workers, and man-days idle in each of the categories. A greater percentage of the larger and longer-than-average strikes, however, resulted in compromise settlements, as is indicated by the fact that, while 24 percent of all strikes were compromised, these involved 36 percent of the workers and 37 percent of the man-days idle.[16]

[16] See table 31, p. 78, for an analysis of strikes in relation to their duration.

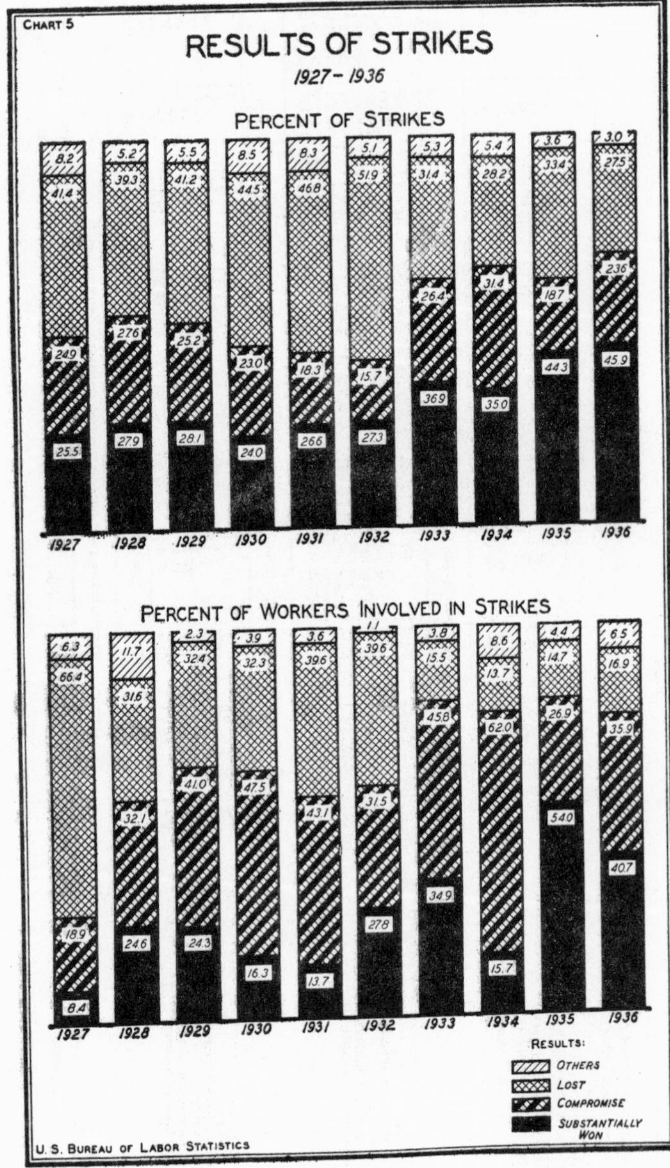
CHART 5
RESULTS OF STRIKES
1927 - 1936
PERCENT OF STRIKES
8.2
41.4
24.9
25.5
5.2
39.3
27.6
27.9
5.5
41.2
25.2
28.1
8.5
44.5
23.0
24.0
8.3
46.8
18.3
26.6
5.1
51.9
15.7
27.3
5.3
31.4
26.4
36.9
5.4
28.2
31.4
35.0
3.6
33.4
18.7
44.3
3.0
27.5
23.6
45.9
1927
1928
1929
1930
1931
1932
1933
1934
1935
1936
PERCENT OF WORKERS INVOLVED IN STRIKES
6.3
66.4
18.9
8.4
11.7
31.6
32.1
24.6
2.3
32.4
41.0
24.3
3.9
32.3
47.5
16.3
3.6
39.6
43.1
13.7
1.1
39.6
31.5
27.8
3.8
15.5
45.8
34.9
8.6
13.7
62.0
15.7
4.4
14.7
26.9
54.0
6.5
16.9
35.9
40.7
1927
1928
1929
1930
1931
1932
1933
1934
1935
1936
RESULTS:
OTHERS
LOST
COMPROMISE
SUBSTANTIALLY WON
U. S. BUREAU OF LABOR STATISTICS

TABLE 29.—*Results of strikes ending 1927–36*

Results	1927	1928	1929	1930	1931	1932	1933	1934	1935	1936
	Number of strikes ending in year									
Total	666	620	924	651	796	852	1,672	1,817	2,003	2,156
Substantial gains to workers	170	173	260	156	212	233	617	634	886	991
Partial gains or compromises	166	171	233	150	146	134	442	571	374	508
Little or no gains	276	244	380	290	372	442	525	512	669	592
Jurisdiction or rival unions	18	24	27	30	29	22	30	37	37	39
Indeterminate	15	6	21	24	35	4	11	17	24	22
Not reported	21	2	3	1	2	17	47	46	13	4
	Percentage of total strikes ending in year									
Total	100.0	100.0	100.0	100.0	100.0	100.0	100.0	100.0	100.0	100.0
Substantial gains to workers	25.5	27.9	28.1	24.0	26.6	27.3	36.9	35.0	44.3	45.9
Partial gains or compromises	24.9	27.6	25.2	23.0	18.3	15.7	26.4	31.4	18.7	23.6
Little or no gains	41.4	39.3	41.2	44.5	46.8	51.9	31.4	28.2	33.4	27.5
Jurisdiction or rival unions	2.7	3.9	2.9	4.6	3.6	2.6	1.8	2.0	1.8	1.8
Indeterminate	2.3	1.0	2.3	3.7	4.4	.5	.7	.9	1.2	1.0
Not reported	3.2	.3	.3	.2	.3	2.0	2.8	2.5	.6	.2
	Number of workers involved in strikes ending in year									
Total	319,442	322,866	286,163	181,901	345,669	324,960	1,143,910	1,480,343	1,101,902	709,748
Substantial gains to workers	26,710	79,278	69,597	29,585	47,287	90,273	399,534	232,484	596,253	288,952
Partial gains or compromises	60,530	103,555	117,191	86,361	149,168	102,495	523,757	918,915	296,885	254,751
Little or no gains	212,063	102,122	92,746	58,792	136,980	128,711	177,192	202,143	161,598	120,288
Jurisdiction or rival unions	7,395	33,990	2,711	2,177	1,986	1,505	27,030	69,600	11,640	8,276
Indeterminate	4,786	3,305	3,742	4,973	10,068	279	3,246	50,237	34,755	36,879
Not reported	7,958	616	176	13	180	1,697	13,151	6,964	771	602

TABLE 29.—*Results of strikes ending 1927–36*—Continued

Results	1927	1928	1929	1930	1931	1932	1933	1934	1935	1936
	Percentage of total workers involved in strikes ending in year									
Total	100.0	100.0	100.0	100.0	100.0	100.0	100.0	100.0	100.0	100.0
Substantial gains to workers	8.4	24.6	24.3	16.3	13.7	27.8	34.9	15.7	54.0	40.7
Partial gains or compromises	18.9	32.1	41.0	47.5	43.1	31.5	45.8	62.0	26.9	35.9
Little or no gains	66.4	31.6	32.4	32.3	39.6	39.6	15.5	13.7	14.7	16.9
Jurisdiction or rival unions	2.3	10.5	.9	1.2	.6	.5	2.4	4.7	1.1	1.2
Indeterminate	1.5	1.0	1.3	2.7	2.9	.1	.3	3.4	3.2	5.2
Not reported	2.5	.2	.1	(1)	.1	.5	1.1	.5	.1	.1
	Number of man-days idle as a result of strikes ending in year									
Total	25, 689, 915	13, 065, 634	5, 304, 638	3, 107, 948	7, 212, 127	10, 521, 437	16, 563, 940	19, 491, 844	14, 918, 234	11, 432, 536
Substantial gains to workers	404, 079	1, 189, 340	1, 135, 479	362, 982	650, 392	1, 108, 851	4, 636, 572	3, 358, 083	4, 515, 596	4, 136, 603
Partial gains or compromises	1, 174, 374	4, 871, 367	1, 742, 488	1, 220, 058	3, 030, 478	2, 530, 081	8, 798, 094	11, 936, 940	6, 883, 118	4, 244, 071
Little or no gains	23, 640, 923	6, 689, 039	2, 279, 884	1, 238, 038	3, 387, 325	6, 841, 306	2, 240, 939	2, 491, 281	3, 155, 827	2, 836, 771
Jurisdiction or rival unions	104, 158	283, 838	98, 578	24, 457	32, 147	16, 903	742, 630	713, 048	266, 628	75, 716
Indeterminate	131, 670	25, 306	45, 456	262, 062	107, 705	1, 189	82, 252	944, 420	84, 349	137, 059
Not reported	234, 711	6, 744	2, 753	351	4, 080	23, 107	63, 453	48, 072	12, 716	2, 316
	Percentage of total man-days idle as a result of strikes ending in year									
Total	100.0	100.0	100.0	100.0	100.0	100.0	100.0	100.0	100.0	100.0
Substantial gains to workers	1.6	9.1	21.4	11.7	9.0	10.5	28.0	17.2	30.3	36.2
Partial gains or compromises	4.6	37.3	32.8	39.3	42.0	24.0	53.1	61.3	46.0	37.1
Little or no gains	92.0	51.1	42.9	39.8	47.0	65.1	13.5	12.8	21.2	24.8
Jurisdiction or rival unions	.4	2.2	1.9	.8	.4	.2	4.5	3.7	1.8	.7
Indeterminate	.5	.2	.9	8.4	1.5	(1)	.5	4.8	.6	1.2
Not reported	.9	.1	.1	(1)	.1	.2	.4	.2	.1	(1)

1 Less than 1/10 of 1 percent.

Results in Relation to Cause

In the 10-year period 1927–36, about 35 percent of the wage and hour strikes brought substantial gains to the workers, 28 percent resulted in compromises, and 36 percent brought little or no gains. In strikes in which the major issues were questions of union organization, 41 percent resulted in gains to workers, 21 percent were compromised, and 36 percent resulted in no gains (see table 30).

There was variation from year to year in the proportionate results of strikes for various causes. Each year from 1927 through 1930 a greater proportion of the union organization than the wage and hour strikes were won and lost and fewer were compromised. In 1931 and 1932 a greater proportion of the wage and hour than the union organization strikes resulted in no gains to workers. In the latter year a considerably greater proportion of the union organization strikes were won and a smaller proportion compromised than wage and hour strikes. From 1933 through 1936 the proportions of wage and hour strikes which resulted in substantial gains, compromises, and losses were approximately the same as those of strikes over union organization matters, there being no greater than a 6-percent difference in any year.

TABLE **30**.—*Results of strikes ending 1927–36, in relation to major issues involved*

STRIKES

Major issues and years	Total strikes		Percentage of strikes resulting in—				
	Number	Percentage	Substantial gains to workers	Partial gains or compromises	Little or no gains to workers	Indeterminate	Not reported
ALL WAGES AND HOURS STRIKES							
1927	273	100.0	22.3	34.1	39.6	2.2	1.8
1928	222	100.0	26.6	40.5	32.4	5.1	-------
1929	373	100.0	21.7	37.0	39.9	1.1	.3
1930	284	100.0	21.8	28.2	48.2	1.8	-------
1931	447	100.0	26.8	17.0	52.6	3.4	.2
1932	560	100.0	24.3	18.0	56.6	.2	.9
1933	926	100.0	39.2	28.9	29.4	.3	2.2
1934	717	100.0	38.2	36.4	24.5	.1	.8
1935	760	100.0	45.7	19.7	33.8	-------	.8
1936	756	100.0	45.9	27.1	26.6	.4	-------
Wage increase:							
1927	147	100.0	22.4	36.1	35.4	3.4	2.7
1928	113	100.0	29.2	39.8	31.0	-------	-------
1929	130	100.0	18.5	41.5	39.2	.8	-------
1930	70	100.0	27.1	25.7	44.3	2.9	-------
1931	90	100.0	37.8	18.9	38.9	3.3	1.1
1932	100	100.0	52.0	12.0	35.0	-------	1.0
1933	543	100.0	39.8	28.2	28.7	.4	2.9
1934	487	100.0	35.3	38.4	25.5	-------	.8
1935	368	100.0	47.2	20.7	30.7	-------	1.4
1936	413	100.0	47.3	28.3	24.2	.2	-------
Wage decrease:							
1927	61	100.0	23.0	29.5	44.3	1.6	1.6
1928	75	100.0	22.7	42.6	34.7	-------	-------
1929	129	100.0	24.8	25.6	47.2	1.6	.8
1930	165	100.0	17.0	23.6	57.6	1.8	-------
1931	329	100.0	23.4	15.8	57.5	3.3	-------
1932	421	100.0	15.0	19.5	64.3	.2	1.0
1933	220	100.0	28.2	28.2	42.6	.5	.5
1934	112	100.0	40.2	26.8	31.2	.9	.9
1935	178	100.0	39.9	17.4	42.7	-------	-------
1936	151	100.0	32.5	25.2	41.6	.7	-------
Wage increase, hour decrease:							
1927	47	100.0	23.4	38.3	38.3	-------	-------
1928	22	100.0	22.7	41.0	31.8	4.5	-------
1929	93	100.0	20.4	48.4	30.1	1.1	-------

TABLE **30.**—*Results of strikes ending 1927–36, in relation to major issues involved*—Continued

STRIKES—Continued

Major issues and years	Total strikes		Percentage of strikes resulting in—				
	Number	Percentage	Substantial gains to workers	Partial gains or compromises	Little or no gains to workers	Indeterminate	Not reported
Wage increase, hour decrease—Con.							
1930	39	100.0	25.6	48.8	25.6		
1931	10	100.0	10.0	60.0	30.0		
1932	24	100.0	66.7	20.8	12.5		
1933	152	100.0	51.9	32.9	13.2		2.0
1934	100	100.0	45.0	40.0	15.0		
1935	96	100.0	46.9	24.0	28.1		1.0
1936	146	100.0	55.4	28.8	15.8		
Wage decrease, hour increase:							
1927	1	100.0			100.0		
1928	2	100.0	100.0				
1929							
1930	3	100.0	66.7		33.3		
1931	9	100.0	55.6	11.1	33.3		
1932	10	100.0	20.0	10.0	70.0		
1933	1	100.0	100.0				
1934	6	100.0	66.7	33.3			
1935	73	100.0	46.6	17.8	35.6		
1936	19	100.0	31.6	26.3	42.1		
Hour increase:							
1927	1	100.0			100.0		
1928	3	100.0		33.3	66.7		
1929	4	100.0		25.0	75.0		
1930	1	100.0		100.0			
1931	4	100.0			75.0	25.0	
1932							
1933	1	100.0			100.0		
1934	2	100.0	50.0		50.0		
1935	33	100.0	54.6	12.1	33.3		
1936	15	100.0	66.7	13.3	20.0		
Hour decrease:							
1927	16	100.0	18.8	25.0	56.2		
1928	7	100.0	28.6	42.8	28.6		
1929	17	100.0	35.3	29.4	35.3		
1930	6	100.0	50.0	50.0			
1931	5	100.0	60.0		40.0		
1932	5	100.0	60.0	20.0	20.0		
1933	9	100.0	55.6	33.3	11.1		
1934	10	100.0	60.0	20.0	10.0		10.0
1935	12	100.0	41.7	25.0	33.3		
1936	12	100.0	50.1	8.3	33.3	8.3	
ALL UNION ORGANIZATION STRIKES							
1927	240	100.0	32.1	17.1	45.8	.8	4.2
1928	226	100.0	37.6	15.9	44.3	1.8	.4
1929	382	100.0	39.0	13.4	45.2	2.1	.3
1930	207	100.0	27.1	17.4	49.7	5.8	
1931	221	100.0	32.1	20.8	41.2	5.4	.5
1932	162	100.0	41.4	8.0	47.5	.6	2.5
1933	533	100.0	37.7	25.9	34.3	.6	1.5
1934	835	100.0	35.9	30.1	30.7	1.0	2.3
1935	945	100.0	46.1	18.1	34.9	.5	.4
1936	1,083	100.0	49.9	21.9	27.3	.7	.2
Recognition:							
1927	74	100.0	33.8	8.1	58.1		
1928	86	100.0	44.2	7.0	45.3	2.3	1.2
1929	102	100.0	43.1	5.9	48.1	2.9	
1930	48	100.0	27.1	6.2	62.5	4.2	
1931	66	100.0	21.2	18.2	51.5	7.6	1.5
1932	34	100.0	29.4	8.8	61.8		
1933	163	100.0	31.9	19.0	46.7	1.8	.6
1934	226	100.0	41.5	19.9	34.1	1.8	2.7
1935	179	100.0	50.2	10.1	38.5	.6	.6
1936	173	100.0	41.6	9.8	46.9	1.7	
Recognition and wages:							
1927	23	100.0	21.7	43.6	30.4		4.3
1928	28	100.0	35.8	32.1	32.1		
1929	62	100.0	53.3	14.5	27.4	3.2	1.6
1930	21	100.0	23.8	19.0	47.7	9.5	
1931	35	100.0	20.0	37.1	34.3	8.6	
1932	29	100.0	34.5	6.9	55.2		3.4
1933	145	100.0	44.1	38.6	16.6		.7
1934	224	100.0	33.0	45.6	21.4		
1935	194	100.0	48.0	23.7	27.8		.5
1936	272	100.0	50.0	29.8	20.2		

TABLE 30.—*Results of strikes ending 1927–36, in relation to major issues involved*—Continued

STRIKES—Continued

Major issues and years	Total strikes		Percentage of strikes resulting in—				
	Number	Percentage	Substantial gains to workers	Partial gains or compromises	Little or no gains to workers	Indeterminate	Not reported
Recognition and hours:							
1927	5	100.0	----	20.0	80.0	----	----
1928	1	100.0	----	----	100.0	----	----
1929	1	100.0	----	----	100.0	----	----
1930	3	100.0	----	66.7	33.3	----	----
1931	3	100.0	66.7	33.3	----	----	----
1932	----	----	----	----	----	----	----
1933	1	100.0	100.0	----	----	----	----
1934	1	100.0	100.0	----	----	----	----
1935	7	100.0	42.9	42.9	14.2	----	----
1936	7	100.0	57.1	----	42.9	----	----
Recognition, wages, and hours:							
1927	10	100.0	10.0	30.0	40.0	----	20.0
1928	19	100.0	21.1	52.6	26.3	----	----
1929	32	100.0	15.6	37.5	43.8	3.1	----
1930	12	100.0	33.3	41.7	25.0	----	----
1931	15	100.0	----	53.3	46.7	----	----
1932	21	100.0	52.4	14.3	33.3	----	----
1933	81	100.0	43.3	37.0	16.0	----	3.7
1934	101	100.0	30.7	49.5	18.8	1.0	----
1935	168	100.0	49.4	24.4	25.6	----	.6
1936	357	100.0	55.8	25.5	17.9	.8	----
Closed shop:							
1927	43	100.0	34.9	7.0	44.2	2.3	11.6
1928	63	100.0	34.9	11.1	52.4	1.6	----
1929	91	100.0	34.1	12.1	52.7	1.1	----
1930	59	100.0	25.4	22.0	44.1	8.5	----
1931	52	100.0	55.8	9.6	30.8	3.8	----
1932	45	100.0	51.1	4.4	35.6	2.2	6.7
1933	41	100.0	24.4	9.8	65.8	----	----
1934	109	100.0	33.0	17.4	44.1	----	5.5
1935	151	100.0	49.0	13.2	36.4	.7	.7
1936	130	100.0	52.2	18.5	28.5	----	.8
Discrimination:							
1927	45	100.0	31.1	20.0	44.5	----	4.4
1928	20	100.0	35.0	5.0	55.0	5.0	----
1929	66	100.0	27.3	16.7	54.5	1.5	----
1930	44	100.0	22.7	15.9	61.4	----	----
1931	38	100.0	34.2	13.2	50.0	2.6	----
1932	28	100.0	35.7	10.7	53.6	----	----
1933	95	100.0	35.8	16.8	45.3	----	2.1
1934	154	100.0	34.4	19.5	40.3	1.9	3.9
1935	232	100.0	35.3	17.2	46.2	1.3	----
1936	120	100.0	37.5	15.8	44.2	1.7	.8
Other:							
1927	40	100.0	42.5	22.5	32.5	2.5	----
1928	9	100.0	44.5	33.3	22.2	----	----
1929	28	100.0	64.3	7.1	28.6	----	----
1930	20	100.0	45.0	10.0	30.0	15.0	----
1931	12	100.0	50.0	16.7	25.0	8.3	----
1932	5	100.0	60.0	----	40.0	----	----
1933	7	100.0	71.4	14.3	----	----	14.3
1934	20	100.0	60.0	25.0	10.0	----	5.0
1935	14	100.0	71.5	21.4	7.1	----	----
1936	24	100.0	66.7	20.8	12.5	----	----
MISCELLANEOUS[1]							
Sympathy:							
1927	18	100.0	16.7	27.8	49.9	----	5.6
1928	7	100.0	28.6	----	71.4	----	----
1929	16	100.0	6.3	31.3	62.4	----	----
1930	14	100.0	28.6	21.4	50.0	----	----
1931	6	100.0	----	----	66.7	33.3	----
1932	3	100.0	33.3	----	66.7	----	----
1933	9	100.0	----	11.2	44.4	44.4	----
1934	45	100.0	24.4	40.1	11.1	11.1	13.3
1935	42	100.0	33.3	26.2	23.8	16.7	----
1936	25	100.0	36.0	20.0	20.0	24.0	----

[1] Other miscellaneous strikes included in previous tables are not listed here. In addition to a few strikes for which no information as to major issues involved is available, these omissions include strikes due to rival unions competing for control, jurisdictional disputes, and other strikes over miscellaneous grievances.

TABLE **30**.—*Results of strikes ending 1927–36, in relation to major issues involved*—Continued

WORKERS INVOLVED

Major issues and years	Total workers		Percentage of workers involved in the strikes resulting in—				
	Number	Percentage	Substantial gains to workers	Partial gains or compromises	Little or no gains to workers	Indeterminate	Not reported
ALL WAGES AND HOURS STRIKES							
1927	232, 217	100. 0	4. 4	13. 3	78. 6	0. 8	2. 9
1928	139, 913	100. 0	13. 0	46. 3	40. 7	([2])	-------
1929	104, 059	100. 0	26. 4	37. 8	35. 7	. 1	([2])
1930	73, 223	100. 0	20. 4	40. 9	38. 5	. 2	-------
1931	155, 308	100. 0	17. 7	30. 5	48. 9	2. 8	. 1
1932	234, 158	100. 0	14. 6	38. 8	46. 0	. 1	. 5
1933	544, 084	100. 0	46. 0	38. 5	14. 0	. 2	1. 3
1934	346, 174	100. 0	25. 4	53. 4	21. 1	([2])	. 1
1935	662, 539	100. 0	73. 0	17. 0	9. 9	-------	. 1
1936	250, 672	100. 0	37. 8	44. 0	17. 5	. 7	-------
Wage increase:							
1927	39, 159	100. 0	12. 4	40. 3	25. 4	4. 7	17. 2
1928	21, 310	100. 0	27. 9	51. 6	20. 5	-------	-------
1929	30, 743	100. 0	15. 9	66. 9	17. 1	. 1	-------
1930	14, 886	100. 0	34. 9	26. 2	38. 7	. 2	-------
1931	31, 791	100. 0	13. 6	65. 7	20. 0	. 4	. 3
1932	19, 064	100. 0	67. 1	4. 6	28. 2	-------	. 1
1933	220, 162	100. 0	42. 2	33. 2	21. 3	. 5	2. 8
1934	207, 868	100. 0	24. 8	52. 8	22. 3	-------	. 1
1935	561, 423	100. 0	80. 0	13. 9	6. 0	-------	. 1
1936	142, 663	100. 0	37. 6	46. 5	15. 8	. 1	-------
Wage decrease:							
1927	172, 442	100. 0	2. 4	. 9	96. 7	([2])	([2])
1928	111, 619	100. 0	8. 8	44. 3	46. 9	-------	-------
1929	26, 160	100. 0	27. 3	16. 7	55. 5	. 3	. 2
1930	38, 091	100. 0	16. 0	28. 4	55. 2	. 4	-------
1931	110, 141	100. 0	18. 8	17. 2	61. 6	2. 4	-------
1932	189, 272	100. 0	7. 0	38. 6	53. 7	. 1	. 6
1933	61, 961	100. 0	32. 9	41. 5	24. 8	. 3	. 5
1934	46, 529	100. 0	16. 8	45. 3	37. 5	. 1	. 3
1935	46, 585	100. 0	21. 3	37. 7	41. 0	-------	-------
1936	45, 031	100. 0	34. 2	31. 4	34. 1	. 3	-------
Wage increase, hour decrease:							
1927	17, 878	100. 0	6. 7	66. 3	27. 0	-------	-------
1928	4, 993	100. 0	23. 6	72. 8	2. 8	. 8	-------
1929	35, 163	100. 0	17. 1	36. 8	46. 0	. 1	-------
1930	17, 091	100. 0	6. 3	87. 0	6. 7	-------	-------
1931	8, 237	100. 0	. 5	87. 5	12. 0	-------	-------
1932	23, 116	100. 0	34. 6	64. 9	. 5	-------	-------
1933	259, 144	100. 0	52. 0	42. 6	5. 2	-------	. 2
1934	79, 796	100. 0	21. 3	67. 1	11. 6	-------	-------
1935	31, 303	100. 0	37. 2	41. 8	20. 8	-------	. 2
1936	37, 178	100. 0	16. 6	75. 8	7. 6	-------	-------
Wage decrease, hour increase:							
1927	26	100. 0	-------	-------	100. 0	-------	-------
1928	445	100. 0	100. 0	-------	-------	-------	-------
1929	-------	-------	-------	-------	-------	-------	-------
1930	364	100. 0	31. 3	-------	68. 7	-------	-------
1931	2, 378	100. 0	85. 3	12. 6	2. 1	-------	-------
1932	2, 611	100. 0	8. 6	76. 6	14. 8	-------	-------
1933	70	100. 0	100. 0	-------	-------	-------	-------
1934	10, 578	100. 0	96. 8	3. 2	-------	-------	-------
1935	16, 309	100. 0	50. 9	18. 4	30. 7	-------	-------
1936	2, 665	100. 0	18. 3	45. 0	36. 7	-------	-------
Hour increase:							
1927	8	100. 0	-------	-------	100. 0	-------	-------
1928	142	100. 0	-------	31. 7	68. 3	-------	-------
1929	225	100. 0	-------	8. 9	91. 1	-------	-------
1930	103	100. 0	-------	100. 0	-------	-------	-------
1931	1, 930	100. 0	-------	-------	19. 2	80. 8	-------
1932	-------	-------	-------	-------	-------	-------	-------
1933	24	100. 0	-------	-------	100. 0	-------	-------
1934	760	100. 0	92. 1	-------	7. 9	-------	-------
1935	6, 068	100. 0	69. 2	14. 9	15. 9	-------	-------
1936	17, 676	100. 0	95. 0	2. 3	2. 7	-------	-------

[2] Less than 1/10 of 1 percent.

TABLE 30.—*Results of strikes ending 1927–36, in relation to major issues involved*—Continued

WORKERS INVOLVED—Continued

Major issues and years	Total workers		Percentage of workers involved in the strikes resulting in—				
	Number	Percentage	Substantial gains to workers	Partial gains or compromises	Little or no gains to workers	Indeterminate	Not reported
Hour decrease:							
1927	2,704	100.0	6.5	62.8	30.7		
1928	1,404	100.0	53.2	42.7	4.1		
1929	11,768	100.0	79.8	12.1	8.1		
1930	2,688	100.0	91.1	8.9			
1931	831	100.0	38.5		61.5		
1932	95	100.0	68.4	15.8	15.8		
1933	2,723	100.0	89.2	9.7	1.1		
1934	643	100.0	79.6	17.6	1.2		1.6
1935	851	100.0	14.8	34.5	50.7		
1936	5,459	100.0	41.7	.4	30.4	27.5	
UNION ORGANIZATION STRIKES							
1927	44,451	100.0	28.5	37.1	31.6	.4	2.4
1928	95,320	100.0	61.6	19.9	15.3	2.6	.6
1929	101,724	100.0	35.0	36.2	28.0	.8	([2])
1930	75,949	100.0	11.7	63.4	20.9	4.0	
1931	115,997	100.0	14.8	57.4	25.4	2.3	.1
1932	72,940	100.0	74.3	4.8	20.8	([2])	.1
1933	465,272	100.0	28.5	56.7	14.1	.2	.5
1934	762,367	100.0	15.4	70.8	10.0	3.5	.3
1935	287,876	100.0	28.8	48.9	21.9	.4	([2])
1936	365,019	100.0	46.5	33.1	15.1	5.2	.1
Recognition:							
1927	6,785	100.0	60.2	5.6	34.2		
1928	51,836	100.0	77.3	8.1	10.0	3.4	1.2
1929	19,901	100.0	46.5	4.9	47.0	1.6	
1930	10,133	100.0	24.1	2.0	72.5	1.4	
1931	40,554	100.0	9.0	42.3	47.6	.9	.2
1932	2,820	100.0	26.2	5.0	68.8		
1933	168,784	100.0	11.2	65.9	22.3	.5	.1
1934	111,446	100.0	29.7	55.9	11.9	1.9	.6
1935	34,271	100.0	39.0	14.6	46.3	.1	([2])
1936	47,347	100.0	37.3	10.9	20.3	31.5	
Recognition and wages:							
1927	6,827	100.0	4.9	68.7	22.7		3.7
1928	14,149	100.0	15.4	66.4	18.2		
1929	16,549	100.0	70.3	10.5	18.4	.5	.3
1930	4,575	100.0	6.4	14.7	30.4	48.5	
1931	47,022	100.0	9.3	87.4	1.0	2.3	
1932	32,137	100.0	68.3	.3	31.4		([2])
1933	162,717	100.0	56.7	40.0	3.2		.1
1934	458,329	100.0	8.2	85.5	6.3		
1935	68,736	100.0	26.0	49.2	24.7		.1
1936	103,521	100.0	52.3	30.9	16.8		
Recognition and hours:							
1927	975	100.0		41.0	59.0		
1928	250	100.0			100.0		
1929	36	100.0			100.0		
1930	2,642	100.0		99.4	.6		
1931	742	100.0	59.6	40.4			
1932							
1933	2,000	100.0	100.0				
1934	125	100.0	100.0				
1935	557	100.0	43.8	40.0	16.2		
1936	325	100.0	69.5		30.5		
Recognition, wages, and hours:							
1927	4,818	100.0	41.5	45.0	11.0		2.5
1928	14,807	100.0	59.7	28.5	11.8		
1929	37,360	100.0	7.9	79.1	12.8	.2	
1930	40,712	100.0	4.3	94.8	.9		
1931	12,453	100.0		61.2	38.8		
1932	32,708	100.0	87.9	8.8	3.3		
1933	102,645	100.0	12.6	74.9	11.5		1.0
1934	131,463	100.0	16.5	55.9	10.9	16.7	
1935	94,879	100.0	29.2	64.1	6.7		([2])
1936	120,820	100.0	43.9	49.3	6.4	.4	

[2] Less than 1/10 of 1 percent.

TABLE 30.—*Results of strikes ending 1927–36, in relation to major issues involved*—Continued

WORKERS INVOLVED—Continued

Major issues and years	Total workers		Percentage of workers involved in the strikes resulting in—				
	Number	Per-cent-age	Substantial gains to workers	Partial gains or compromises	Little or no gains to workers	Indeterminate	Not reported
Closed shop:							
1927	7,417	100.0	20.1	45.1	27.0	0.2	7.6
1928	6,282	100.0	40.4	12.7	46.6	.3	
1929	8,009	100.0	42.1	20.2	36.5	1.2	
1930	7,898	100.0	31.5	27.7	32.8	8.0	
1931	5,784	100.0	36.2	3.8	59.1	.9	
1932	2,047	100.0	68.8	4.4	23.5	1.0	2.3
1933	6,090	100.0	8.1	8.5	83.4		
1934	16,586	100.0	23.6	24.1	48.4		3.9
1935	46,213	100.0	17.3	66.5	16.1	.1	(2)
1936	42,543	100.0	30.8	32.5	35.8		.9
Discrimination:							
1927	8,051	100.0	11.8	20.6	66.1		1.5
1928	7,197	100.0	65.4	3.7	21.3	9.6	
1929	16,608	100.0	37.2	16.7	44.6	1.5	
1930	9,309	100.0	16.0	41.1	42.9		
1931	7,695	100.0	67.7	1.4	16.5	14.4	
1932	2,055	100.0	37.0	15.4	47.6		
1933	21,118	100.0	23.9	44.2	28.1		3.8
1934	39,304	100.0	42.7	20.0	28.8	6.3	2.2
1935	34,883	100.0	28.4	21.9	46.3	3.4	
1936	26,019	100.0	54.9	11.6	18.7	14.4	.4
Other:							
1927	9,578	100.0	39.8	40.1	18.2	1.9	
1928	799	100.0	43.2	16.0	40.8		
1929	3,261	100.0	68.4	2.3	29.3		
1930	680	100.0	59.6	12.6	21.6	6.2	
1931	1,747	100.0	81.6	3.4	11.6	3.4	
1932	1,173	100.0	47.3		52.7		
1933	1,918	100.0	41.3	52.2			6.5
1934	5,114	100.0	79.9	15.9	.8		3.4
1935	8,337	100.0	70.7	27.7	1.6		
1936	24,444	100.0	69.5	30.0	.5		
MISCELLANEOUS[1]							
Sympathy:							
1927	12,634	100.0	4.9	64.7	30.2		.2
1928	255	100.0	67.5		32.5		
1929	14,268	100.0	.3	6.8	92.9		
1930	1,521	100.0	30.4	3.9	65.7		
1931	1,474	100.0			15.2	84.8	
1932	366	100.0	2.7		97.3		
1933	1,892	100.0		26.3	9.9	63.8	
1934	207,897	100.0	1.2	73.6	13.0	10.7	1.5
1935	61,066	100.0	8.9	41.7	1.4	48.0	
1936	4,976	100.0	24.9	26.9	3.5	44.7	

[1] See footnote p. 73. [2] Less than 1/10 of 1 percent.

Results in Relation to Duration

Strike experience during the 10 years 1927–36 indicates that a larger proportion of the short strikes are successful than of the long drawn-out disputes. Table 31 shows that the ratio of those lost to those which were successful reversed with strikes lasting 1 month or more. Out of every 100 strikes lasting less than 1 month 39 were won and 33 were lost, from the workers point of view. Of each 100 strikes which lasted a month or more, on the other hand, only 25 were won while 43 were lost. In the longest strikes, those lasting 3 months or longer, the proportion of failures was even greater. Almost half of these strikes resulted in no gains, 26 percent were compromised, while 22 percent brought substantial gains to workers.

Very short strikes, those of less than a week's duration, had a greater tendency to result either in gains (39.7 percent) or losses (35.5 percent) than in compromises (19.3 percent). With this exception, the proportion of compromised strikes showed little fluctuation in relation to the duration of the strikes, varying from 24 to 30 percent throughout the period.

The proportion of short and long strikes to the total successful, compromise, and unsuccessful strikes each year was about the same as the average for the 10-year period.

Table 31.—*Results of strikes ending 1927–36, in relation to their duration*

Years and duration of strikes	Total	Number of strikes resulting in—				Total	Percentage of strikes resulting in—			
		Substantial gains to workers	Partial gains or compromises	Little or no gains to workers	Other[1]		Substantial gains to workers	Partial gains or compromises	Little or no gains to workers	Other[1]
10-year period—Total	12,157	4,332	2,894	4,302	629	100.0	35.6	23.8	35.4	5.2
Less than 1 week	4,532	1,797	876	1,608	251	100.0	39.7	19.3	35.5	5.5
1 week and less than ½ month	2,663	1,045	704	795	119	100.0	39.2	26.4	29.9	4.5
½ and less than 1 month	2,147	781	582	686	98	100.0	36.3	27.1	32.0	4.6
1 and less than 2 months	1,748	458	431	753	106	100.0	26.2	24.7	43.0	6.1
2 and less than 3 months	602	149	181	236	36	100.0	24.8	30.1	39.1	6.0
3 months or over	465	102	120	224	19	100.0	21.9	25.8	48.2	4.1
1927—Total	666	170	166	276	54	100.0	25.5	24.9	41.5	8.1
Less than 1 week	181	50	45	73	13	100.0	27.6	24.9	40.3	7.2
1 week and less than ½ month	152	42	44	53	13	100.0	27.6	28.9	34.9	8.6
½ and less than 1 month	138	43	29	54	12	100.0	31.2	21.0	39.1	8.7
1 and less than 2 months	118	23	37	50	8	100.0	19.5	31.4	42.3	6.8
2 and less than 3 months	47	8	8	26	5	100.0	17.0	17.0	55.4	10.6
3 months or over	30	4	3	20	3	100.0	13.3	10.0	66.7	10.0
1928—Total	620	173	171	244	32	100.0	27.9	27.6	39.3	5.2
Less than 1 week	235	67	58	102	8	100.0	28.5	24.7	43.4	3.4
1 week and less than ½ month	131	43	43	39	6	100.0	32.8	32.8	29.8	4.6
½ and less than 1 month	98	29	28	36	5	100.0	29.6	28.6	36.7	5.1
1 and less than 2 months	75	18	24	25	8	100.0	24.0	32.0	33.3	10.7
2 and less than 3 months	30	5	8	12	5	100.0	16.7	26.7	39.9	16.7
3 months or over	51	11	10	30	-------	100.0	21.6	19.6	58.8	-------
1929—Total	924	260	233	380	51	100.0	28.1	25.2	41.2	5.5
Less than 1 week	360	116	82	149	13	100.0	32.2	22.8	41.4	3.6
1 week and less than ½ month	218	69	61	79	9	100.0	31.7	28.0	36.2	4.1
½ and less than 1 month	143	37	39	56	11	100.0	25.9	27.3	39.1	7.7
1 and less than 2 months	127	24	36	54	13	100.0	18.9	28.3	42.6	10.2
2 and less than 3 months	33	5	10	17	1	100.0	15.2	30.3	51.5	3.0
3 months or over	43	9	5	25	4	100.0	20.9	11.6	58.2	9.3
1930—Total	651	156	150	290	55	100.0	24.0	23.0	44.6	8.4
Less than 1 week	238	65	30	124	19	100.0	27.3	12.6	52.1	8.0
1 week and less than ½ month	157	44	52	49	12	100.0	28.0	33.2	31.2	7.6
½ and less than 1 month	111	26	34	45	6	100.0	23.4	30.6	40.6	5.4
1 and less than 2 months	80	13	18	39	10	100.0	16.3	22.5	48.7	12.5
2 and less than 3 months	41	7	11	19	4	100.0	17.1	26.8	46.3	9.8
3 months or over	24	1	5	14	4	100.0	4.2	20.8	58.3	16.7

[1] Includes strikes for which sufficient information was not available as well as those involving rival unions and questions of jurisdiction, the results of which cannot be evaluated in terms of their effect on the welfare of all workers concerned.

TABLE **31.**—*Results of strikes ending 1927–36, in relation to their duration*—Con.

Years and duration of strikes	Number of strikes resulting in—					Percentage of strikes resulting in—				
	Total	Substantial gains to workers	Partial gains or compromises	Little or no gains to workers	Other	Total	Substantial gains to workers	Partial gains or compromises	Little or no gains to workers	Other
1931—Total	796	212	146	372	66	100.0	26.6	18.3	46.8	8.3
Less than 1 week	319	90	49	158	22	100.0	28.2	15.4	49.5	6.9
1 week and less than ½ month	169	55	32	64	18	100.0	32.5	18.9	37.9	10.7
½ and less than 1 month	136	42	28	56	10	100.0	30.9	20.6	41.1	7.4
1 and less than 2 months	116	17	16	72	11	100.0	14.7	13.8	62.0	9.5
2 and less than 3 months	39	4	16	14	5	100.0	10.3	41.0	35.9	12.8
3 months or over	17	4	5	8	------	100.0	23.5	29.4	47.1	------
1932—Total	852	233	134	442	43	100.0	27.3	15.7	52.0	5.0
Less than 1 week	334	101	46	172	15	100.0	30.2	13.8	51.5	4.5
1 week and less than ½ month	165	51	31	67	16	100.0	30.9	18.8	40.6	9.7
½ and less than 1 month	149	44	23	75	7	100.0	29.5	15.4	50.4	4.7
1 and less than 2 months	146	23	19	100	4	100.0	15.8	13.0	68.5	2.7
2 and less than 3 months	35	11	7	16	1	100.0	31.4	20.0	45.7	2.9
3 months or over	23	3	8	12	------	100.0	13.0	34.8	52.2	------
1933—Total	1,672	617	441	525	89	100.0	36.9	26.4	31.4	5.3
Less than 1 week	700	255	145	242	58	100.0	36.4	20.7	34.6	8.3
1 week and less than ½ month	362	147	106	99	10	100.0	40.7	29.3	27.3	2.7
½ and less than 1 month	307	118	95	87	7	100.0	38.5	30.9	28.3	2.3
1 and less than 2 months	222	71	65	78	8	100.0	32.0	29.3	35.1	3.6
2 and less than 3 months	56	16	20	16	4	100.0	28.6	35.7	28.6	7.1
3 months or over	25	10	10	3	2	100.0	40.0	40.0	12.0	8.0
1934—Total	1,817	634	571	512	100	100.0	34.9	31.4	28.2	5.5
Less than 1 week	703	279	170	209	45	100.0	39.7	24.2	29.7	6.4
1 week and less than ½ month	360	140	117	91	12	100.0	38.9	32.5	25.3	3.3
½ and less than 1 month	337	103	133	85	16	100.0	30.6	39.5	25.2	4.7
1 and less than 2 months	288	77	96	96	19	100.0	26.7	33.3	33.4	6.6
2 and less than 3 months	88	23	36	25	4	100.0	26.1	41.0	28.4	4.5
3 months or over	41	12	19	6	4	100.0	29.3	46.3	14.6	9.8
1935—Total	2,003	886	374	669	74	100.0	44.2	18.7	33.4	3.7
Less than 1 week	709	376	106	198	29	100.0	53.0	15.0	27.9	4.1
1 week and less than ½ month	437	209	82	130	16	100.0	47.8	18.8	29.7	3.7
½ and less than 1 month	346	164	70	100	12	100.0	47.4	20.2	28.9	3.5
1 and less than 2 months	285	89	50	136	10	100.0	31.2	17.5	47.8	3.5
2 and less than 3 months	127	31	33	58	5	100.0	24.4	26.0	45.7	3.9
3 months or over	99	17	33	47	2	100.0	17.2	33.3	47.5	2.0
1936—Total	2,156	991	508	592	65	100.0	45.9	23.6	27.5	3.0
Less than 1 week	753	398	145	181	29	100.0	52.8	19.3	24.0	3.9
1 week and less than ½ month	512	245	136	124	7	100.0	47.8	26.6	24.2	1.4
½ and less than 1 month	382	175	103	92	12	100.0	45.9	26.9	24.1	3.1
1 and less than 2 months	291	103	70	103	15	100.0	35.3	24.1	35.4	5.2
2 and less than 3 months	106	39	32	33	2	100.0	36.7	30.2	31.2	1.9
3 months or over	112	31	22	59	------	100.0	27.7	19.6	52.7	------

Results in Relation to Size

The most significant fact revealed in table 32, "Results of strikes ending 1927–36 in relation to the number of workers involved," is that compromise settlements are more numerous in the larger strikes. During the 10-year period, only 13 percent of the strikes involving fewer than 20 workers resulted in compromises. This percentage consistently increased with the size of the strikes, approximately 50 percent of those involving 5,000 or more workers resulting in compromise settlements.

Conversely, the proportion of successful and unsuccessful strikes decreased as the size of the strike increased. The reduction, however, was more marked with the unsuccessful strikes, a greater proportion of the very small strikes and a lesser proportion of the largest strikes resulting in failures than in gains. Of the strikes involving 6 to 20 workers, 45 percent were lost. This proportion steadily declined with the increase in size, about 15 percent of those involving 10,000 or more workers resulting in failure. Approximately 35 to 36 percent of the strikes involving from 6 to 1,000 workers were won, about 30 percent of those involving from 1,000 to 5,000, and approximately 21 to 22 percent of the largest strikes resulted in substantial gains to workers.

There was no uniform difference in the proportion of successful and unsuccessful strikes of various sizes. A greater percentage of the strikes involving fewer than 100 workers were lost than won. In each of the classifications from 100 to 5,000 workers more of the strikes were won than lost. About the same proportion of the strikes involving from 5,000 to 10,000 workers were successful and unsuccessful, and 5 percent more of the largest strikes resulted in substantial gains than in little or no gains.

TABLE 32.—*Results of strikes ending 1927–36, in relation to the number of workers involved*

Years and number of workers involved	Total	Number of strikes resulting in—				Total	Percentage of strikes resulting in—			
		Substantial gains to workers	Partial gains or compromises	Little or no gains to workers	Other [1]		Substantial gains to workers	Partial gains or compromises	Little or no gains to workers	Other [1]
10-year period—Total	12,157	4,332	2,894	4,302	629	100.0	35.6	23.8	35.4	5.2
6 and under 20	2,106	764	277	950	115	100.0	36.3	13.2	45.0	5.5
20 and under 100	4,495	1,627	884	1,719	265	100.0	36.2	19.7	38.2	5.9
100 and under 250	2,343	860	601	767	115	100.0	36.7	25.7	32.7	4.9
250 and under 500	1,374	499	422	410	43	100.0	36.4	30.7	29.8	3.1
500 and under 1,000	900	317	310	233	40	100.0	35.3	34.4	25.9	4.4
1,000 and under 5,000	755	225	308	186	36	100.0	29.8	40.8	24.6	4.8
5,000 and under 10,000	113	25	56	26	6	100.0	22.1	49.6	23.0	5.3
10,000 workers and over	71	15	36	11	9	100.0	21.1	50.7	15.5	12.7
1927—Total	666	170	166	276	54	100.0	25.5	24.9	41.5	8.1
6 and under 20	149	46	21	67	15	100.0	30.9	14.1	44.9	10.1
20 and under 100	275	73	60	118	24	100.0	26.5	21.8	43.0	8.7
100 and under 250	96	16	29	46	5	100.0	16.7	30.2	47.9	5.2
250 and under 500	64	18	24	19	3	100.0	28.1	37.5	29.7	4.7
500 and under 1,000	44	13	16	12	3	100.0	29.5	36.4	27.3	6.8
1,000 and under 5,000	34	4	15	13	2	100.0	11.8	44.1	38.2	5.9
5,000 and under 10,000	3		1		2	(2)				
10,000 workers and over	1			1		(2)				
1928—Total	620	173	171	244	32	100.0	27.9	27.6	39.3	5.2
6 and under 20	119	45	13	56	5	100.0	37.8	10.9	47.1	4.2
20 and under 100	259	69	72	103	15	100.0	26.6	27.8	39.8	5.8
100 and under 250	89	25	22	35	7	100.0	28.1	24.7	39.3	7.9
250 and under 500	56	14	20	22		100.0	25.0	35.7	39.3	
500 and under 1,000	45	8	21	13	3	100.0	17.8	46.6	28.9	6.7
1,000 and under 5,000	43	9	20	13	1	100.0	20.9	46.6	30.2	2.3
5,000 and under 10,000	4	2	1	1		(2)				
10,000 workers and over	5	1	2	1	1	(2)				

[1] Includes strikes for which sufficient information was not available as well as those involving rival unions and questions of jurisdiction, the results of which cannot be evaluated in terms of their effect on the welfare of all workers concerned.

[2] Too few to give percentage.

TABLE 32.—*Results of strikes ending 1927–36, in relation to the number of workers involved*—Continued

Years and number of workers involved	Total	Number of strikes resulting in—				Total	Percentage of strikes resulting in—			
		Substantial gains to workers	Partial gains or compromises	Little or no gains to workers	Other		Substantial gains to workers	Partial gains or compromises	Little or no gains to workers	Other
1929—Total	924	260	233	380	51	100.0	28.1	25.2	41.2	5.5
6 and under 20	167	42	22	95	8	100.0	25.1	13.2	56.9	4.8
20 and under 100	361	96	84	154	27	100.0	26.6	23.3	42.6	7.5
100 and under 250	174	55	49	62	8	100.0	31.6	28.2	35.6	4.6
250 and under 500	90	23	29	33	5	100.0	25.6	32.2	36.6	5.6
500 and under 1,000	62	24	23	13	2	100.0	38.7	37.1	21.0	3.2
1,000 and under 5,000	62	20	22	19	1	100.0	32.3	35.5	30.6	1.6
5,000 and under 10,000	7		3	4		(2)				
10,000 workers and over	1		1			(2)				
1930—Total	651	156	150	290	55	100.0	24.0	23.0	44.6	8.4
6 and under 20	130	30	18	72	10	100.0	23.1	13.8	55.4	7.7
20 and under 100	268	64	55	122	27	100.0	23.9	20.5	45.5	10.1
100 and under 250	122	32	33	44	13	100.0	26.2	27.0	36.1	10.7
250 and under 500	65	16	21	25	3	100.0	24.6	32.3	38.5	4.6
500 and under 1,000	32	7	8	17		100.0	21.9	25.0	53.1	
1,000 and under 5,000	31	7	12	10	2	100.0	22.6	38.6	32.3	6.5
5,000 and under 10,000	2		2			(2)				
10,000 workers and over	1		1			(2)				
1931—Total	796	212	146	372	66	100.0	26.6	18.3	46.8	8.3
6 and under 20	169	35	22	101	11	100.0	20.7	13.0	59.8	6.5
20 and under 100	317	94	65	127	31	100.0	29.7	20.5	40.0	9.8
100 and under 250	152	44	23	73	12	100.0	28.9	15.1	48.1	7.9
250 and under 500	59	17	13	25	4	100.0	28.8	22.0	42.4	6.8
500 and under 1,000	40	9	5	23	3	100.0	22.5	12.5	57.5	7.5
1,000 and under 5,000	46	13	11	17	5	100.0	28.3	23.9	36.9	10.9
5,000 and under 10,000	7		2	5		(2)				
10,000 workers and over	6		5	1		(2)				
1932—Total	852	233	134	442	43	100.0	27.3	15.7	52.0	5.0
6 and under 20	208	65	19	114	10	100.0	31.2	9.1	54.9	4.8
20 and under 100	334	93	51	170	20	100.0	27.8	15.3	50.9	6.0
100 and under 250	148	36	20	81	11	100.0	24.3	13.5	54.8	7.4
250 and under 500	79	17	19	42	1	100.0	21.5	24.1	53.1	1.3
500 and under 1,000	34	8	7	18	1	100.0	23.5	20.6	53.0	2.9
1,000 and under 5,000	38	11	14	13		100.0	28.9	36.9	34.2	
5,000 and under 10,000	4	1	1	2		(2)				
10,000 workers and over	7	2	3	2		(2)				
1933—Total	1,672	617	441	525	89	100.0	36.9	26.4	31.4	5.3
6 and under 20	176	55	29	87	5	100.0	31.2	16.5	49.5	2.8
20 and under 100	523	188	100	202	33	100.0	35.9	19.1	38.7	6.3
100 and under 250	363	134	104	105	20	100.0	36.9	28.7	28.9	5.5
250 and under 500	251	107	74	61	9	100.0	42.6	29.5	24.3	3.6
500 and under 1,000	160	61	52	34	13	100.0	38.1	32.5	21.3	8.1
1,000 and under 5,000	157	61	60	30	6	100.0	38.9	38.2	19.1	3.8
5,000 and under 10,000	26	7	14	4	1	100.0	26.9	53.9	15.4	3.8
10,000 workers and over	16	4	8	2	2	100.0	25.0	50.0	12.5	12.5
1934—Total	1,817	634	571	512	100	100.0	34.9	31.4	28.2	5.5
6 and under 20	245	109	36	83	17	100.0	44.5	14.7	33.9	6.9
20 and under 100	575	225	120	195	35	100.0	39.1	20.9	33.9	6.1
100 and under 250	373	122	138	93	20	100.0	32.7	37.0	24.9	5.4
250 and under 500	255	75	98	72	10	100.0	29.4	38.5	28.2	3.9
500 and under 1,000	187	58	88	35	6	100.0	31.0	47.1	18.7	3.2
1,000 and under 5,000	135	37	63	27	8	100.0	27.4	46.7	20.0	5.9
5,000 and under 10,000	28	6	18	4		100.0	21.4	64.3	14.3	
10,000 workers and over	19	2	10	3	4	100.0	10.5	52.6	15.8	21.1

[2] Too few to give percentage.

TABLE 32.—*Results of strikes ending 1927–36, in relation to the number of workers involved*—Continued

Years and number of workers involved	Total	Number of strikes resulting in—				Total	Percentage of strikes resulting in—			
		Substantial gains to workers	Partial gains or compromises	Little or no gains to workers	Other		Substantial gains to workers	Partial gains or compromises	Little or no gains to workers	Other
1935—Total	2,003	886	374	669	74	100.0	44.2	18.7	33.4	3.7
6 and under 20	348	164	41	123	20	100.0	47.2	11.8	35.3	5.7
20 and under 100	749	330	106	283	30	100.0	44.0	14.2	37.8	4.0
100 and under 250	416	191	81	134	10	100.0	45.9	19.5	32.2	2.4
250 and under 500	219	105	42	69	3	100.0	47.9	19.2	31.5	1.4
500 and under 1,000	139	53	48	34	4	100.0	38.1	34.5	24.5	2.9
1,000 and under 5,000	109	38	45	21	5	100.0	34.9	41.2	19.3	4.6
5,000 and under 10,000	14	3	6	4	1	100.0	21.4	42.9	28.6	7.1
10,000 workers and over	9	2	5	1	1	(2)	-------	-------	-------	-------
1936—Total	2,156	991	508	592	65	100.0	45.9	23.6	27.5	3.0
6 and under 20	395	173	56	152	14	100.0	43.8	14.2	38.5	3.5
20 and under 100	834	395	171	245	23	100.0	47.3	20.5	29.4	2.8
100 and under 250	410	205	102	94	9	100.0	50.0	24.9	22.9	2.2
250 and under 500	236	107	82	42	5	100.0	45.4	34.7	17.8	2.1
500 and under 1,000	157	76	42	34	5	100.0	48.3	26.8	21.7	3.2
1,000 and under 5,000	100	25	46	23	6	100.0	25.0	46.0	23.0	6.0
5,000 and under 10,000	18	6	8	2	2	100.0	33.3	44.5	11.1	11.1
10,000 workers and over	6	4	1	-------	1	(2)	-------	-------	-------	-------

[2] Too few to give percentage.

Strikes In Various Cities [17]

Greater New York had nearly three times as many strikes (1,652) during the 10-year period 1927–36 as Philadelphia, which had the second highest number (568). Almost one million workers were involved in the strikes in New York City. This does not necessarily mean that a million different persons engaged in strikes, since some of these workers may have been involved in more than one strike. Chicago had the third highest number of strikes (330), the number of workers involved being almost two-thirds as great as the number involved in Philadelphia. Cleveland had 241 strikes during the 10-year period, and the San Francisco Bay area had 224. Other cities which had more than 100 strikes were Boston; Los Angeles; St. Louis; Detroit; Pittsburgh; Paterson and Newark, N. J.; Milwaukee; and Baltimore.

[17] It should be noted that the data in table 33 pertain to local strikes only. In other words, the incidence of intercity strikes is not shown in this table. It was not possible accurately to determine how many workers in intercity strikes were employed in each of the cities affected, hence the figures in this table are exclusive of intercity strikes.

TABLE 33.—*Strikes beginning in 1927–36, in cities which had 10 or more local strikes in any year*

City and year	Number of strikes beginning in year	Number of workers involved	Man-days idle during year
Akron:			
1927	----	----	----
1928	1	150	600
1929	1	20	80
1930	1	72	2,160
1931	----	----	----
1932	----	----	----
1933	5	536	5,780
1934	13	4,310	94,683
1935	3	352	20,574
1936	43	70,797	488,346
Allentown:			
1927	4	337	3,479
1928	2	237	9,762
1929	10	471	5,365
1930	1	35	70
1931	3	3,137	257,939
1932	----	----	----
1933	8	984	9,557
1934	8	963	27,950
1935	9	1,172	24,135
1936	5	811	11,114
Baltimore:			
1927	7	8,651	109,643
1928	7	737	20,863
1929	10	1,833	16,148
1930	8	5,535	67,084
1931	5	243	6,114
1932	5	5,165	36,924
1933	9	1,575	30,903
1934	16	2,317	16,677
1935	20	6,231	31,821
1936	15	2,961	33,887
Birmingham:			
1927	----	----	----
1928	----	----	----
1929	----	----	----
1930	1	50	1,150
1931	1	72	10,512
1932	2	27	328
1933	1	62	1,028
1934	14	8,999	227,759
1935	8	1,401	33,668
1936	3	1,455	5,005
Boston:			
1927	21	4,185	48,326
1928	25	4,764	118,476
1929	20	5,517	328,105
1930	8	2,797	32,162
1931	15	6,776	240,977
1932	14	3,446	55,897
1933	22	11,317	118,113
1934	16	4,200	58,611
1935	16	3,694	29,127
1936	17	7,226	63,504
Buffalo:			
1927	3	414	11,216
1928	8	2,623	21,157
1929	8	460	6,761
1930	2	97	1,354
1931	3	262	2,124
1932	2	156	156
1933	21	8,833	45,865
1934	12	4,366	147,808
1935	16	2,676	40,037
1936	13	1,683	36,815
Chattanooga:			
1927	2	1,115	37,865
1928	1	6	12
1929	1	15	285
1930	1	8	8
1931	----	----	----
1932	1	44	968
1933	2	18	326
1934	11	2,755	45,221
1935	8	434	16,772
1936	2	123	1,701
Chicago:			
1927	29	8,572	177,182
1928	11	6,456	82,950
1929	32	11,586	189,784
1930	18	1,414	27,711
1931	21	7,257	79,961
1932	27	8,414	165,048
1933	58	28,206	347,949
1934	48	21,310	196,930
1935	47	17,891	440,782
1936	39	3,221	66,418
Cincinnati:			
1927	1	127	11,303
1928	----	----	----
1929	4	1,036	36,785
1930	2	550	2,400
1931	4	534	5,323
1932	5	492	10,816
1933	6	358	11,252
1934	13	2,382	57,289
1935	17	6,288	95,834
1936	7	600	7,506
Cleveland:			
1927	5	817	15,172
1928	9	711	36,796
1929	11	1,518	43,194
1930	12	3,866	72,991
1931	3	330	3,280
1932	3	163	4,113
1933	26	5,550	67,503
1934	67	30,727	428,956
1935	66	28,490	538,022
1936	39	13,918	124,926
Columbus:			
1927	4	72	3,604
1928	2	43	283
1929	3	156	356
1930	1	250	1,250
1931	2	108	888
1932	----	----	----
1933	5	411	7,356
1934	13	3,391	13,757
1935	6	1,544	46,367
1936	2	489	23,705
Detroit:			
1927	6	376	2,498
1928	3	199	18,510
1929	10	1,972	21,664
1930	11	650	9,860
1931	1	190	1,520
1932	4	314	2,489
1933	13	10,398	174,915
1934	44	16,954	227,542
1935	26	6,514	113,968
1936	18	12,603	102,690
Easton:			
1927	4	506	18,586
1928	1	90	90
1929	----	----	----
1930	2	475	10,325
1931	3	510	4,490
1932	1	100	600
1933	1	61	915
1934	----	----	----
1935	3	176	1,158
1936	14	1,586	144,254
Elizabeth:			
1927	2	130	1,580
1928	1	50	200
1929	----	----	----
1930	2	45	285
1931	5	81	530
1932	1	16	908
1933	5	2,896	53,725
1934	2	132	1,548
1935	10	1,748	12,344
1936	8	2,200	24,739

TABLE 33.—*Strikes beginning in 1927-36, in cities which had 10 or more local strikes in any year*—Continued

City and year	Number of strikes beginning in year	Number of workers involved	Man-days idle during year
Erie:			
1927	1	100	800
1928	---	---	---
1929	---	---	---
1930	1	10	60
1931	10	658	23,848
1932	1	100	700
1933	2	386	2,216
1934	---	---	---
1935	2	160	2,124
1936	3	92	1,909
Fall River:			
1927	8	718	7,502
1928	17	4,141	68,482
1929	2	17	25
1930	5	875	6,719
1931	4	611	12,444
1932	5	645	8,450
1933	14	5,497	64,739
1934	12	6,385	45,774
1935	7	632	1,844
1936	9	4,010	49,631
Haverhill:			
1927	1	3,000	36,000
1928	7	5,023	44,370
1929	8	5,835	369,495
1930	2	51	894
1931	3	181	2,133
1932	3	671	2,844
1933	16	9,454	149,845
1934	6	7,195	184,358
1935	8	916	9,686
1936	---	---	---
Houston:[1]			
1927	2	25	290
1929	2	180	720
1931	1	150	2,250
1932	1	60	180
1934	4	565	12,388
1935	2	68	68
1936	11	1,056	14,467
Jersey City:			
1927	3	791	11,307
1928	3	41	1,663
1929	3	272	8,277
1930	6	555	6,750
1931	4	447	1,497
1932	7	765	11,779
1933	2	288	288
1934	4	308	3,355
1935	10	431	10,600
1936	5	812	3,632
Kansas City:			
1927	2	22	1,321
1928	1	14	14
1929	1	415	415
1930	5	497	4,812
1931	1	200	200
1932	5	540	4,370
1933	6	146	3,692
1934	12	1,540	7,377
1935	10	582	8,347
1936	2	2,472	24,940
Los Angeles:			
1927	6	200	8,521
1928	8	624	5,812
1929	9	1,648	27,864
1930	3	906	25,391
1931	5	228	2,519
1932	2	20	200
1933	20	13,029	211,297
1934	18	4,738	60,994
1935	42	3,790	70,938
1936	50	10,502	239,497
Lynn:			
1927	2	35	520
1928	9	4,070	35,812
1929	8	6,484	80,956
1930	3	143	1,933
1931	3	170	822
1932	6	984	9,749
1933	7	8,175	47,606
1934	3	3,353	34,668
1935	7	1,881	22,735
1936	11	3,638	25,464
Milwaukee:			
1927	---	---	---
1928	2	365	4,525
1929	1	100	4,400
1930	4	182	2,650
1931	6	1,973	44,027
1932	1	100	600
1933	6	482	8,489
1934	42	13,980	307,002
1935	21	3,952	69,587
1936	24	4,512	60,360
Minneapolis:			
1927	7	568	28,420
1928	1	120	4,380
1929	8	387	6,200
1930	3	80	3,318
1931	3	241	5,503
1932	2	525	5,845
1933	4	628	28,985
1934	12	19,127	258,404
1935	16	2,706	131,320
1936	30	5,230	194,642
Newark:			
1927	3	1,218	9,342
1928	8	621	11,725
1929	13	1,690	8,355
1930	11	234	5,781
1931	8	2,583	110,606
1932	9	723	10,054
1933	24	2,494	43,931
1934	22	2,399	51,205
1935	13	4,406	134,878
1936	7	888	12,073
New Bedford:			
1927	8	868	20,925
1928	6	25,749	3,689,221
1929	4	180	6,519
1930	1	44	1,531
1931	1	13	26
1932	---	---	---
1933	9	7,126	19,350
1934	11	2,191	10,814
1935	4	545	6,061
1936	7	1,852	38,684
New York (Greater):			
1927	117	42,757	1,111,780
1928	87	75,021	908,966
1929	125	60,673	1,212,180
1930	86	51,745	602,732
1931	169	59,976	624,342
1932	171	110,441	2,192,451
1933	152	187,582	2,957,224
1934	201	133,465	1,628,422
1935	257	102,267	955,210
1936	287	128,644	1,368,813
Paterson:			
1927	6	422	11,540
1928	10	6,481	250,451
1929	24	726	13,642
1930	8	930	19,694
1931	5	8,273	499,919
1932	12	2,067	40,773
1933	15	25,069	936,167

[1] No strikes during 1928, 1930, and 1933.

TABLE 33.—*Strikes beginning in 1927–36, in cities which had 10 or more local strikes in any year*—Continued

City and year	Number of strikes beginning in year	Number of workers involved	Man-days idle during year
Paterson—Continued.			
1934	7	1,541	26,815
1935	18	16,661	282,044
1936	14	2,302	26,508
Philadelphia:			
1927	23	2,502	71,350
1928	22	1,729	19,470
1929	75	13,293	184,435
1930	33	5,314	183,511
1931	31	8,672	536,234
1932	34	2,946	46,299
1933	106	60,122	601,975
1934	68	36,076	496,814
1935	74	14,873	161,656
1936	102	31,901	347,198
Pittsburgh:			
1927	8	2,429	20,324
1928	6	530	3,046
1929	12	1,884	66,923
1930	9	1,975	193,346
1931	16	2,684	33,989
1932	10	2,860	80,854
1933	20	5,061	87,775
1934	18	2,399	40,974
1935	17	1,246	49,279
1936	16	3,256	54,807
Portland (Oreg.):			
1927	4	396	10,542
1928	---	---	---
1929	5	276	3,558
1930	1	40	720
1931	4	126	396
1932	4	590	3,865
1933	1	15	15
1934	16	2,807	25,207
1935	10	403	7,970
1936	31	3,632	75,294
Providence:			
1927	7	571	16,884
1928	2	550	15,500
1929	4	359	1,514
1930	5	270	1,970
1931	3	1,150	20,350
1932	5	205	1,794
1933	12	2,364	17,789
1934	2	81	81
1935	7	427	2,450
1936	10	2,070	30,474
Reading:			
1927	2	462	13,832
1928	3	271	10,618
1929	5	792	12,182
1930	4	742	7,144
1931	3	148	780
1932	4	252	7,059
1933	22	3,204	69,515
1934	7	730	14,427
1935	8	829	25,844
1936	6	5,784	153,144
Rochester:			
1927	11	377	4,794
1928	3	89	435
1929	6	190	2,826
1930	3	322	3,321
1931	5	863	1,178
1932	8	1,219	14,117
1933	6	7,618	32,650
1934	14	2,116	13,096
1935	7	306	2,782
1936	10	3,941	36,662
St. Louis:			
1927	11	1,325	25,162
1928	5	640	50,379
1929	14	6,660	184,210
St. Louis—Continued.			
1930	4	1,334	26,052
1931	10	354	9,965
1932	10	2,319	26,503
1933	29	13,428	340,272
1934	20	6,184	90,691
1935	21	2,673	64,429
1936	20	2,369	26,311
San Francisco (Bay area):			
1927	7	174	4,446
1928	3	90	1,270
1929	8	3,651	22,103
1930	3	66	282
1931	10	846	18,324
1932	7	478	4,290
1933	8	1,001	18,468
1934	42	97,665	328,826
1935	60	11,549	142,291
1936	76	18,882	422,737
Seattle:			
1927	1	15	105
1928	4	155	2,107
1929	2	68	915
1930	1	18	270
1931	6	1,851	75,375
1932	3	1,150	14,600
1933	5	327	5,327
1934	6	331	1,291
1935	22	3,340	33,918
1936	21	2,775	105,698
Scranton:			
1927	5	1,751	150,794
1928	6	1,783	119,504
1929	10	1,887	7,174
1930	3	373	4,775
1931	5	375	16,055
1932	3	82	1,374
1933	13	6,922	39,312
1934	10	1,625	25,353
1935	3	233	1,785
1936	5	681	8,266
Terre Haute:			
1927	1	125	125
1928	1	125	4,000
1929	2	80	4,262
1930	1	45	2,070
1931	---	---	---
1932	2	496	2,504
1933	---	---	---
1934	7	1,082	12,055
1935	10	27,896	135,855
1936	2	114	765
Toledo:			
1927	---	---	---
1928	1	22	22
1929	2	140	3,920
1930	2	17	449
1931	3	122	792
1932	3	102	502
1933	7	245	1,599
1934	14	5,147	58,545
1935	18	8,034	125,949
1936	22	4,811	117,561
Washington, D. C.:			
1927	---	---	---
1928	2	20	100
1929	5	281	12,024
1930	4	225	2,669
1931	6	249	1,479
1932	6	249	2,286
1933	14	1,914	19,767
1934	22	3,175	60,329
1935	13	4,401	10,521
1936	16	1,231	22,474

TABLE 33.—*Strikes beginning in 1927-36, in cities which had 10 or more local strikes in any year*—Continued

City and year	Number of strikes beginning in year	Number of workers involved	Man-days idle during year	City and year	Number of strikes beginning in year	Number of workers involved	Man-days idle during year
Woonsocket:				Worcester—Continued.			
1927	4	1,655	59,533	1932	2	132	257
1928	-----	-----	-----	1933	2	705	10,514
1929	1	50	100	1934	2	220	3,968
1930	1	23	92	1935	11	468	3,838
1931	2	335	335	1936	4	93	4,083
1932	1	118	1,652	York:			
1933	14	3,257	41,249	1927	-----	-----	-----
1934	1	350	29,050	1928	-----	-----	-----
1935	4	501	2,620	1929	-----	-----	-----
1936	7	1,437	19,243	1930	3	97	934
Worcester:				1931	1	174	696
1927	2	55	1,210	1932	-----	-----	-----
1928	2	36	1,308	1933	2	61	103
1929	1	50	150	1934	11	1,384	23,013
1930	1	18	90	1935	5	272	8,802
1931	2	65	1,430	1936	2	88	354

Strikes in Each State [18]

In 7 of the 10 years from 1927 to 1936, Pennsylvania had more workers involved in strikes than any other State. In the other 3 years—1930, 1932, and 1936—the greatest number were in New York.

In 1930 New York had 31 percent of the total number of workers involved in all strikes, in 1932 over 42 percent, and in 1936 over 20 percent. The years in which Pennsylvania had the greatest number of workers involved, the proportion varied from 17 to 30 percent of the total.

There were 2,333 strikes in New York State from 1927 to 1936. Almost 1¼ million workers were involved in these strikes. Although there were fewer strikes in Pennsylvania (2,135), more workers (1,389,-482) were involved. Massachusetts had 903 strikes during this period, which involved almost one-half million workers. Other States having more than 500 strikes were Ohio, 850; New Jersey, 818; Illinois, 706; California, 594.

---

[18] In table 34 the interstate strikes have been broken down, insofar as possible, and regarded as separate strikes in each State affected, with the proper allocation of workers involved and man-days of idleness. Because of this division the sum of the strikes in all States for any year would amount to more than the total number of strikes for the year as shown in other tables. Strikes for which information was lacking wth respect to number of workers affected in each State have been listed at the end of the table.

Table 34.—*Strikes beginning in 1927–36, by States*

State and year	Number of strikes beginning in year	Workers involved			Man-days idle during year	
		Number	Percentage of total for all States	Average per strike	Number	Percentage of total for all States
Alabama:						
1927	1	30	(1)	30	120	(1)
1928	-----	-----	-----	-----	-----	-----
1929	1	14	(1)	14	14	(1)
1930	1	50	(1)	50	1,150	(1)
1931	1	72	(1)	72	10,512	0.2
1932	5	702	0.2	140	4,878	(1)
1933	21	6,799	.6	324	93,781	.6
1934	45	84,228	5.7	1,872	1,722,993	8.8
1935	59	38,275	3.4	649	1,124,392	7.3
1936	31	10,126	1.3	327	278,674	2.0
Arizona:						
1927	-----	-----	-----	-----	-----	-----
1928	3	66	(1)	22	730	(1)
1929	-----	-----	-----	-----	-----	-----
1930	-----	-----	-----	-----	-----	-----
1931	2	43	(1)	22	172	(1)
1932	-----	-----	-----	-----	-----	-----
1933	3	2,807	.2	936	13,904	.1
1934	2	400	(1)	200	4,300	(1)
1935	2	260	(1)	130	6,650	(1)
1936	2	940	.1	470	1,880	(1)
Arkansas:						
1927	1	400	.1	400	45,600	.2
1928	1	22	(1)	22	22	(1)
1929	2	185	.1	93	2,015	(1)
1930	1	400	.2	400	3,600	.1
1931	2	324	.1	162	1,824	(1)
1932	-----	-----	-----	-----	-----	-----
1933	8	1,263	.1	158	15,317	.1
1934	2	1,388	(1)	694	55,208	.3
1935	7	6,371	.6	910	49,168	.3
1936	4	2,825	.4	706	64,602	.5
California:						
1927	20	1,464	.4	73	18,005	.1
1928	16	1,119	.4	70	9,017	.1
1929	28	6,719	2.3	240	57,009	1.1
1930	14	4,272	2.3	305	79,231	2.4
1931	23	5,769	1.7	251	37,398	.5
1932	23	2,090	.6	91	28,796	.3
1933	47	38,950	3.3	829	638,435	3.8
1934	92	130,456	8.9	1,418	1,110,254	5.7
1935	137	29,487	2.6	215	479,677	3.0
1936	194	70,027	8.9	361	2,038,101	14.7
Colorado:						
1927	6	4,856	1.5	809	233,293	.9
1928	5	480	.2	06	168,421	1.3
1929	1	45	(1)	45	315	(1)
1930	-----	-----	-----	-----	-----	-----
1931	4	105	(1)	26	224	(1)
1932	3	340	.1	113	3,810	(1)
1933	4	499	(1)	125	3,630	(1)
1934	12	1,914	.1	160	13,947	.1
1935	5	8,170	.7	1,634	56,764	.4
1936	8	1,707	.2	213	13,084	.1
Connecticut:						
1927	27	4,302	1.3	159	75,445	.3
1928	10	2,368	.8	237	40,772	.3
1929	13	3,365	1.2	259	47,354	.9
1930	13	1,138	.6	88	16,886	.5
1931	17	3,201	.9	188	78,307	1.1
1932	22	1,330	.4	60	21,157	.2
1933	61	26,061	2.2	427	230,610	1.4
1934	56	31,635	2.2	565	409,791	2.1
1935	44	12,656	1.1	288	194,291	1.[illegible]
1936	45	9,435	1.2	210	178,674	1.[illegible]
Delaware:						
1927	3	237	.1	79	1,513	(1)
1928	-----	-----	-----	-----	-----	-----
1929	3	59	(1)	20	185	(1)
1930	3	307	.2	102	6,646	.2
1931	1	40	(1)	40	80	(1)
1932	-----	-----	-----	-----	-----	-----
1933	2	310	(1)	155	1,310	(1)
1934	3	450	(1)	150	1,800	(1)
1935	2	345	(1)	173	1,965	(1)
1936	6	249	(1)	42	2,823	(1)

1 Less than 1/10 of 1 percent.

TABLE 34.—*Strikes beginning in 1927–36, by States*—Continued

State and year	Number of strikes beginning in year	Workers involved			Man-days idle during year	
		Number	Percentage of total for all States	Average per strike	Number	Percentage of total for all States
District of Columbia:						
1927	-----	-----	-----	-----	-----	-----
1928	2	20	(1)	10	100	(1)
1929	5	281	0.1	56	12,024	0.2
1930	4	225	.1	56	2,669	.1
1931	6	249	.1	42	1,479	(1)
1932	6	249	.1	42	2,286	(1)
1933	14	1,914	.2	137	19,767	.1
1934	22	3,175	.2	144	60,329	.3
1935	13	4,401	.4	339	10,521	.1
1936	16	1,231	.2	77	22,474	.2
Florida:						
1927	6	516	.2	86	21,046	.1
1928	2	70	(1)	35	7,640	.1
1929	2	275	.1	138	18,325	.3
1930	3	168	.1	56	1,668	.1
1931	4	8,812	2.6	2,203	110,067	1.6
1932	2	17	(1)	9	29	(1)
1933	8	12,207	1.0	1,526	129,315	.8
1934	4	246	(1)	62	18,264	.1
1935	9	7,046	.6	783	290,070	1.9
1936	7	1,491	.2	213	13,864	.1
Georgia:						
1927	1	7	(1)	7	434	(1)
1928	2	62	(1)	31	1,457	(1)
1929	3	893	.3	298	10,053	.2
1930	2	61	(1)	30	1,187	(1)
1931	3	482	.1	161	4,232	.1
1932	2	81	(1)	41	1,287	(1)
1933	17	11,219	1.0	660	73,401	.4
1934	18	38,637	2.6	2,147	503,974	2.6
1935	16	6,692	.6	418	182,236	1.2
1936	10	2,558	.3	256	64,850	.5
Idaho:						
1927	-----	-----	-----	-----	-----	-----
1928	-----	-----	-----	-----	-----	-----
1929	-----	-----	-----	-----	-----	-----
1930	2	124	.1	62	744	(1)
1931	1	25	(1)	25	250	(1)
1932	-----	-----	-----	-----	-----	-----
1933	1	13	(1)	13	91	(1)
1934	-----	-----	-----	-----	-----	-----
1935	5	1,623	.1	325	6,373	(1)
1936	5	2,617	.3	523	123,375	.9
Illinois:						
1927	44	77,770	23.6	1,768	7,882,094	30.1
1928	40	39,382	12.5	985	2,302,617	18.2
1929	65	22,591	7.8	348	290,706	5.4
1930	45	12,022	6.6	267	378,127	11.4
1931	42	17,790	5.2	424	455,226	6.6
1932	52	40,270	12.4	774	3,530,524	33.6
1933	104	38,457	3.3	370	480,705	2.8
1934	110	44,900	3.1	408	455,950	2.3
1935	106	73,538	6.6	694	834,043	5.4
1936	98	24,094	3.1	246	409,748	2.9
Indiana:						
1927	17	18,534	5.6	1,090	2,036,077	7.8
1928	15	4,179	1.3	279	450,385	3.6
1929	40	10,760	3.7	269	398,577	7.4
1930	27	3,930	2.1	146	56,867	1.7
1931	19	7,124	2.1	375	97,802	1.4
1932	17	6,083	1.9	358	442,075	4.2
1933	23	6,590	.6	287	69,577	.4
1934	40	9,600	.7	240	194,852	1.0
1935	41	46,448	4.2	1,133	350,207	2.3
1936	34	11,726	1.5	345	153,596	1.1
Iowa:						
1927	7	5,825	1.8	832	640,645	2.4
1928	12	6,037	1.9	503	241,474	1.9
1929	7	806	.3	115	4,505	.1
1930	4	414	.2	104	12,052	.4
1931	10	942	.3	94	9,808	.1
1932	8	599	.2	75	8,809	.1
1933	12	7,378	.6	615	248,446	1.5
1934	14	8,289	.6	592	64,765	.3
1935	13	11,129	1.0	856	79,796	.5
1936	10	1,210	.2	121	45,297	.3

1 Less than 1/10 of 1 percent.

TABLE 34.—*Strikes beginning in 1927–36, by States*—Continued

State and year	Number of strikes beginning in year	Workers involved			Man-days idle during year	
		Number	Percentage of total for all States	Average per strike	Number	Percentage of total for all States
Kansas:						
1927	2	3,014	0.9	1,507	342,644	1.3
1928	3	2,352	.7	784	144,952	1.1
1929	5	352	.1	70	2,566	(1)
1930	2	2,109	1.2	1,055	84,619	2.6
1931	1	75	(1)	75	300	(1)
1932	3	59	(1)	20	672	(1)
1933	3	62	(1)	21	614	(1)
1934	6	2,767	.2	461	88,711	.5
1935	7	4,854	.4	693	39,507	.3
1936	5	265	(1)	53	998	(1)
Kentucky:						
1927	13	4,073	1.2	313	60,182	.2
1928	4	452	.1	113	39,177	.3
1929	7	923	.3	132	10,559	.2
1930	13	9,190	5.0	707	411,304	12.4
1931	5	6,314	1.8	1,263	172,803	2.5
1932	9	1,339	.4	149	27,642	.3
1933	16	6,568	.6	411	94,467	.6
1934	14	15,667	1.1	1,119	191,367	1.0
1935	13	14,894	1.3	1,146	403,116	2.6
1936	9	1,305	.2	145	358,713	2.6
Louisiana:						
1927	3	212	.1	71	14,372	.1
1928	3	67	(1)	22	10,606	.1
1929	8	3,302	1.1	413	201,976	3.8
1930	5	412	.2	82	6,424	.2
1931	3	2,140	.6	713	5,705	.1
1932	6	2,976	.9	496	7,116	.1
1933	10	10,967	.9	1,097	72,221	.4
1934	9	1,566	.1	174	18,539	.1
1935	12	5,355	.5	446	138,251	.9
1936	17	3,082	.4	181	31,858	.2
Maine:						
1927	3	383	.1	128	3,053	(1)
1928	5	2,046	.7	409	14,556	.1
1929	7	550	.2	79	9,917	.2
1930	7	1,196	.7	171	22,236	.7
1931	3	34	(1)	11	215	(1)
1932	4	2,246	.7	562	38,736	.4
1933	6	654	.1	109	3,716	(1)
1934	3	9,796	.7	3,265	98,386	.5
1935	7	2,299	.2	328	25,717	.2
1936	7	831	.1	119	5,811	(1)
Maryland:						
1927	9	8,803	2.7	978	110,295	.4
1928	8	772	.2	96	21,108	.2
1929	13	2,070	.7	159	17,249	.3
1930	10	6,585	3.6	659	86,684	2.6
1931	6	923	.3	154	13,594	.2
1932	6	5,365	1.7	894	41,924	.4
1933	12	6,601	.6	550	57,841	.3
1934	19	2,507	.2	132	18,477	.1
1935	27	9,456	.8	350	49,694	.3
1936	27	19,131	2.4	709	203,300	1.5
Massachusetts:						
1927	68	10,779	3.3	159	162,157	.6
1928	90	46,865	14.9	521	4,008,413	31.7
1929	78	23,673	8.2	304	862,300	16.1
1930	45	5,274	2.9	117	61,563	1.9
1931	63	47,954	14.0	761	1,106,746	16.1
1932	65	9,763	3.0	150	130,996	1.2
1933	161	88,754	7.6	551	1,411,408	8.4
1934	112	116,422	7.9	1,039	1,339,084	6.8
1935	110	26,321	2.4	239	605,188	3.9
1936	111	34,193	4.3	308	432,223	3.1
Michigan:						
1927	8	411	.1	51	3,163	(1)
1928	7	351	.1	50	21,806	.2
1929	16	2,706	.9	169	37,005	.7
1930	15	5,401	3.0	360	64,366	1.9
1931	9	532	.2	59	10,565	.2
1932	11	1,014	.3	92	9,835	.1
1933	25	17,531	1.5	701	346,831	2.1
1934	63	25,447	1.7	404	290,481	1.5
1935	55	17,226	1.5	313	187,325	1.2
1936	45	26,986	3.4	600	214,182	1.5

[1] Less than 1/10 of 1 percent.

Table 34.—*Strikes beginning in 1927–36, by States*—Continued

State and year	Number of strikes beginning in year	Workers involved			Man-days idle during year	
		Number	Percentage of total for all States	Average per strike	Number	Percentage of total for all States
Minnesota:						
1927	11	1,695	0.5	154	75,964	0.3
1928	3	305	.1	102	5,120	(1)
1929	9	417	.1	46	6,440	.1
1930	7	250	.1	36	4,869	.1
1931	7	602	.2	86	11,928	.2
1932	5	581	.2	116	6,723	.1
1933	9	5,103	.4	567	48,475	.3
1934	22	23,437	1.6	1,065	286,381	1.5
1935	35	6,028	.5	172	177,135	1.1
1936	54	14,214	1.8	263	249,744	1.8
Mississippi:						
1927	1	35	(1)	35	70	(1)
1928						
1929	1	35	(1)	35	35	(1)
1930	1	100	.1	100	300	(1)
1931	2	256	.1	128	376	(1)
1932	2	1,700	.5	850	72,400	.7
1933	8	2,212	.2	276	6,624	(1)
1934	7	3,018	.2	431	45,480	.2
1935	8	3,601	.3	450	62,378	.4
1936	3	285	(1)	95	2,800	(1)
Missouri:						
1927	16	4,040	1.2	253	324,914	1.2
1928	9	1,781	.6	198	145,520	1.2
1929	17	7,214	2.5	424	184,931	3.5
1930	13	8,749	4.8	673	64,320	1.9
1931	18	1,716	.5	95	29,147	.4
1932	19	3,313	1.0	174	41,495	.4
1933	48	17,077	1.5	356	360,457	2.1
1934	42	15,762	1.1	375	223,204	1.1
1935	45	16,438	1.5	365	230,291	1.5
1936	35	9,821	1.2	281	158,194	1.1
Montana:						
1927	3	89	(1)	29	2,379	(1)
1928	2	2,400	.8	1,200	16,400	.1
1929	4	586	.2	147	10,544	.2
1930	7	1,434	.8	205	19,743	.6
1931	2	24	(1)	12	296	(1)
1932	5	3,041	.9	608	117,384	1.1
1933	1	18	(1)	18	378	(1)
1934	8	6,923	.5	865	549,483	2.8
1935	7	2,130	.2	304	26,892	.2
1936	6	1,215	.2	203	10,628	.1
Nebraska:						
1927	2	37	(1)	19	162	(1)
1928						
1929	2	75	(1)	38	115	(1)
1930						
1931						
1932						
1933	1	8	(1)	8	48	(1)
1934	5	1,288	.1	258	4,603	(1)
1935	2	282	(1)	141	2,613	(1)
1936	5	290	(1)	58	1,715	(1)
Nevada:						
1927	2	88	(1)	44	388	(1)
1928						
1929						
1930						
1931	1	1,470	.4	1,470	14,700	.2
1932	1	70	(1)	70	70	(1)
1933						
1934						
1935	2	1,287	.1	644	12,888	.1
1936	3	169	(1)	56	247	(1)
New Hampshire:						
1927	4	286	.1	72	6,964	(1)
1928	4	525	.2	131	2,405	(1)
1929	4	1,190	.4	298	54,439	1.0
1930	1	165	.1	165	1,880	.1
1931	3	252	.1	84	1,874	(1)
1932	9	1,216	.4	135	5,978	.1
1933	26	19,116	1.6	735	343,104	2.0
1934	13	30,838	2.1	2,372	251,087	1.3
1935	8	1,547	.1	193	30,844	.2
1936	5	1,093	.1	219	13,288	.1

1 Less than 1/10 of 1 percent.

TABLE 34.—*Strikes beginning in 1927–36, by States*—Continued

State and year	Number of strikes beginning in year	Workers involved			Man-days idle during year	
		Number	Percentage of total for all States	Average per strike	Number	Percentage of total for all States
New Jersey:						
1927	61	8,905	2.7	146	138,143	0.5
1928	43	11,754	3.7	273	364,160	2.9
1929	77	13,713	4.8	178	170,256	3.2
1930	55	5,625	3.1	102	91,583	2.8
1931	60	24,015	7.0	400	856,904	12.4
1932	75	13,802	4.3	184	212,548	2.0
1933	112	66,259	5.7	592	1,802,331	10.7
1934	86	50,758	3.5	590	938,563	4.8
1935	123	47,233	4.2	384	1,090,083	7.1
1936	126	30,024	3.8	238	560,953	4.0
New Mexico:						
1927	1	10	(1)	10	30	(1)
1928						
1929						
1930						
1931	1	14	(1)	14	28	(1)
1932	1	350	.1	350	10,841	.1
1933	2	1,151	.1	576	61,426	.4
1934	5	1,385	.1	277	4,528	(1)
1935	3	2,504	.2	835	16,902	.1
1936	4	885	.1	221	35,165	.3
New York:						
1927	159	47,993	14.5	302	1,220,602	4.7
1928	127	81,741	26.0	644	980,724	7.8
1929	176	66,765	23.1	379	1,382,912	25.8
1930	140	56,027	30.6	400	646,206	19.5
1931	227	67,997	19.9	300	727,702	10.6
1932	241	137,347	42.4	570	2,504,541	23.8
1933	240	300,308	25.7	1,251	3,880,929	23.0
1934	281	190,376	13.0	677	2,465,475	12.6
1935	349	140,299	12.6	402	1,498,133	9.7
1936	393	160,734	20.5	409	1,943,992	14.0
North Carolina:						
1927	6	979	.3	163	27,616	.1
1928	1	50	(1)	50	1,150	(1)
1929	18	4,797	1.7	267	90,673	1.7
1930	6	938	.5	156	6,474	.2
1931	2	306	.1	153	2,078	(1)
1932	22	14,092	4.3	641	185,062	1.8
1933	28	10,689	.9	382	179,676	1.1
1934	22	48,413	3.3	2,201	538,558	2.7
1935	16	5,215	.5	326	46,893	.3
1936	13	5,319	.7	409	85,707	.6
North Dakota:						
1927						
1928						
1929						
1930						
1931						
1932						
1933	1	175	(1)	175	2,800	(1)
1934	2	211	(1)	106	211	(1)
1935	3	1,622	.1	541	7,861	.1
1936	4	647	.1	162	1,878	(1)
Ohio:						
1927	21	28,487	8.6	1,357	4,520,822	17.2
1928	27	11,825	3.8	438	1,627,136	12.9
1929	44	6,387	2.2	145	174,161	3.3
1930	33	8,278	4.5	251	115,735	3.5
1931	42	12,289	3.6	293	142,801	2.1
1932	37	18,888	5.8	510	1,814,682	17.3
1933	96	24,904	2.1	259	279,587	1.7
1934	200	80,635	5.5	403	1,380,664	7.0
1935	173	88,620	7.9	512	1,301,504	8.4
1936	177	124,803	15.9	705	1,742,788	12.5
Oklahoma:						
1927	4	373	.1	93	30,876	.1
1928	3	58	(1)	19	601	(1)
1929	3	419	.1	140	729	(1)
1930	1	10	(1)	10	10	(1)
1931	6	1,231	.4	205	36,397	.5
1932	6	1,043	.3	174	22,049	.2
1933	2	1,700	.1	850	10,700	.1
1934	11	5,218	.4	474	119,110	.6
1935	15	5,638	.5	376	121,450	.8
1936	6	871	.1	145	40,396	.3

[1] Less than 1/10 of 1 percent.

TABLE 34.—*Strikes beginning in 1927–36, by States*—Continued

State and year	Number of strikes beginning in year	Workers involved			Man-days idle during year	
		Number	Percentage of total for all States	Average per strike	Number	Percentage of total for all States
Oregon:						
1927	9	525	0.2	58	11,989	(1)
1928	6	372	.1	62	1,957	(1)
1929	7	311	.1	44	4,053	0.1
1930	2	140	.1	70	820	(1)
1931	7	954	.3	136	1,248	(1)
1932	4	590	.2	148	3,865	(1)
1933	10	10,067	.9	1,007	171,755	1.0
1934	36	17,941	1.2	498	146,966	.8
1935	21	13,829	1.2	659	539,201	3.5
1936	53	16,009	2.0	302	391,174	2.8
Pennsylvania:						
1927	119	81,132	24.6	682	7,624,735	29.1
1928	110	90,432	28.8	822	1,910,801	15.1
1929	184	80,792	28.0	439	661,187	12.4
1930	115	34,556	18.9	300	621,353	18.7
1931	130	100,950	29.5	777	2,069,603	30.0
1932	115	36,505	11.3	317	444,142	4.2
1933	381	347,244	29.7	911	4,632,545	27.5
1934	296	254,478	17.3	860	2,691,252	13.7
1935	320	245,189	21.9	766	2,326,961	15.1
1936	365	118,204	15.0	324	2,016,541	14.5
Rhode Island:						
1927	23	5,583	1.7	243	248,628	.9
1928	9	1,368	.4	152	29,079	.2
1929	17	2,920	1.0	172	86,946	1.6
1930	10	533	.3	53	3,423	.1
1931	20	4,836	1.4	242	120,030	1.7
1932	11	1,402	.4	127	26,661	.3
1933	49	12,509	1.1	255	203,160	1.2
1934	14	30,198	2.1	2,157	334,398	1.7
1935	21	3,512	.3	167	79,622	.5
1936	27	5,810	.7	215	82,289	.6
South Carolina:						
1927						
1928						
1929	14	11,907	4.1	851	302,034	5.6
1930	1	48	(1)	48	240	(1)
1931	1	8	(1)	8	8	(1)
1932	4	1,857	.6	464	72,897	.7
1933	32	15,276	1.3	477	111,327	.7
1934	17	42,414	2.9	2,495	544,358	2.8
1935	11	5,050	.5	459	183,760	1.2
1936	16	4,445	.6	278	257,375	1.9
South Dakota:						
1927						
1928						
1929	1	17	(1)	17	68	(1)
1930						
1931	1	150	(1)	150	900	(1)
1932						
1933						
1934	1	1,200	.1	1,200	6,000	(1)
1935	3	2,522	.2	841	25,777	.2
1936						
Tennessee:						
1927	4	1,372	.4	343	41,657	.2
1928	6	462	.1	77	7,374	.1
1929	8	8,456	2.9	1,057	149,391	2.8
1930	1	8	(1)	8	8	(1)
1931	6	872	.3	145	8,462	
1932	4	635	.2	159	51,723	.1
1933	20	4,019	.3	201	55,984	.5
1934	17	10,866	.7	639	145,484	.3
1935	27	4,145	.4	154	125,815	.7
1936	23	2,760	.3	120	62,322	.8
						4

[1] Less than 1/10 of 1 percent.

Table 34.—*Strikes beginning in 1927–36, by States*—Continued

State and year	Number of strikes beginning in year	Workers involved			Man-days idle during year	
		Number	Percentage of total for all States	Average per strike	Number	Percentage of total for all States
Texas:						
1927	8	131	(1)	16	7,863	(1)
1928	5	311	0.1	62	10,432	0.1
1929	6	501	.2	84	8,972	.2
1930	6	3,229	1.8	538	7,513	.2
1931	13	3,134	.9	241	52,660	.8
1932	7	353	.1	50	7,481	.1
1933	7	3,102	.3	443	14,375	.1
1934	22	8,222	.6	374	111,707	.6
1935	24	7,615	.7	317	156,408	1.0
1936	38	7,058	.9	186	93,641	.7
Utah:						
1927	1	90	(1)	90	6,930	(1)
1928						
1929	1	45	(1)	45	45	(1)
1930						
1931						
1932	1	10	(1)	10	70	(1)
1933	1	453	(1)	453	2,868	(1)
1934	3	281	(1)	94	896	(1)
1935	3	2,828	.3	943	13,692	.1
1936	4	3,382	.4	846	136,995	1.0
Vermont:						
1927	1	14	(1)	14	56	(1)
1928	1	130	(1)	130	9,360	.1
1929	1	75	(1)	75	75	(1)
1930	1	50	(1)	50	1,300	(1)
1931						
1932						
1933	5	1,916	.2	383	81,908	.5
1934	3	3,613	.2	1,204	55,430	.3
1935	6	1,960	.2	327	32,809	.2
1936	3	168	(1)	56	57,044	.4
Virginia:						
1927	1	6	(1)	6	402	(1)
1928	3	314	.1	105	2,129	(1)
1929	5	751	.3	150	4,848	.1
1930	3	4,081	2.2	1,360	316,361	9.5
1931	2	611	.2	306	99,611	1.4
1932	2	275	.1	138	1,625	(1)
1933	15	5,183	.4	346	89,917	.5
1934	7	2,907	.2	415	109,928	.6
1935	12	12,765	1.1	1,064	85,342	.6
1936	7	1,659	.2	237	8,311	.1
Washington:						
1927	9	1,292	.4	144	44,184	.2
1928	13	647	.2	50	12,219	.1
1929	10	582	.2	58	63,985	1.2
1930	6	542	.3	90	28,876	.9
1931	15	3,585	1.0	239	102,012	1.5
1932	7	1,734	.5	248	19,109	.2
1933	23	3,223	.3	140	96,234	.6
1934	28	7,665	.5	274	265,153	1.4
1935	61	33,830	3.0	555	1,043,066	6.7
1936	82	28,073	3.6	342	846,825	6.1
West Virginia:						
1927	6	2,963	.9	494	210,988	.8
1928					3,230	(1)
1929	2	365	.1	183	3,010	.1
1930	10	4,105	2.2	411	79,155	2.4
1931	8	8,662	2.5	1,083	388,795	5.6
1932	7	7,284	2.2	1,041	528,709	5.0
1933	15	25,766	2.2	1,718	380,621	2.3
1934	23	35,095	2.4	1,526	556,517	2.8
1935	17	104,431	9.3	6,143	570,426	3.7
1936	30	7,333	.9	244	140,968	1.0
Wisconsin:						
1927	3	621	.2	207	11,089	(1)
1928	8	1,245	.4	156	12,305	.1
1929	6	283	.1	47	7,837	.1
1930	9	759	.4	84	7,846	.2
1931	15	4,933	1.4	329	108,375	1.6
1932	8	588	.2	74	7,321	.1
1933	17	4,670	.4	275	42,312	.3
1934	77	33,085	2.3	430	791,377	4.0
1935	46	10,275	.9	223	266,703	1.7
1936	50	16,417	2.1	328	233,200	1.7

[1] Less than 1/10 of 1 percent.

TABLE 34.—*Strikes beginning in 1927–36, by States*—Continued

State and year	Number of strikes beginning in year	Workers involved			Man-days idle during year	
		Number	Percentage of total for all States	Average per strike	Number	Percentage of total for all States
Wyoming:						
1927						
1928	3	1,418	0.5	473	4,034	(1)
1929						
1930	1	70	(1)	70	770	(1)
1931						
1932	1	11	(1)	11	1,078	(1)
1933	2	520	(1)	260	7,200	(1)
1934	2	180	(1)	90	2,160	(1)
1935	2	3,690	.3	1,845	18,420	0
1936	3	800	.1	267	12,120	1
Extended across State lines:[2]						
1927	2	1,577	.5	789	11,039	(1)
1928	2	362	.1	181	2,474	(1)
1929	2	400	.1	200	1,200	(1)
1930						
1931						
1932	4	3,000	.9	750	43,007	4
1933						
1934	11	30,798	2.1	2,800	361,504	1.8
1935	25	16,282	1.5	651	247,517	1.6
1936	2	131	(1)	66	57,529	4

[1] Less than 1/10 of 1 percent.
[2] Unable to determine number of workers involved in each State.

Twenty-four States had fewer than 25 strikes each year between 1927 and 1936 and therefore are not included in table 35, which shows strikes by industry group. In general, the number of strikes in each industry varied with the importance of the industry in each State. Exceptions are most marked in the automobile, petroleum, paper, and textile industries. The first three experienced fewer and textiles many more strikes in relation to the size of the industry in most of the States.

In half of the 24 States having 25 or more strikes in any year between 1927 and 1936, the greatest number occurred in the textile and clothing industries. In seven of these States (Illinois, Indiana, Minnesota, Missouri, Ohio, Texas, and Wisconsin) the largest number of strikes took place in the building-construction trades.

During the 10-year period, the greatest number of strikes in Alabama occurred in textiles (37) and mining (35); in California, in transportation (144) and agriculture (69); in Connecticut, in textiles (141); in Illinois, in building-construction trades (129) and mining (91); in Indiana, in building-construction trades (80); and in Maryland, in textiles (30).

Massachusetts had 305 strikes in the textile industries and 231 in leather and shoes; Michigan had 42 strikes in the manufacture of transportation equipment; Minnesota and Missouri experienced the greatest number of strikes in the building trades, 26 and 66, respectively; New Hampshire had 30 strikes each in the textile and leather industries; and New Jersey had 303 strikes in the textile industries.

In New York State the greatest number of strikes occurred in the textile and clothing industries (617) and the next largest number was in the building trades (327); a majority of the strikes in North Carolina occurred in the textile industries (94); Ohio had the greatest number in the building trades (107), the next highest being in steel manufacturing (64); and in Oregon the greatest number occurred in transportation (38), the next highest being in lumber (25).

The greatest number of strikes in Pennsylvania was in the textile and clothing industries (666), the second greatest number was in mining (442). The greatest number of strikes occurred in the textile and clothing industries in Rhode Island (136), South Carolina (81), and Tennessee (32). Texas had 38 strikes in the building trades and 24 in transportation, Washington had 86 in the lumber industry, West Virginia 44 in mining, and Wisconsin 43 in the building trades.

Table 35.—*Strikes beginning in 1927–36, in States having 25 or more strikes in any year, by industry group*

ALABAMA

Industry group and year	Number of strikes	Number of workers involved	Man-days idle during year
Iron and steel and their products, not including machinery:			
1927–29			
1930	1	50	1,150
1931–32			
1933	1	600	6,000
1934	6	2,101	36,581
1935	3	599	2,766
1936	1	160	1,120
Lumber and allied products:			
1927–32			
1933	1	38	608
1934	2	665	1,720
1935	12	1,320	33,058
1936	3	190	10,403
Stone, clay, and glass products:			
1927–34			
1935	5	314	5,325
1936			
Textiles and their products:			
1927–31			
1932	1	125	3,000
1933	9	3,076	59,329
1934	11	38,207	910,850
1935	12	5,725	203,334
1936	4	3,838	154,862
Leather and its manufactures:			
1927–35			
1936	2	124	1,555
Food and kindred products:			
1927–32			
1933	1	40	240
1934	1	450	4,050
1935	3	200	5,260
1936			1 690
Paper and printing:			
1927–31			
1932	1	10	260
1933			
Paper and printing—Con.			
1934	1	750	7,500
1935	2	756	43,518
1936			
Chemicals and allied products:			
1927–32			
1933	1	108	216
1934	1	52	104
1935–36			
Rubber products:			
1927–28			
1929	1	14	14
1930–36			
Miscellaneous manufacturing:			
1927–31			
1932	1	17	68
1933	1	62	1,028
1934–36			
Extraction of minerals:			
1927–31			
1932	1	500	1,500
1933	6	2,855	26,080
1934	12	38,197	714,782
1935	9	22,239	672,240
1936	7	3,909	99,771
Transportation and communication:			
1927–33			
1934	2	1,060	17,780
1935	3	1,066	46,822
1936	3	233	3,320
Trade:			
1927–33			
1934	1	216	2,376
1935			
1936	1	18	18
Domestic and personal service:			
1927	1	30	120
1928–33			
1934	6	2,198	25,309
1935	1	286	15,444
1936	1	20	1,720

TABLE 35.—*Strikes beginning in 1927–36, in States having 25 or more strikes in any year, by industry group*—Continued

ALABAMA—Continued

Industry group and year	Number of strikes	Number of workers involved	Man-days idle during year
Professional service:			
1927–30			
1931	1	72	10,512
1932	1	50	50
1933–36			
Building and construction:			
1927–32			
1933	1	20	280
1934			
1935	1	25	275
1936	5	234	750

Industry group and year	Number of strikes	Number of workers involved	Man-days idle during year
Agriculture and fishing:			
1927–34			
1935	5	2,074	52,029
1936			
Relief work and W. P. A.:			
1927–33			
1934	2	332	1,941
1935	3	3,671	44,321
1936	4	1,400	4,465

CALIFORNIA

Industry group and year	Number of strikes	Number of workers involved	Man-days idle during year
Iron and steel and their products, not including machinery:			
1927–32			
1933	1	279	1,674
1934	1	30	840
1935	1	370	4,070
1936	10	893	15,534
Machinery, not including transportation equipment:			
1927–28			
1929	1	150	150
1930			
1931	1	15	360
1932	1	43	2,193
1933	1	80	1,600
1934	1	46	506
1935	1	130	390
1936	6	1,664	19,091
Transportation equipment:			
1927–28			
1929	1	75	75
1930	1	30	30
1931	1	35	175
1932			
1933	1	65	845
1934	1	540	17,820
1935	1	75	150
1936	10	5,384	241,204
Nonferrous metals and their products:			
1927–30			
1931	1	26	26
1932			
1933	1	12	48
1934			
1935	1	450	4,950
1936	3	108	424
Lumber and allied products:			
1927	5	112	7,689
1928	5	134	5,192
1929	2	548	20,374
1930	1	22	88
1931–32			
1933	1	535	3,745
1934	5	1,622	24,900
1935	6	2,416	80,334
1936	12	1,814	137,954
Stone, clay, and glass products:			
1927–31			
1932	1	55	55
1933–34			
1935	1	9	270
1936	1	57	285

Industry group and year	Number of strikes	Number of workers involved	Man-days idle during year
Textiles and their products:			
1927			
1928	4	510	1,700
1929	3	234	4,580
1930	4	941	25,576
1931	4	223	2,283
1932	1	11	1,207
1933	10	4,071	48,790
1934	8	1,994	10,906
1935	8	959	5,233
1936	22	5,938	83,513
Leather and its manufactures:			
1927–32			
1933	2	50	388
1934–36			
Food and kindred products:			
1927	1	6	12
1928	1	75	75
1929			
1930	2	704	3,104
1931	2	3,995	11,970
1932	2	142	142
1933	2	1,160	11,960
1934	5	561	929
1935	11	4,163	28,416
1936	10	2,488	12,547
Tobacco manufactures:			
1927–32			
1933	1	30	240
1934–35			
1936	2	418	3,936
Paper and printing:			
1927	2	43	941
1928			
1929	1	253	5,313
1930			
1931	5	161	4,378
1932	1	45	53
1933	1	10	10
1934	1	14	14
1935	1	8	24
1936	1	10	50
Chemicals and allied products:			
1927–28			
1929	1	100	1,400
1930–31			
1932	1	40	40
1933	2	270	1,380
1934–35			
1936	2	246	4,380
Rubber products:			
1927–35			
1936	1	136	2,040

[1] Man-days idle as a result of strikes which began in the preceding year and continued into this year.

TABLE 35.—*Strikes beginning in 1927–36, in States having 25 or more strikes in any year, by industry group*—Continued

CALIFORNIA—Continued

Industry group and year	Number of strikes	Number of workers involved	Man-days idle during year
Miscellaneous manufacturing:			
1927	1	12	84
1928–34	---	---	---
1935	3	135	2,055
1936	4	905	30,689
Extraction of minerals:			
1927–33	---	---	---
1934	5	604	39,366
1935	---	---	[1] 15,507
1936	1	60	120
Transportation and communication:			
1927–31	---	---	---
1932	2	157	497
1933	1	200	1,000
1934	34	15,747	605,086
1935	70	10,698	249,605
1936	37	29,131	1,122,659
Trade:			
1927	2	815	4,075
1928	---	---	---
1929	2	193	193
1930–31	---	---	---
1932	2	66	66
1933	1	12	36
1934	2	230	880
1935	7	1,233	17,677
1936	19	5,465	91,056
Domestic and personal service:			
1927	3	166	1,606
1928	---	---	---
1929	4	3,646	16,292
1930	---	---	---
1931	3	621	13,621
1932	1	46	460
1933	2	750	11,250
1934	10	1,564	8,687
1935	6	3,694	20,073
1936	15	1,462	11,571
Professional service:			
1927	---	---	---
1928	1	10	10
1929	5	242	1,899
1930	2	39	579
Professional service—Con.			
1931	2	36	232
1932	2	16	196
1933	2	5,462	145,533
1934	2	14	14
1935	3	111	172
1936	2	33	983
Building and construction:			
1927	5	280	3,388
1928	2	90	480
1929	7	278	1,733
1930	2	236	32,954
1931	2	82	403
1932	4	472	1,590
1933	4	244	2,676
1934	2	209	6,418
1935	1	30	150
1936	11	391	5,877
Agriculture and fishing:			
1927	1	30	210
1928	3	300	1,560
1929	1	1,000	5,000
1930	2	2,300	16,900
1931	2	575	3,950
1932	5	997	22,297
1933	12	24,470	405,170
1934	12	17,212	122,858
1935	9	4,873	50,018
1936	22	13,301	253,989
Relief work and W. P. A.:			
1927–32	---	---	---
1933	1	1,230	1,230
1934	2	69	810
1935	4	63	423
1936	2	116	192
Other nonmanufacturing industries:			
1927–32	---	---	---
1933	1	20	860
1934	---	---	[1] 220
1935	3	70	160
1936	1	7	7
Interindustry:			
1927–33	---	---	---
1934	[2] 1	90,000	270,000
1935–36	---	---	---

[1] Man-days idle as a result of a strike which began in the preceding year and continued into this year.
[2] General strike of all organized workers in San Francisco Bay area.

CONNECTICUT

Industry group and year	Number of strikes	Number of workers involved	Man-days idle during year
Iron and steel and their products, not including machinery:			
1927–28	---	---	---
1929	1	21	252
1930–32	---	---	---
1933	2	172	5,955
1934	2	207	3,285
1935	2	1,046	53,806
1936	2	852	4,832
Machinery, not including transportation equipment:			
1927–28	---	---	---
1929	1	1,050	19,950
1930	2	78	1,271
1931–32	---	---	---
1933	3	481	7,531
1934	5	3,352	78,476
Machinery, not including transportation equipment—Continued.			
1935	---	---	---
1936	2	1,500	78,300
Transportation equipment:			
1927–32	---	---	---
1933	1	88	1,760
1934	2	1,224	33,000
1935	1	1,700	6,800
1936	---	---	---
Nonferrous metals and their products:			
1927	1	20	260
1928–32	---	---	---
1933	2	197	10,697
1934	1	172	5,676
1935	---	---	---
1936	3	371	2,070

TABLE 35.—*Strikes beginning in 1927–36, in States having 25 or more strikes in any year, by industry group*—Continued

CONNECTICUT—Continued

Industry group and year	Number of strikes	Number of workers involved	Man-days idle during year
Lumber and allied products:			
1927	1	41	492
1928–32	----	----	----
1933	1	14	70
1934	1	68	1, 174
1935	1	13	13
1936	2	59	540
Textiles and their products:			
1927	6	568	6, 816
1928	3	779	6, 032
1929	3	918	7, 504
1930	4	595	9, 270
1931	7	1, 995	63, 745
1932	6	472	1, 006
1933	30	15, 510	170, 467
1934	35	24, 977	276, 787
1935	27	8, 461	127, 271
1936	20	5, 074	81, 557
Leather and its manufactures:			
1927–30	----	----	----
1931	2	105	1, 480
1932	----	----	----
1933	2	57	1, 570
1934–35	----	----	----
1936	1	120	240
Food and kindred products:			
1927	1	27	1, 728
1928–29	----	----	----
1930	1	40	40
1931	1	75	75
1932	2	15	393
1933	2	118	1, 632
1934	1	43	1, 333
1935	1	19	19
1936	----	----	----
Tobacco manufactures:			
1927–32	----	----	----
1933	1	61	122
1934	----	----	----
1935	1	325	2, 755
1936	----	----	----
Paper and printing:			
1927	1	80	800
1928–33	----	----	----
1934	1	75	75
1935	1	35	140
1936	----	----	----
Rubber products:			
1927	1	64	576
1928–32	----	----	----
1933	1	190	760
1934	2	202	2, 970
1935	----	----	----
1936	1	14	14
Miscellaneous manufacturing:			
1927–30	----	----	----
1931	2	569	4, 293
Miscellaneous manufacturing—Continued.			
1932–35	----	----	----
1936	3	327	1, 739
Extraction of minerals:			
1927–30	----	----	----
1931	1	40	280
1932–36	----	----	----
Transportation and communication:			
1927–32	----	----	----
1933	3	7, 500	15, 000
1934	2	66	374
1935	3	218	361
1936	6	590	6, 030
Trade:			
1927–34	----	----	----
1935	2	50	1, 260
1936	1	46	46
Domestic and personal service:			
1927	1	21	63
1928	1	210	2, 520
1929	1	14	14
1930	----	----	----
1931	1	32	64
1932	----	----	----
1933	4	1, 147	11, 442
1934	----	----	----
1935	1	500	500
1936	----	----	----
Professional service:			
1927	1	40	40
1928–31	----	----	----
1932	3	120	180
1933	2	90	90
1934–36	----	----	----
Building and construction:			
1927	14	3, 441	64, 670
1928	6	1, 379	32, 220
1929	7	1, 362	19, 634
1930	6	425	6, 305
1931	3	385	8, 370
1932	11	723	19, 578
1933	3	244	2, 476
1934	2	275	3, 475
1935	2	70	230
1936	3	128	2, 244
Agriculture and fishing:			
1927–32	----	----	----
1933	4	192	1, 038
1934	1	174	1, 566
1935	----	----	----
1936	1	354	1, 062
Relief work and W. P. A.:			
1927–33	----	----	----
1934	1	800	1, 600
1935	2	219	1, 136
1936	----	----	----

TABLE 35.—*Strikes beginning in 1927–36, in States having 25 or more strikes in any year, by industry group*—Continued

ILLINOIS

Industry group and year	Number of strikes	Number of workers involved	Man-days idle during year
Iron and steel and their products, not including machinery:			
1927	2	57	97
1928	2	129	6,253
1929	2	90	8,690
1930	---	---	---
1931	2	318	5,246
1932	---	---	---
1933	8	1,927	41,286
1934	5	890	7,070
1935	2	875	5,900
1936	2	1,250	28,250
Machinery, not including transportation equipment:			
1927	2	56	4,679
1928	1	10	340
1929	---	---	---
1930	1	50	1,250
1931	---	---	---
1932	1	26	1,118
1933	6	1,022	4,239
1934	11	2,970	37,140
1935	6	1,117	26,602
1936	7	845	17,130
Transportation equipment:			
1927–29	---	---	---
1930	1	44	88
1931–32	---	---	---
1933	2	283	2,774
1934	---	---	---
1935	2	624	9,120
1936	---	---	[1] 41,000
Nonferrous metals and their products:			
1927	---	---	---
1928	2	104	4,336
1929	---	---	---
1930	1	435	1,305
1931–32	---	---	---
1933	5	1,093	8,632
1934	5	2,835	85,767
1935	7	658	14,840
1936	1	300	13,725
Lumber and allied products:			
1927	3	1,275	29,292
1928	---	---	---
1929	1	500	5,500
1930	1	18	522
1931	2	36	168
1932	2	1,061	108,183
1933	4	1,329	39,332
1934	5	1,298	29,375
1935	10	1,174	16,610
1936	4	1,071	20,381
Stone, clay, and glass products:			
1927–32	---	---	---
1933	1	54	270
1934	1	405	1,215
1935	1	530	2,120
1936	1	1,300	32,500
Textiles and their products:			
1927	6	314	3,610
1928	1	700	3,500
1929	8	1,056	24,186
1930	4	380	22,647
1931	5	1,073	45,612
Textiles and their products—Continued.			
1932	5	615	6,277
1933	17	17,693	203,307
1934	6	902	15,532
1935	12	11,151	375,974
1936	12	1,625	32,768
Leather and its manufactures:			
1927–28	---	---	---
1929	1	50	2,350
1930	1	60	2,820
1931	1	48	624
1932	3	197	694
1933	2	1,179	22,517
1934	2	3,250	42,273
1935	8	1,203	61,278
1936	2	76	1,908
Food and kindred products:			
1927	1	500	500
1928	1	10	70
1929	6	274	2,873
1930	2	180	1,350
1931	3	154	484
1932	3	121	651
1933	10	3,039	40,421
1934	16	4,717	51,070
1935	6	353	5,493
1936	5	873	13,939
Tobacco manufactures:			
1927–32	---	---	---
1933	1	28	532
1934–35	---	---	---
1936	1	450	4,338
Paper and printing:			
1927	2	267	24,726
1928	---	---	---
1929	1	1,000	28,000
1930	2	31	404
1931	1	25	150
1932	2	818	3,218
1933	4	502	4,103
1934	4	345	2,831
1935	1	12	1,368
1936	3	372	5,538
Chemicals and allied products:			
1927–32	---	---	---
1933	1	600	600
1934	1	315	1,890
1935	1	16	256
1936	4	2,645	66,475
Rubber products:			
1927–33	---	---	---
1934	2	1,715	5,337
1935	---	---	---
1936	1	35	840
Miscellaneous manufacturing:			
1927	1	140	2,520
1928	1	100	800
1929–30	---	---	---
1931	2	144	6,624
1932	2	165	2,095
1933	5	753	11,616
1934	3	122	3,386
1935	4	317	13,905
1936	9	973	35,508
Extraction of minerals:			
1927	5	68,183	7,641,159
1928	14	30,960	2,176,631

[1] Man-days idle as a result of a strike which began in the preceding year and continued into this year.

TABLE 35.—*Strikes beginning in 1927–36, in States having 25 or more strikes in any year, by industry group*—Continued

ILLINOIS—Continued

Industry group and year	Number of strikes	Number of workers involved	Man-days idle during year
Extraction of minerals—Continued.			
1929	17	10,095	68,032
1930	13	8,650	311,150
1931	10	9,591	350,139
1932	11	31,231	3,356,078
1933	7	2,110	27,434
1934	5	2,756	5,876
1935	6	45,001	225,663
1936	3	4,118	50,793
Transportation and communication:			
1927	----	----	----
1928	1	21	84
1929	1	46	598
1930	1	10	610
1931	2	1,320	1,340
1932	2	1,843	20,204
1933	3	329	3,007
1934	5	636	36,371
1935	4	180	2,505
1936	6	395	4,165
Trade:			
1927	4	4,670	92,230
1928	----	----	----
1929	3	26	584
1930	----	----	----
1931	2	12	18
1932	3	516	1,887
1933	7	1,686	5,414
1934	11	7,727	18,267
1935	8	4,133	49,921
1936	3	337	823
Domestic and personal service:			
1927	1	20	80
1928	2	145	13,484
1929	3	2,917	84,347
1930	----	----	----
1931	2	33	99
1932	2	17	281
1933	3	112	692
1934	6	6,361	77,580
1935	5	202	5,578
1936	5	188	2,533
Professional service:			
1927	2	694	6,928
1928	4	759	4,168
1929	1	10	200
1930	1	18	18
1931	1	400	30,000
Professional service—Continued.			
1932	2	55	237
1933	2	74	1,686
1934	2	69	461
1935	1	15	195
1936	1	13	702
Building and construction:			
1927	12	1,220	74,803
1928	9	1,684	35,941
1929	20	4,727	58,146
1930	16	2,041	30,503
1931	6	236	1,422
1932	13	605	8,601
1933	11	2,187	52,741
1934	10	1,103	10,353
1935	15	742	9,167
1936	17	1,739	18,533
Agriculture and fishing:			
1927	1	272	544
1928	1	110	1,210
1929	----	----	----
1930	1	105	5,460
1931–32	----	----	----
1933	1	48	48
1934–36	----	----	----
Relief work and W. P. A.:			
1927–32	----	----	----
1933	2	850	1,000
1934	6	1,174	16,646
1935	5	2,228	4,506
1936	5	3,791	8,707
Other nonmanufacturing industries:			
1927	2	102	926
1928	1	4,650	55,800
1929	1	1,800	7,200
1930	----	----	----
1931	3	4,400	13,300
1932	1	3,000	21,000
1933	2	1,559	9,054
1934	2	110	2,310
1935	1	7	42
1936	5	198	4,692
Interindustry strikes:			
1927–33	----	----	----
1934	2	5,200	5,200
1935	1	3,000	3,000
1936	[2] 1	1,500	4,500

INDIANA

Industry group and year	Number of strikes	Number of workers involved	Man-days idle during year
Iron and steel and their products, not including machinery:			
1927	1	19	630
1928–32	----	----	----
1933	1	500	10,500
1934	1	100	2,400
1935	3	339	3,598
1936	----	----	----
Machinery, not including transportation equipment:			
1927	1	120	1,080
1928	1	9	459
1929	----	----	[1] 405
1930	2	121	795
1931	1	12	24
Machinery, not including transportation equipment—Continued.			
1932	1	13	312
1933	2	517	3,442
1934	1	278	834
1935	3	1,901	29,611
1936	4	517	15,926
Transportation equipment:			
1927–28	----	----	----
1929	3	175	4,513
1930	3	1,230	10,530
1931–33	----	----	----
1934	1	415	415
1935	----	----	----
1936	4	6,125	39,677

[1] Man-days idle as a result of a strike which began in the preceding year and continued into this year.
[2] General strike of all organized workers in Pekin, Ill.

TABLE 35.—*Strikes beginning in 1927–36, in States having 25 or more strikes in any year, by industry group*—Continued

INDIANA—Continued

Industry group and year	Number of strikes	Number of workers involved	Man-days idle during year
Nonferrous metals and their products:			
1927	1	6	672
1928			[1] 120
1929	1	10	10
1930–31			
1932	1	470	1,880
1933			
1934	1	70	560
1935	3	932	82,724
1936	1	556	2,780
Lumber and allied products:			
1927–30			
1931	1	25	300
1932			
1933	4	850	10,535
1934	1	33	132
1935	4	2,129	17,243
1936			
Stone, clay, and glass products:			
1927–30			
1931	1	85	255
1932–33			
1934	1	95	3,800
1935	1	90	4,320
1936	4	551	14,228
Textiles and their products:			
1927	2	270	3,120
1928	1	140	840
1929	1	300	3,600
1930			
1931	1	71	710
1932			
1933	2	216	4,826
1934	3	1,602	23,794
1935	6	3,055	89,945
1936			[1] 12,300
Leather and its manufactures:			
1927–30			
1931	1	2,800	50,400
1932			
1933	1	670	3,350
1934	2	1,200	9,777
1935–36			
Food and kindred products:			
1927–28			
1929	1	15	75
1930–32			
1933	2	69	789
1934	6	745	8,854
1935	2	138	3,014
1936	2	80	2,525
Paper and printing:			
1927–29			
1930	1	6	624
1931	1	12	84
1932	1	16	16
1933	1	37	518
1934	3	373	3,619
1935	3	208	1,208
1936			
Chemicals and allied products:			
1927–33			
1934	2	1,090	16,580
1935–36			
Rubber products:			
1927–31			
1932	1	1,268	5,072
1933–36			
Miscellaneous manufacturing:			
1927–32			
1933	1	160	3,200
1934–36			
Extraction of minerals:			
1927	2	17,425	1,972,325
1928	2	3,325	429,600
1929	13	3,845	53,841
1930	5	1,718	31,779
1931	3	1,353	12,860
1932	1	3,800	429,400
1933	3	3,150	28,050
1934	4	1,396	5,788
1935	1	10,614	53,070
1936	4	2,387	44,009
Transportation and communication:			
1927–28			
1929	1	20	240
1930	1	7	14
1931	1	160	320
1932			
1933	3	271	1,007
1934	3	433	6,414
1935	3	293	2,612
1936	2	150	600
Trade:			
1927–29			
1930	1	359	5,385
1931–33			
1934	3	245	955
1935	4	412	8,984
1936	2	67	5,890
Domestic and personal service:			
1927–33			
1934	1	6	150
1935	2	134	456
1936	1	54	756
Professional service:			
1927	1	28	6,832
1928			[1] 2,548
1929	4	101	4,424
1930	2	34	1,667
1931	1	12	660
1932	3	53	438
1933			
1934	1	11	22
1935	1	25	50
1936	1	11	44
Building and construction:			
1927	9	666	51,418
1928	10	685	16,758
1929	16	6,294	331,469
1930	12	455	6,073
1931	8	2,594	32,189
1932	9	463	4,957
1933	3	150	3,360
1934	3	1,049	107,410
1935	2	22	736
1936	8	715	14,348
Agriculture and fishing:			
1927–33			
1934	1	35	1,050
1935–36			
Relief work and W. P. A.:			
1927–33			
1934	2	424	2,298
1935	2	156	636
1936	1	513	513

[1] Man-days idle as a result of a strike which began in the preceding year and continued into this year.

TABLE 35.—*Strikes beginning in 1927–36, in States having 25 or more strikes in any year, by industry group*—Continued

INDIANA—Continued

Industry group and year	Number of strikes	Number of workers involved	Man-days idle during year
Other nonmanufacturing industries:			
1927	-----	-----	-----
1928	1	20	60
1929–36	-----	-----	-----
Interindustry:			
1927–34	-----	-----	-----
1935	[4] 1	26,000	52,000
1936	-----	-----	-----

MARYLAND

Industry group and year	Number of strikes	Number of workers involved	Man-days idle during year
Iron and steel and their products, not including machinery:			
1927–31	-----	-----	-----
1932	1	200	5,000
1933	-----	-----	-----
1934	1	66	330
1935	1	989	1,063
1936	2	1,392	10,805
Machinery, not including transportation equipment:			
1927–28	-----	-----	-----
1929	1	17	476
1930	1	80	1,840
1931	-----	-----	-----
1932	1	17	17
1933–35	-----	-----	-----
1936	1	7	42
Transportation equipment:			
1927–33	-----	-----	-----
1934	1	105	1,050
1935	-----	-----	-----
1936	1	200	5,200
Nonferrous metals and their products:			
1927–35	-----	-----	-----
1936	1	11	297
Lumber and allied products:			
1927	1	160	6,080
1928–32	-----	-----	-----
1933	1	392	5,880
1934	-----	-----	-----
1935	2	159	1,542
1936	4	143	7,393
Stone, clay, and glass products:			
1927	1	100	600
1928–31	-----	-----	-----
1932	1	57	570
1933–36	-----	-----	-----
Textiles and their products:			
1927	2	1,991	13,973
1928	1	50	200
1929	3	1,239	9,971
1930	3	5,090	55,450
1931	1	92	3,220
1932	1	5,000	35,000
1933	5	5,323	33,579
1934	4	465	2,375
1935	8	3,490	18,769
1936	2	200	3,357
Leather and its manufactures:			
1927–28	-----	-----	-----
1929	2	163	2,203
1930	1	27	216
1931–32	-----	-----	-----
1933	2	660	17,244
1934–35	-----	-----	-----
1936	1	450	3,600
Food and kindred products:			
1927	-----	-----	-----
1928	1	35	245
1929	1	8	40
1930	-----	-----	-----
1931	1	680	7,480
1932	-----	-----	-----
1933	1	50	350
1934	1	1,200	9,600
1935	-----	-----	-----
1936	1	28	1,596
Tobacco manufactures:			
1927–33	-----	-----	-----
1934	1	55	660
1935–36	-----	-----	-----
Paper and printing:			
1927	1	370	9,250
1928	1	49	147
1929	1	6	258
1930–36	-----	-----	-----
Chemicals and allied products:			
1927–34	-----	-----	-----
1935	1	334	3,006
1936	1	8,800	114,400
Rubber products:			
1927–35	-----	-----	-----
1936	1	1,700	11,900
Miscellaneous manufacturing:			
1927–35	-----	-----	-----
1936	2	600	6,900
Extraction of minerals:			
1927	1	52	52
1928	-----	-----	-----
1929	1	190	190
1930	2	1,050	19,600
1931–34	-----	-----	-----
1935	1	2,928	14,640
1936	-----	-----	-----
Transportation and communication:			
1927	-----	-----	-----
1928	1	350	2,100
1929	-----	-----	-----
1930	1	23	23
1931	1	50	250
1932	-----	-----	-----
1933	2	164	764
1934	7	389	2,836
1935	5	778	5,560
1936	7	5,501	37,486
Trade:			
1927	-----	-----	-----
1928	1	48	96
1929–33	-----	-----	-----
1934	1	16	208
1935	-----	-----	-----
1936	1	14	28
Professional service:			
1927–29	-----	-----	-----
1930	1	15	855
1931	1	6	114

[4] General strike of all organized workers in Terre Haute, Ind.

Table 35.—*Strikes beginning in 1927–36, in States having 25 or more strikes in any year, by industry group*—Continued

MARYLAND—Continued

Industry group and year	Number of strikes	Number of workers involved	Man-days idle during year
Professional service—Con.			
1932	2	91	1,337
1933			
1934	1	100	1,100
1935–36			
Building and construction:			
1927	3	6,130	80,340
1928	3	240	18,320
1929	4	447	4,111
1930	1	300	8,700
1931	2	95	2,530
1932–33			
1934	2	111	318
Building and construction—Continued.			
1935	4	228	1,024
1936			
Agriculture and fishing:			
1927–32			
1933	1	12	24
1934			
1935	2	300	500
1936			[1] 200
Relief work and W. P. A.:			
1927–34			
1935	3	240	3,590
1936	2	85	96

MASSACHUSETTS

Industry group and year	Number of strikes	Number of workers involved	Man-days idle during year
Iron and steel and their products, not including machinery:			
1927	2	46	648
1928			
1929	1	42	42
1930	1	40	400
1931	2	64	1,666
1932			
1933	4	238	3,636
1934	1	52	104
1935	3	172	416
1936	1	57	3,800
Machinery, not including transportation equipment:			
1927–28			
1929	2	191	1,241
1930	3	96	1,556
1931	3	107	627
1932			
1933	1	2,991	61,611
1934–35			
1936	1	69	690
Transportation equipment:			
1927–28			
1929	1	116	232
1930–31			
1932	1	300	3,900
1933	1	87	522
1934	1	1,680	40,320
1935–36			
Nonferrous metals and their products:			
1927–35			
1936	1	606	18,180
Lumber and allied products:			
1927	5	150	3,368
1928	9	223	12,499
1929	5	174	5,621
1930	3	400	13,505
1931			
1932	2	52	446
1933	7	807	13,440
1934	8	457	7,847
1935	1	102	1,194
1936	3	382	4,924
Stone, clay, and glass products:			
1927–31			
1932	2	430	15,800
1933–36			
Textiles and their products:			
1927	26	4,773	77,497
1928	34	32,039	3,784,064
1929	20	1,685	36,914
1930	14	3,482	28,792
1931	25	42,271	891,612
1932	17	4,575	66,245
1933	46	24,280	306,895
1934	39	85,395	856,562
1935	38	15,546	469,807
1936	46	17,318	302,513
Leather and its manufactures:			
1927	8	3,673	51,100
1928	21	9,786	92,498
1929	20	18,217	774,112
1930	8	355	5,569
1931	7	642	4,501
1932	17	2,663	24,205
1933	58	52,140	964,671
1934	33	22,864	350,900
1935	33	7,485	91,257
1936	26	10,971	56,935
Food and kindred products:			
1927	1	44	44
1928	2	70	132
1929			
1930	1	80	4,640
1931			
1932	2	92	6,807
1933	3	475	6,350
1934	2	61	151
1935	5	221	1,119
1936	1	400	3,900
Tobacco manufactures:			
1927			
1928	1	24	1,032
1929–32			
1933	1	121	363
1934–36			
Paper and printing:			
1927	1	17	1,326
1928	1	101	303
1929–31			
1932	1	12	12
1933	1	6	12
1934	1	225	675
1935	3	521	19,947
1936	1	394	12,608
Chemicals and allied products:			
1927–32			

[1] Man-days idle as a result of a strike which began in the preceding year and continued into this year.

Table 35.—*Strikes beginning in 1927–36, in States having 25 or more strikes in any year, by industry group*—Continued

MASSACHUSETTS—Continued

Industry group and year	Number of strikes	Number of workers involved	Man-days idle during year
Chemicals and allied products—Continued.			
1933	1	75	375
1934–36	----	----	----
Rubber products:			
1927	----	----	----
1928	1	900	5,400
1929–32	----	----	----
1933	4	3,855	18,030
1934	1	63	504
1935	2	210	650
1936	4	1,371	4,525
Miscellaneous manufacturing:			
1927–28	----	----	----
1929	2	47	262
1930	----	----	----
1931	1	11	132
1932	----	----	----
1933	6	564	7,409
1934	2	139	5,520
1935	1	34	238
1936	1	89	89
Extraction of minerals:			
1927–28	----	----	----
1929	1	150	300
1930	2	87	619
1931	1	60	360
1932	2	185	1,755
1933	2	144	972
1934–36	----	----	----
Transportation and communication:			
1927	1	380	3,800
1928	----	----	----
1929	5	839	6,861
1930	----	----	----
1931	4	3,352	195,529
1932	2	26	226
1933	2	317	4,216
1934	5	811	1,005
1935	5	137	973
1936	11	800	7,569
Trade:			
1927	----	----	----
1928	1	15	315
1929	1	80	560
1930–32	----	----	----
1933	1	11	77
1934	4	527	2,999
1935	6	423	5,161
1936	----	----	----
Domestic and personal service:			
1927	3	92	1,132

Industry group and year	Number of strikes	Number of workers involved	Man-days idle during year
Domestic and personal service—Continued.			
1928	2	422	9,754
1929–31	----	----	----
1932	1	500	2,000
1933	3	291	3,710
1934	1	7	28
1935	1	500	9,500
1936	----	----	----
Professional service:			
1927	3	95	1,306
1928	3	1,232	65,296
1929	2	139	139
1930–31	----	----	----
1932	1	20	20
1933	3	475	2,475
1934	1	75	75
1935	----	----	----
1936	3	100	923
Building and construction:			
1927	18	1,509	21,936
1928	14	1,978	36,895
1929	17	1,978	35,791
1930	13	734	6,332
1931	17	1,180	11,672
1932	17	908	9,580
1933	9	650	11,528
1934	8	807	7,711
1935	11	930	4,846
1936	10	1,470	15,301
Agriculture and fishing:			
1927	----	----	----
1928	1	75	225
1929–30	----	----	----
1931	1	230	460
1932	----	----	----
1933	2	510	3,340
1934	3	3,045	64,395
1935	----	----	----
1936	2	166	266
Relief work and W. P. A.:			
1927–32	----	----	----
1933	5	681	1,524
1934	2	214	288
1935	1	40	80
1936	----	----	----
Other nonmanufacturing industries:			
1927–28	----	----	----
1929	1	15	225
1930	----	----	[1] 150
1931	2	37	187
1932	----	----	----
1933	1	36	252
1934–36	----	----	----

MICHIGAN

Industry group and year	Number of strikes	Number of workers involved	Man-days idle during year
Iron and steel and their products, not including machinery:			
1927	----	----	----
1928	1	87	9,222
1929	1	55	2,915
1930	2	220	8,620
1931	1	40	80
1932	----	----	----
1933	3	974	2,568
1934	4	880	13,320
1935	3	1,976	23,962
1936	4	1,383	11 649

Industry group and year	Number of strikes	Number of workers involved	Man-days idle during year
Machinery, not including transportation equipment:			
1927	----	----	----
1928	1	20	100
1929	----	----	----
1930	2	84	3,794
1931	----	----	----
1932	1	286	1,144
1933	----	----	----
1934	7	6,804	159,973
1935	3	372	2,598
1936	3	324	1,623

[1] Man-days idle as a result of a strike which began in the preceding year and continued into this year.

TABLE 35.—*Strikes beginning in 1927–36, in States having 25 or more strikes in any year, by industry group*—Continued

MICHIGAN—Continued

Industry group and year	Number of strikes	Number of workers involved	Man-days idle during year
Transportation equipment:			
1927	2	235	1,905
1928	1	52	156
1929	4	1,911	15,372
1930	2	4,650	40,250
1931–32	----	----	----
1933	10	14,807	321,313
1934	4	11,226	48,650
1935	8	8,042	96,950
1936	11	17,345	97,679
Nonferrous metals and their products:			
1927	----	----	----
1928	1	60	2,520
1929	----	----	----
1930	2	30	756
1931–33	----	----	----
1934	1	102	204
1935	2	36	269
1936	2	967	9,023
Lumber and allied products:			
1927	----	----	----
1928	2	39	615
1929	1	150	900
1930–32	----	----	----
1933	2	86	1,238
1934	3	260	5,616
1935	2	792	5,360
1936	5	1,947	30,930
Stone, clay, and glass products:			
1927–31	----	----	----
1932	1	65	325
1933	----	----	----
1934	1	6	66
1935–36	----	----	----
Textiles and their products:			
1927–29	----	----	----
1930	1	48	3,312
1931–32	----	----	----
1933	1	625	1,250
1934	2	206	2,196
1935	3	395	2,885
1936	----	----	----
Leather and its manufactures:			
1927–32	----	----	----
1933	2	181	1,417
1934	1	60	300
1935	----	----	----
1936	1	695	41,005
Food and kindred products:			
1927	1	6	288
1928–31	----	----	----
1932	2	229	449
1933	----	----	----
1934	6	524	5,700
1935	4	119	1,299
1936	1	300	2,400
Tobacco manufactures:			
1927–33	----	----	----
1934	1	696	8,548
1935–36	----	----	----
Paper and printing:			
1927–31	----	----	----
1932	2	24	480
1933	----	----	----
1934	3	777	11,289
1935	2	64	152
1936	1	20	700
Chemicals and allied products:			
1927–35	----	----	----
1936	1	147	1,617
Rubber products:			
1927–28	----	----	----
1929	1	200	1,000
1930–36	----	----	----
Miscellaneous manufacturing:			
1927–29	----	----	----
1930	1	70	1,680
1931–33	----	----	----
1934	1	300	3,200
1935	1	53	338
1936	1	6	144
Extraction of minerals:			
1927–33	----	----	----
1934	1	50	250
1935	2	2,864	19,920
1936	----	----	----
Transportation and communication:			
1927	----	----	----
1928	1	93	93
1929	1	20	20
1930–31	----	----	----
1932	2	287	4,447
1933	----	----	----
1934	10	1,873	21,419
1935	3	162	1,526
1936	1	291	6,095
Trade:			
1927–31	----	----	----
1932	1	75	1,950
1933	1	200	400
1934	9	584	1,931
1935	8	687	13,913
1936	2	25	235
Domestic and personal service:			
1927	1	13	39
1928	----	----	----
1929	2	30	90
1930–31	----	----	----
1932	1	10	90
1933	1	340	7,480
1934	7	985	7,265
1935	3	256	5,262
1936	2	2,013	3,026
Professional service:			
1927	1	7	301
1928	----	----	----
1929	3	49	309
1930	1	115	2,185
1931–33	----	----	----
1934	1	44	484
1935	1	11	77
1936	----	----	----
Building and construction:			
1927	3	150	630
1928	----	----	[1]9,100
1929	2	191	8,699
1930	4	184	3,769
1931	8	492	10,485
1932	1	38	950
1933	5	318	11,165
1934	----	----	----
1935	6	438	2,396
1936	4	511	4,738

[1] Man-days idle as a result of a strike which began in the preceding year and continued into this year.

Table 35.—*Strikes beginning in 1927–36, in States having 25 or more strikes in any year, by industry group*

MICHIGAN—Continued

Industry group and year	Number of strikes	Number of workers involved	Man-days idle during year
Relief work and W. P. A.:			
1927–33	----	----	----
1934	1	70	70
1935	4	959	10,418
1936	5	997	3,288
Other nonmanufacturing industries:			
1927–28	----	----	----
1929	1	100	7,700
1930–35	----	----	----
1936	1	15	30

MINNESOTA

Industry group and year	Number of strikes	Number of workers involved	Man-days idle during year
Iron and steel and their products, not including machinery:			
1927–33	----	----	----
1934	1	8	435
1935	1	300	16,228
1936	1	161	1,288
Machinery, not including transportation equipment:			
1927–32	----	----	----
1933	1	20	560
1934	1	415	4,565
1935	1	35	175
1936	3	751	10,122
Transportation equipment:			
1927–33	----	----	----
1934	1	300	2,700
1935–36	----	----	----
Nonferrous metals and their products:			
1927–35	----	----	----
1936	1	95	1,520
Lumber and allied products:			
1927	2	340	16,700
1928	----	----	[1] 3,780
1929–32	----	----	----
1933	3	695	34,170
1934	----	----	[1] 3,000
1935	2	579	20,495
1936	11	2,059	60,234
Textiles and their products:			
1927	3	145	11,848
1928	1	35	140
1929	6	257	6,070
1930	3	160	1,051
1931–32	----	----	----
1933	2	117	441
1934	1	28	392
1935	5	1,216	104,909
1936	3	35	73,986
Leather and its manufactures:			
1927–31	----	----	----
1932	1	185	2,105
1933–36	----	----	----
Food and kindred products:			
1927–30	----	----	----
1931	1	70	2,870
1932	----	----	----
1933	3	4,271	13,304
1934	----	----	----
1935	2	254	1,291
1936	5	2,125	48,656
Paper and printing:			
1927	1	18	1,800
1928–29	----	----	----
1930	1	30	480
1931–33	----	----	----
1934	1	600	6,000
Paper and printing—Con.			
1935–36	----	----	----
Chemicals and allied products:			
1927	1	48	528
1928–34	----	----	----
1935	1	38	304
1936	----	----	----
Miscellaneous manufacturing:			
1927–30	----	----	----
1931	1	22	484
1932–34	----	----	----
1935	2	205	6,413
1936	4	167	1,259
Transportation and communication:			
1927	----	----	----
1928	1	120	600
1929	1	110	110
1930	----	----	----
1931	1	75	75
1932–33	----	----	----
1934	5	13,176	243,466
1935	2	31	181
1936	----	----	----
Trade:			
1927–33	----	----	----
1934	4	934	3,342
1935	6	1,025	11,200
1936	7	1,970	20,903
Domestic and personal service:			
1927–28	----	----	----
1929	1	20	20
1930	----	----	----
1931	1	19	19
1932–33	----	----	----
1934	2	2,018	2,018
1935	2	99	4,551
1936	5	424	3,639
Professional service:			
1927	2	1,075	43,500
1928	1	150	600
1929	----	----	----
1930	3	60	3,338
1931	----	----	----
1932	1	13	429
1933	----	----	----
1934	1	81	243
1935	----	----	----
1936	1	225	2,475
Building and construction:			
1927	2	69	1,588
1928	----	----	----
1929	1	30	240
1930	----	----	----
1931	3	416	8,480
1932	3	383	4,189
1933	----	----	----
1934	3	5,054	10,206
1935	7	795	3,850
1936	7	804	6,250

[1] Man-days idle as a result of a strike which began in the preceding year and continued into this year.

TABLE 35.—*Strikes beginning in 1927–36, in States having 25 or more strikes in any year, by industry group*—Continued

MINNESOTA—Continued

Industry group and year	Number of strikes	Number of workers involved	Man-days idle during year
Agriculture and fishing:			
1927–35	------	------	------
1936	1	30	30
Relief work and W. P. A.:			
1927–33	------	------	------
1934	1	800	9,600
1935	3	1,435	7,490
1936	3	5,274	19,180
Other nonmanufacturing industries:			
1927–33	------	------	------
1934	1	23	414
1935	1	16	48
1936	2	94	202

MISSOURI

Industry group and year	Number of strikes	Number of workers involved	Man-days idle during year
Iron and steel and their products, not including machinery:			
1927	------	------	------
1928	3	81	173
1929–32	------	------	------
1933	1	150	2,100
1934	------	------	------
1935	1	67	201
1936	------	------	------
Machinery, not including transportation equipment:			
1927–28	------	------	------
1929	3	178	698
1930–32	------	------	------
1933	2	34	986
1934	1	1,200	21,600
1935	1	27	1,404
1936	2	240	1,800
Transportation equipment:			
1927–32	------	------	------
1933	1	156	312
1934	2	3,579	30,369
1935	------	------	------
1936	1	2,450	24,500
Nonferrous metals and their products:			
1927–29	------	------	------
1930	1	24	192
1931	1	11	264
1932–36	------	------	------
Lumber and allied products:			
1927	2	62	734
1928	1	12	72
1929	1	150	5,250
1930	------	------	------
1931	1	11	11
1932	1	6	90
1933	2	127	678
1934	3	252	2,710
1935	2	105	1,995
1936	4	307	5,164
Stone, clay, and glass products:			
1927–33	------	------	------
1934	2	19	151
1935–36	------	------	------
Textiles and their products:			
1927	2	76	1,276
1928	------	------	------
1929	1	90	270
1930	------	------	------
1931	2	210	250
1932	2	215	1,840
1933	11	4,856	140,803
1934	4	121	2,044
1935	6	192	13,285
1936	8	764	5,358
Leather and its manufactures:			
1927	------	------	------
1928	1	100	100
1929–32	------	------	------
1933	7	3,901	22,711
1934	3	2,401	23,126
1935–36	------	------	------
Food and kindred products:			
1927	------	------	------
1928	1	63	378
1929	2	1,615	4,015
1930–31	------	------	------
1932	1	625	1,875
1933	5	1,242	11,320
1934	4	1,368	21,030
1935	5	2,803	7,447
1936	------	------	------
Tobacco manufactures:			
1927–32	------	------	------
1933	1	185	1,110
1934–36	------	------	------
Paper and printing:			
1927–32	------	------	------
1933	1	18	18
1934	------	------	------
1935	1	6	6
1936	------	------	------
Miscellaneous manufacturing:			
1927	2	32	3,216
1928	------	------	[1] 3,750
1929	------	------	------
1930	1	30	300
1931	1	25	100
1932	------	------	------
1933	2	107	1,198
1934	2	93	1,641
1935	5	733	45,268
1936	3	137	137
Extraction of minerals:			
1927	2	2,650	297,700
1928	2	1,511	96,533
1929	1	125	250
1930	1	80	2,880
1931	4	1,034	13,812
1932	------	------	------
1933	1	150	600
1934	4	2,327	90,571
1935	4	9,742	129,194
1936	4	4,550	102,486
Transportation and communication:			
1927–29	------	------	------
1930	1	645	12,255
1931	------	------	------
1932	2	1,000	8,000
1933	3	548	38,288
1934	4	520	2,100
1935	2	80	860
1936	1	125	1,750

[1] Man-days idle as a result of a strike which began in the preceding year and continued into this year.

TABLE 35.—*Strikes beginning in 1927-36, in States having 25 or more strikes in any year, by industry group*—Continued

MISSOURI—Continued

Industry group and year	Number of strikes	Number of workers involved	Man-days idle during year
Trade:			
1927	1	15	1,230
1928-32	------	------	------
1933	1	2,000	10,000
1934	2	1,715	11,960
1935	2	135	999
1936	1	6	6
Domestic and personal service:			
1927	2	455	13,340
1928	------	------	------
1929	2	220	2,220
1930	------	------	------
1931	1	8	888
1932	1	36	2,520
1933	4	3,362	128,686
1934	1	139	2,502
1935	1	13	3,805
1936	------	------	------
Professional service:			
1927	1	43	731
1928	------	------	------
1929	1	316	26,228
1930	1	85	7,225
1931	2	103	5,070
1932	2	330	930

Industry group and year	Number of strikes	Number of workers involved	Man-days idle during year
Professional service—Con.			
1933	4	145	1,055
1934-36	------	------	------
Building and construction:			
1927	4	707	6,687
1928	1	14	44,514
1929	6	4,520	146,000
1930	8	7,885	41,468
1931	5	195	8,395
1932	8	1,019	24,412
1933	2	96	592
1934	8	1,782	13,108
1935	14	1,556	20,932
1936	10	1,228	16,503
Relief work and W. P. A.:			
1927-33	------	------	------
1934	2	246	292
1935	1	979	4,895
1936	1	14	490
Other nonmanufacturing industries:			
1927-30	------	------	------
1931	1	119	357
1932	2	82	1,828
1933-36	------	------	------

NEW HAMPSHIRE

Industry group and year	Number of strikes	Number of workers involved	Man-days idle during year
Lumber and allied products:			
1927-33	------	------	------
1934	1	70	280
1935	1	53	848
1936	------	------	------
Stone, clay, and glass products:			
1927-30	------	------	------
1931	1	200	1,600
1932-34	------	------	------
1935	1	80	1,840
1936	------	------	------
Textiles and their products:			
1927	1	210	5,040
1928	------	------	------
1929	1	1,000	52,000
1930-31	------	------	------
1932	4	477	2,294
1933	11	10,406	108,611
1934	8	29,380	212,264
1935	3	679	11,979
1936	2	467	4,776
Leather and its manufactures:			
1927	------	------	------
1928	1	75	975
1929	1	11	66
1930	1	165	1,880
1931	2	52	274
1932	2	700	3,450
1933	13	8,342	212,477
1934	4	1,388	38,543

Industry group and year	Number of strikes	Number of workers involved	Man-days idle during year
Leather and its manufactures—Continued.			
1935	3	735	16,177
1936	3	626	8,512
Food and kindred products:			
1927-31	------	------	------
1932	1	7	7
1933-36	------	------	------
Extraction of minerals:			
1927	------	------	------
1928	2	410	1,230
1929-32	------	------	------
1933	1	360	21,960
1934-36	------	------	------
Professional service:			
1927-28	------	------	------
1929	1	9	333
1930-31	------	------	------
1932	1	20	20
1933-36	------	------	------
Building and construction:			
1927	3	76	1,924
1928	1	40	200
1929	1	170	2,040
1930-32	------	------	------
1933	1	8	56
1934-36	------	------	------
Other nonmanufacturing industries:			
1927-31	------	------	------
1932	1	12	207
1933-36	------	------	------

Table 35.—*Strikes beginning in 1927–36, in States having 25 or more strikes in any year, by industry group*—Continued

NEW JERSEY

Industry group and year	Number of strikes	Number of workers involved	Man-days idle during year
Iron and steel and their products, not including machinery:			
1927	2	441	1,507
1928	1	50	40,600
1929	2	56	798
1930	----	----	----
1931	3	156	1,120
1932	1	300	7,800
1933	2	1,270	22,270
1934	1	257	5,654
1935	1	80	1,440
1936	1	125	500
Machinery, not including transportation equipment:			
1927	1	93	372
1928	----	----	----
1929	2	794	4,910
1930	1	19	19
1931–32	----	----	----
1933	2	571	15,991
1934	2	830	3,560
1935	2	112	1,030
1936	2	7,700	161,900
Transportation equipment:			
1927–29	----	----	----
1930	1	600	9,600
1931	----	----	[1] 6,600
1932	----	----	----
1933	1	3,500	59,500
1934	1	2,967	100,878
1935	2	3,928	292,040
1936	3	996	6,938
Nonferrous metals and their products:			
1927–28	----	----	----
1929	1	2,500	27,500
1930–32	----	----	----
1933	2	694	25,302
1934	----	----	[1] 12,000
1935	----	----	----
1936	1	1,600	6,400
Lumber and allied products:			
1927	1	17	1,020
1928	1	8	640
1929	1	20	380
1930–31	----	----	----
1932	1	300	600
1933	3	73	518
1934	6	356	4,067
1935	2	176	4,598
1936	4	346	4,454
Stone, clay, and glass products:			
1927	----	----	----
1928	1	14	14
1929–32	----	----	----
1933	3	230	2,240
1934	----	----	----
1935	1	195	3,705
1936	1	116	1,276
Textiles and their products:			
1927	15	951	27,603
1928	10	3,588	229,426
1929	34	2,222	47,351
1930	11	504	13,112
1931	20	15,530	634,995
1932	15	8,134	131,946
1933	44	53,517	1,590,774
1934	26	36,179	673,136
Textiles and their products—Continued.			
1935	69	31,733	608,049
1936	59	12,270	304,763
Leather and its manufactures:			
1927	2	113	1,470
1928	2	102	2,092
1929	1	20	60
1930	1	17	238
1931	----	----	----
1932	2	141	3,846
1933	9	1,034	24,491
1934	4	360	9,290
1935	4	364	7,850
1936	4	348	5,097
Food and kindred products:			
1927	2	46	648
1928	2	108	1,188
1929	----	----	----
1930	3	35	68
1931	3	177	483
1932	6	71	241
1933	8	869	7,278
1934	5	3,027	63,966
1935	6	654	21,800
1936	3	324	2,312
Tobacco manufactures:			
1927–28	----	----	----
1929	1	350	17,850
1930–32	----	----	----
1933	1	610	10,380
1934–36	----	----	----
Paper and printing:			
1927	1	50	450
1928	----	----	----
1929	1	8	224
1930	----	----	----
1931	1	150	4,050
1932	5	834	13,215
1933	2	163	3,141
1934	4	303	3,152
1935	1	50	3,310
1936	3	365	11,770
Chemicals and allied products:			
1927	----	----	----
1928	1	1,479	8,874
1929	2	17	24
1930–33	----	----	----
1934	3	315	2,533
1935	----	----	----
1936	1	50	100
Rubber products:			
1927	----	----	----
1928	1	800	5,600
1929	2	445	1,335
1930–31	----	----	----
1932	1	60	420
1933	1	132	1,320
1934–36	----	----	----
Miscellaneous manufacturing:			
1927	1	94	94
1928	----	----	----
1929	1	45	135
1930	----	----	----
1931	1	26	156
1932	3	987	13,428
1933	5	1,233	20,832
1934	1	46	92
1935	6	839	33,047
1936	5	1,496	21,042

[1] Man-days idle as a result of a strike which began in the preceding year and continued into this year.

TABLE 35.—*Strikes beginning in 1927–36, in States having 25 or more strikes in any year, by industry group*—Continued

NEW JERSEY—Continued

Industry group and year	Number of strikes	Number of workers involved	Man-days idle during year
Transportation and communication:			
1927	7	1,069	16,051
1928	1	450	4,050
1929	6	1,027	5,146
1930	6	538	3,247
1931	3	445	2,545
1932	5	365	1,711
1933	5	651	4,217
1934	3	790	6,180
1935	7	386	5,886
1936	7	702	6,195
Trade:			
1927	1	150	450
1928	2	64	1,266
1929	3	380	830
1930	6	358	8,346
1931	2	13	13
1932	4	75	726
1933	3	93	403
1934	1	11	110
1935	2	698	5,490
1936	8	714	5,328
Domestic and personal service:			
1927	7	1,788	14,948
1928	2	316	4,976
1929	1	70	70
1930	1	113	2,486
1931	3	926	4,680
1932	5	866	8,468
1933	5	944	7,390
1934	6	352	2,629
1935	7	379	1,040
1936	10	946	7,970
Professional service:			
1927	3	34	668
1928	1	24	600
1929	1	16	128
Professional service—Continued.			
1930	3	176	9,640
1931	1	56	392
1932	5	60	1,594
1933	3	152	2,151
1934	1	200	400
1935	-	-	-
1936	1	40	200
Building and construction:			
1927	17	3,459	71,062
1928	18	4,751	64,834
1929	18	5,743	63,515
1930	22	3,265	44,827
1931	23	6,536	201,870
1932	21	1,509	27,853
1933	10	419	3,802
1934	8	890	11,341
1935	8	1,112	21,714
1936	10	959	5,841
Agriculture and fishing:			
1927–31	-	-	-
1932	1	100	700
1933	-	-	-
1934	3	1,500	6,400
1935–36	-	-	-
Relief work and W. P. A.:			
1927–32	-	-	-
1933	3	104	323
1934	11	2,375	33,175
1935	4	6,440	73,790
1936	2	900	7,800
Other nonmanufacturing industries:			
1927	1	600	1,800
1928–34	-	-	-
1935	1	87	5,294
1936	1	27	1,067

NEW YORK

Industry group and year	Number of strikes	Number of workers involved	Man-days idle during year
Iron and steel and their products, not including machinery:			
1927	1	405	1,215
1928	1	20	60
1929	1	2,000	122,000
1930	1	14	42
1931	2	191	1,383
1932	2	179	1,916
1933	9	1,154	7,199
1934	3	212	2,582
1935	6	643	16,820
1936	10	1,195	10,268
Machinery, not including transportation equipment:			
1927	1	55	1,430
1928	1	33	132
1929–30	-	-	-
1931	2	105	455
1932	2	99	2,407
1933	10	3,443	19,479
1934	9	4,768	120,529
1935	12	1,947	56,234
1936	11	4,988	217,315
Transportation equipment:			
1927	-	-	-
1928	3	1,104	21,994
Transportation equipment—Continued.			
1929	1	116	696
1930–31	-	-	-
1932	1	45	90
1933	2	3,950	133,900
1934	5	4,273	136,738
1935	1	140	5,600
1936	3	1,742	12,261
Nonferrous metals and their products:			
1927	1	14	266
1928	-	-	[1] 350
1929	-	-	-
1930	1	14	168
1931	5	118	1,275
1932	4	429	652
1933	8	5,038	82,200
1934	7	1,958	45,544
1935	12	2,620	48,691
1936	9	1,582	39,953
Lumber and allied products:			
1927	11	300	5,907
1928	5	436	14,221
1929	13	999	22,430
1930	8	364	8,991
1931	8	876	5,522
1932	15	352	4,231

[1] Man-days idle as a result of a strike which began in the preceding year and continued into this year.

TABLE 35.—*Strikes beginning in 1927–36, in States having 25 or more strikes in any year, by industry group*—Continued

NEW YORK—Continued

Industry group and year	Number of strikes	Number of workers involved	Man-days idle during year
Lumber and allied products—Continued.			
1933	17	11,279	356,324
1934	18	2,001	70,207
1935	24	1,761	31,439
1936	16	1,309	13,629
Stone, clay, and glass products:			
1927	1	137	7,398
1928	-----	-----	-----
1929	2	690	1,560
1930	2	210	835
1931	2	240	858
1932	1	7	98
1933	2	445	6,775
1934	1	13	143
1935	1	70	1,190
1936	3	107	920
Textiles and their products:			
1927	60	4,828	113,420
1928	38	29,257	254,677
1929	43	28,388	334,681
1930	35	42,022	466,333
1931	76	45,144	492,050
1932	70	62,726	639,082
1933	64	190,096	1,826,682
1934	56	64,599	681,856
1935	88	58,210	469,759
1936	87	38,201	397,859
Leather and its manufactures:			
1927	8	518	12,537
1928	6	283	12,585
1929	21	7,792	240,669
1930	8	729	53,310
1931	24	4,050	47,380
1932	18	1,625	32,209
1933	17	16,276	591,082
1934	18	9,010	176,460
1935	19	3,318	49,010
1936	14	2,033	29,470
Food and kindred products:			
1927	8	1,632	32,825
1928	2	95	755
1929	2	56	856
1930	2	27	258
1931	10	1,889	11,988
1932	10	151	3,579
1933	12	9,842	255,242
1934	13	1,064	16,603
1935	12	6,198	337,570
1936	15	376	22,392
Tobacco manufactures:			
1927	1	97	7,372
1928	1	22	66
1929–30	-----	-----	-----
1931	5	289	4,777
1932	1	14	210
1933	5	978	19,611
1934	1	10	70
1935	1	22	418
1936	2	22	299
Paper and printing:			
1927	2	44	646
1928	6	1,674	19,124
1929	5	315	5,431
1930	5	123	742
1931	3	76	714
1932	9	478	12,393
1933	10	5,339	34,367
1934	14	484	9,570
1935	18	433	6,691
1936	23	1,526	30,942

Industry group and year	Number of strikes	Number of workers involved	Man-days idle during year
Chemicals and allied products:			
1927–28	-----	-----	-----
1929	2	219	1,343
1930–32	-----	-----	-----
1933	1	170	510
1934	1	1,100	40,700
1935	1	22	154
1936	2	143	657
Rubber products:			
1927–32	-----	-----	-----
1933	1	200	600
1934–35	-----	-----	-----
1936	2	257	1,011
Miscellaneous manufacturing:			
1927	7	1,317	14,788
1928	6	1,174	51,656
1929	7	427	12,239
1930	7	1,719	14,874
1931	9	2,044	27,616
1932	12	4,062	55,608
1933	15	7,374	123,922
1934	17	4,147	35,477
1935	28	4,559	94,706
1936	24	3,034	78,766
Extraction of minerals:			
1927	1	764	3,056
1928	-----	-----	-----
1929	1	175	7,000
1930	1	40	360
1931–35	-----	-----	-----
1936	2	69	252
Transportation and communication:			
1927	4	8,225	29,775
1928	4	7,526	21,874
1929	10	3,661	16,239
1930	5	1,011	13,814
1931	14	1,197	9,664
1932	7	3,004	89,112
1933	7	1,313	13,663
1934	19	45,724	515,625
1935	16	21,805	66,492
1936	30	12,632	108,664
Trade:			
1927	9	2,176	57,638
1928	4	1,955	28,675
1929	7	6,935	140,695
1930	7	1,039	9,059
1931	6	1,126	16,891
1932	10	1,899	9,376
1933	11	9,733	56,828
1934	20	1,625	30,352
1935	29	1,845	29,740
1936	43	12,112	65,969
Domestic and personal service:			
1927	12	6,328	146,100
1928	16	29,007	465,708
1929	5	3,832	209,958
1930	9	3,506	18,397
1931	9	4,210	27,574
1932	18	10,831	157,502
1933	20	8,250	185,390
1934	34	25,698	283,207
1935	35	19,783	163,189
1936	43	62,359	768,467
Professional service:			
1927	3	42	1,602
1928	4	105	321
1929	3	662	2,566
1930	2	415	7,190
1931	2	61	1,436
1932	8	1,268	5,572

TABLE 35.—*Strikes beginning in 1927–36, in States having 25 or more strikes in any year, by industry group*—Continued

NEW YORK—Continued

Industry group and year	Number of strikes	Number of workers involved	Man-days idle during year
Professional service—Continued.			
1933	5	835	34,423
1934	9	1,648	23,327
1935	6	385	8,302
1936	7	265	6,458
Building and construction:			
1927	28	21,081	784,417
1928	30	9,050	88,526
1929	45	9,530	256,013
1930	44	4,294	48,633
1931	48	5,134	64,781
1932	43	48,467	1,470,533
1933	14	12,646	81,109
1934	24	12,652	249,563
1935	17	5,465	63,737
1936	34	12,854	113,677
Agriculture and fishing:			
1927–30	---	---	---
1931	1	1,200	10,800
1932	---	---	---
1933	1	100	300
1934	---	---	---
Agriculture and fishing—Continued.			
1935	3	1,066	2,042
1936	1	87	348
Relief work and W. P. A.:			
1927–31	---	---	---
1932	3	518	3,182
1933	3	10,015	36,515
1934	11	9,361	26,197
1935	15	9,869	45,447
1936	4	2,715	17,895
Other nonmanufacturing industries:			
1927	1	30	210
1928	---	---	---
1929	8	968	8,536
1930	3	500	3,200
1931	1	47	2,538
1932	7	1,193	16,789
1933	6	1,832	14,808
1934	1	29	725
1935	5	138	902
1936	8	1,126	6,520

NORTH CAROLINA

Industry group and year	Number of strikes	Number of workers involved	Man-days idle during year
Lumber and allied products:			
1927–28	---	---	---
1929	1	60	120
1930	1	8	8
1931	---	---	---
1932	5	1,750	29,500
1933	4	1,465	11,970
1934	2	456	4,017
1935	2	533	5,972
1936	---	---	---
Textiles and their products:			
1927	2	809	21,843
1928	---	---	---
1929	14	4,656	90,016
1930	3	811	5,822
1931	2	306	2,078
1932	15	12,223	155,291
1933	19	7,919	140,880
1934	17	47,651	532,345
1935	12	4,635	38,595
1936	10	5,209	84,941
Food and kindred products:			
1927–35	---	---	---
1936	1	26	338
Paper and printing:			
1927–31	---	---	---
1932	1	19	171
1933–34	---	---	---
1935	1	40	1,920
1936	---	---	---
Chemicals and allied products:			
1927–29	---	---	---
1930	1	44	44
1931–36	---	---	---
Miscellaneous manufacturing:			
1927–33	---	---	---
1934	1	175	875
1935–36	---	---	---
Extraction of minerals:			
1927	---	---	---
1928	1	50	1,150
1929–33	---	---	---
1934	1	11	121
1935–36	---	---	---
Transportation and communication:			
1927–35	---	---	---
1936	1	32	64
Trade:			
1927–28	---	---	---
1929	1	10	10
1930–36	---	---	---
Professional service:			
1927	1	23	345
1928	---	---	---
1929	1	11	407
1930–31	---	---	---
1932	1	100	100
1933–36	---	---	---
Building and construction:			
1927	3	147	5,428
1928	---	---	---
1929	1	60	120
1930	1	75	600
1931–32	---	---	---
1933	2	47	68
1934	1	120	1,200
1935–36	---	---	---
Relief work and W. P. A.:			
1927–32	---	---	---
1933	3	1,258	26,758
1934–35	---	---	---
1936	1	52	364
Other nonmanufacturing industries:			
1927–34	---	---	---
1935	1	7	406
1936	---	---	---

TABLE 35.—*Strikes beginning in 1927–36, in States having 25 or more strikes in any year, by industry group*—Continued

OHIO

Industry group and year	Number of strikes	Number of workers involved	Man-days idle during year
Iron and steel and their products, not including machinery:			
1927	1	26	26
1928	1	300	5,100
1929	2	160	680
1930	4	250	7,119
1931	1	1,500	6,000
1932	1	230	6,210
1933	10	2,917	29,327
1934	20	12,458	308,546
1935	14	2,855	99,902
1936	10	9,054	296,482
Machinery, not including transportation equipment:			
1927–28	----	----	----
1929	3	83	280
1930–32	----	----	----
1933	6	694	4,416
1934	13	4,482	70,673
1935	12	7,875	126,691
1936	14	5,989	272,866
Transportation equipment:			
1927–28	----	----	----
1929	2	69	157
1930	1	23	46
1931–32	----	----	----
1933	6	1,498	4,239
1934	12	13,681	119,583
1935	19	20,045	170,957
1936	8	10,158	119,573
Nonferrous metals and their products:			
1927	----	----	----
1928	1	16	96
1929	3	69	1,731
1930–31	----	----	----
1932	1	300	1,800
1933	2	876	13,308
1934	10	2,224	16,277
1935	7	1,040	11,988
1936	5	1,190	32,910
Lumber and allied products:			
1927	1	15	60
1928	----	----	----
1929	1	145	145
1930–31	----	----	----
1932	1	7	7
1933	4	426	2,896
1934	7	1,938	35,776
1935	6	4,362	35,449
1936	6	3,309	95,714
Stone, clay, and glass products:			
1927	----	----	----
1928	1	250	500
1929	1	133	2,128
1930–31	----	----	----
1932	1	95	2,565
1933	6	1,662	20,862
1934	9	4,777	104,778
1935	8	4,052	190,980
1936	12	9,067	185,494
Textiles and their products:			
1927	1	8	368
1928	----	----	----
1929	4	1,010	9,025
1930	3	2,656	63,922
1931	2	99	678
1932	3	175	3,425
1933	10	2,858	53,647
1934	15	7,773	170,643
1935	13	4,021	125,709
Textiles and their products—Continued.			
1936	5	910	43,769
Leather and its manufactures:			
1927–28	----	----	----
1929	1	546	30,030
1930–31	----	----	----
1932	1	300	900
1933	3	922	7,956
1934	5	2,400	44,240
1935	2	856	11,265
1936	3	1,263	37,232
Food and kindred products:			
1927	----	----	----
1928	1	45	2,115
1929	1	120	960
1930	1	50	300
1931	1	15	15
1932	1	7	7
1933	8	501	4,399
1934	21	4,056	33,092
1935	11	2,861	163,817
1936	11	878	10,696
Tobacco manufactures:			
1927	1	790	4,740
1928	----	----	----
1929	1	100	300
1930–33	----	----	----
1934	1	31	496
1935–36	----	----	----
Paper and printing:			
1927	4	224	12,168
1928	2	63	707
1929–32	----	----	----
1933	1	40	80
1934	3	1,626	7,856
1935	7	628	16,482
1936	4	1,020	57,720
Chemicals and allied products:			
1927–31	----	----	----
1932	1	30	180
1933	2	131	131
1934	6	1,097	5,113
1935	1	13	65
1936	3	1,094	28,787
Rubber products:			
1927–32	----	----	----
1933	9	2,624	22,111
1934	11	5,987	134,986
1935	4	1,037	18,210
1936	24	67,724	438,738
Miscellaneous manufacturing:			
1927	----	----	----
1928	1	12	24
1929	----	----	----
1930	1	147	147
1931–32	----	----	----
1933	1	12	12
1934	5	1,246	31,331
1935	7	1,364	10,119
1936	8	494	4,335
Extraction of minerals:			
1927	5	26,344	4,481,754
1928	5	9,626	1,576,415
1929	7	768	45,138
1930	3	1,150	13,400
1931	13	6,885	110,161
1932	10	16,660	1,772,930
1933	9	7,536	87,591
1934	4	1,205	26,267
1935	1	27,816	139,080
1936	1	900	1,800

TABLE 35.—*Strikes beginning in 1927–36, in States having 25 or more strikes in any year, by industry group*—Continued

OHIO—Continued

Industry group and year	Number of strikes	Number of workers involved	Man-days idle during year
Transportation and communication:			
1927–28	----	----	----
1929	2	190	2,440
1930	3	326	1,948
1931	2	300	2,200
1932	2	193	11,218
1933	4	235	1,631
1934	13	4,189	90,372
1935	14	2,522	39,607
1936	8	3,774	16,646
Trade:			
1927–28	----	----	----
1929	1	22	1,496
1930–32	----	----	----
1933	1	30	60
1934	12	5,987	108,829
1935	24	2,744	41,595
1936	20	2,340	28,194
Domestic and personal service:			
1927–28	----	----	----
1929	1	41	164
1930	5	1,050	7,803
1931	1	30	1,080
1932	----	----	----
1933	3	60	611
1934	9	624	6,367
1935	5	1,465	31,335
1936	9	457	6,271
Professional service:			
1927	3	39	3,551
1928	1	22	22
1929	1	16	16
1930	----	----	----
1931	3	66	432
1932	4	94	2,040
1933	1	148	3,108
1934	2	28	316
1935	2	164	342
1936	----	----	----
Building and construction:			
1927	5	1,041	18,155
1928	14	1,491	42,157
1929	12	2,887	79,247
1930	11	2,596	20,082
1931	18	3,387	22,228
1932	10	762	13,365
1933	5	576	13,926
1934	10	530	6,817
1935	8	347	3,677
1936	14	1,552	29,778
Agriculture and fishing:			
1927–29	----	----	----
1930	1	30	660
1931–32	----	----	----
1933	1	180	360
1934	3	870	38,610
1935	1	23	394
1936	1	37	111
Relief work and W. P. A.:			
1927–31	----	----	----
1932	1	35	35
1933	3	678	2,616
1934	7	3,370	17,456
1935	7	2,530	63,850
1936	6	2,677	21,933
Other nonmanufacturing industries:			
1927–28	----	----	----
1929	1	28	224
1930	----	----	[1] 308
1931	1	7	7
1932	----	----	----
1933	1	300	6,300
1934	2	56	2,240
1935	----	----	----
1936	5	916	13,739

OREGON

Industry group and year	Number of strikes	Number of workers involved	Man-days idle during year
Iron and steel and their products, not including machinery:			
1927–35	----	----	----
1936	1	81	324
Machinery, not including transportation equipment:			
1927–34	----	----	----
1935	1	36	3,996
1936	1	207	2,466
Lumber and allied products:			
1927–28	----	----	----
1929	1	150	2,100
1930	----	----	----
1931	1	50	250
1932	----	----	----
1933	2	3,200	22,500
1934	4	487	5,080
1935	6	13,259	529,674
1936	11	6,818	150,320
Textiles and their products:			
1927	----	----	----
1928	1	37	37
1929–31	----	----	----
Textiles and their products—Continued.			
1932	2	190	1,465
1933	----	----	----
1934	1	180	3,600
1935	----	----	----
1936	4	1,275	35,578
Leather and its manufactures:			
1927	----	----	----
1928	1	20	20
1929–36	----	----	----
Food and kindred products:			
1927	1	139	5,143
1928–30	----	----	----
1931	2	815	815
1932	----	----	----
1933	2	5,025	140,125
1934	3	4,458	21,590
1935	2	109	1,418
1936	7	764	7,183
Paper and printing:			
1927	2	47	479
1928–30	----	----	----
1931	1	7	7
1932–36	----	----	----

[1] Man-days idle as a result of a strike which began in the preceding year and continued into this year.

TABLE 35.—*Strikes beginning in 1927–36, in States having 25 or more strikes in any year, by industry group*—Continued

OREGON—Continued

Industry group and year	Number of strikes	Number of workers involved	Man-days idle during year
Miscellaneous manufacturing:			
1927–33			
1934	1	29	319
1935–36			
Extraction of minerals:			
1927–35			
1936	2	170	2,218
Transportation and communication:			
1927–28			
1929	1	20	200
1930			
1931	2	70	140
1932	1	200	400
1933			
1934	18	3,923	98,765
1935	7	324	1,563
1936	9	4,081	168,516
Trade:			
1927–34			
1935	1	31	1,054
1936	5	401	12,003
Domestic and personal service:			
1927–28			
1929	1	62	62
1930			
1931	1	12	36
1932			
1933	2	92	1,780
1934			
1935	3	45	1,471
1936	3	65	1,040
Professional service:			
1927–28			
1929	2	44	1,196
1930–36			
Building and construction:			
1927	6	339	6,367
1928	3	165	1,450
1929	2	35	495
1930	1	40	720
1931			
1932	1	200	2,000
1933	1	15	15
1934–35			
1936	3	221	774
Agriculture and fishing:			
1927			
1928	1	150	450
1929			
1930	1	100	100
1931–32			
1933	3	1,735	7,335
1934	7	8,673	17,261
1935	1	25	25
1936	4	1,374	1,764
Relief work and W. P. A.:			
1927–33			
1934	2	191	351
1935			
1936	2	482	8,288
Other nonmanufacturing industries:			
1927–35			
1936	1	70	700

PENNSYLVANIA

Industry group and year	Number of strikes	Number of workers involved	Man-days idle during year
Iron and steel and their products, not including machinery:			
1927	3	950	6,100
1928	3	153	2,215
1929	9	1,692	35,480
1930	4	1,476	11,260
1931	4	1,005	9,210
1932	2	95	695
1933	17	11,505	71,511
1934	5	2,054	27,917
1935	16	3,157	21,767
1936	14	3,446	39,079
Machinery, not including transportation equipment:			
1927	3	71	4,566
1928	3	129	753
1929	5	832	53,930
1930	1	26	286
1931	2	28	224
1932			
1933	9	6,127	39,504
1934	3	1,030	33,585
1935	2	59	823
1936	13	1,517	41,380
Transportation equipment:			
1927–28			
1929	1	1,500	6,000
1930			
1931	1	2,000	22,000
1932			
1933	4	1,624	22,812
1934	3	352	41,296
1935	1	85	595
1936	8	6,326	82,046
Nonferrous metals and their products:			
1927			
1928	1	90	1,080
1929			[1] 270
1930–32			
1933	3	1,427	14,332
1934	7	9,356	143,090
1935	6	509	4,579
1936	1	352	3,887
Lumber and allied products:			
1927	10	906	24,896
1928	4	67	6,654
1929	4	71	6,711
1930	4	79	3,786
1931	3	61	470
1932	2	35	1,157
1933	9	1,089	33,912
1934	4	289	11,516
1935	9	889	7,605
1936	13	1,695	16,483
Stone, clay, and glass products:			
1927	4	1,205	26,085
1928	3	658	25,541
1929	2	140	4,700
1930	1	100	1,400
1931	3	562	3,034
1932	3	391	13,382
1933	13	4,239	26,717
1934	10	1,699	49,232
1935	9	5,685	87,799
1936	12	9,033	363,525
Textiles and their products:			
1927	23	3,075	42,109

[1] Man-days idle as a result of a strike which began in the preceding year and continued into this year.

TABLE 35.—*Strikes beginning in 1927–36, in States having 25 or more strikes in any year, by industry group*—Continued

PENNSYLVANIA—Continued

Industry group and year	Number of strikes	Number of workers involved	Man-days idle during year
Textiles and their products—Continued.			
1928	26	2,413	36,660
1929	59	9,500	205,688
1930	41	6,282	231,736
1931	37	13,194	794,068
1932	28	3,979	26,028
1933	126	77,160	1,484,320
1934	77	69,920	888,426
1935	124	30,089	427,589
1936	125	24,440	741,213
Leather and its manufactures:			
1927	2	656	21,487
1928	------	------	------
1929	5	571	19,229
1930	2	116	2,555
1931	3	423	8,898
1932	1	60	480
1933	20	4,130	63,742
1934	10	1,368	44,223
1935	5	1,192	2,306
1936	10	2,617	24,433
Food and kindred products:			
1927	3	144	1,557
1928	4	121	597
1929	3	159	1,279
1930	1	8	24
1931	3	24	102
1932	5	396	8,857
1933	16	5,189	68,131
1934	19	1,324	23,906
1935	13	1,960	106,167
1936	24	2,573	63,755
Tobacco manufactures:			
1927–28	------	------	------
1929	1	200	1,200
1930–31	------	------	------
1932	1	22	154
1933	6	2,678	39,629
1934	6	3,474	122,312
1935	1	200	11,902
1936	1	200	4,000
Paper and printing:			
1927	1	15	90
1928	1	45	45
1929	3	88	3,068
1930	------	------	------
1931	1	110	660
1932	3	631	5,418
1933	8	1,081	4,457
1934	7	691	3,885
1935	6	1,213	25,794
1936	6	633	9,486
Chemicals and allied products:			
1927–28	------	------	------
1929	2	32	369
1930–32	------	------	------
1933	2	470	9,830
1934	3	923	71,097
1935	1	39	117
1936	4	427	4,594
Rubber products:			
1927–32	------	------	------
1933	2	119	680
1934	1	9	45
1935	1	61	122
1936	3	1,115	5,470
Miscellaneous manufacturing:			
1927	2	21	280
1928	------	------	------
1929	1	300	1,200
1930	1	34	3,468
1931	3	133	4,547

Industry group and year	Number of strikes	Number of workers involved	Man-days idle during year
Miscellaneous manufacturing—Continued.			
1932	1	11	33
1933	10	3,640	17,963
1934	4	845	9,875
1935	6	734	13,627
1936	7	665	23,847
Extraction of minerals:			
1927	37	69,202	7,305,032
1928	44	85,174	1,671,554
1929	37	58,051	243,006
1930	25	21,025	129,535
1931	25	79,183	1,129,379
1932	31	25,151	277,415
1933	74	190,264	2,353,720
1934	76	125,785	1,057,546
1935	55	186,313	1,474,885
1936	38	30,284	320,800
Transportation and communication:			
1927	3	119	1,542
1928	1	155	23,715
1929	8	1,248	5,547
1930	5	1,844	189,954
1931	3	903	8,267
1932	------	------	------
1933	13	10,616	103,691
1934	6	467	11,639
1935	9	3,030	45,742
1936	12	5,971	43,753
Trade:			
1927	1	32	1,696
1928	1	29	58
1929	5	354	8,671
1930	3	358	4,677
1931	1	18	18
1932	2	165	265
1933	7	14,963	67,405
1934	9	743	19,081
1935	10	750	9,419
1936	17	4,120	41,910
Domestic and personal service:			
1927	------	------	------
1928	3	540	2,254
1929	------	------	------
1930	1	150	900
1931	2	210	835
1932	1	370	2,590
1933	15	7,124	129,523
1934	18	3,779	76,220
1935	13	1,513	17,169
1936	10	3,845	48,861
Professional service:			
1927	2	22	476
1928	1	11	121
1929	8	408	4,460
1930	1	300	9,000
1931	4	194	14,536
1932	7	880	5,148
1933	10	792	8,716
1934	7	326	3,751
1935	5	151	1,078
1936	4	295	2,036
Building and construction:			
1927	25	4,714	188,819
1928	15	847	139,554
1929	31	5,646	60,379
1930	25	2,758	32,772
1931	33	2,537	55,140
1932	25	3,679	101,280
1933	14	2,437	70,770
1934	10	3,046	20,467
1935	10	1,090	11,150
1936	23	3,941	47,956

TABLE 35.—*Strikes beginning in 1927–36, in States having 25 or more strikes in any year, by industry group*—Continued

PENNSYLVANIA—Continued

Industry group and year	Number of strikes	Number of workers involved	Man-days idle during year
Agriculture and fishing:			
1927–30	------	------	------
1931	2	365	18,215
1932	1	100	700
1933	1	300	300
1934	------	------	------
1935	2	154	1,799
1936	------	------	------
Relief work and W. P. A.:			
1927–31	------	------	------
1932	1	500	500
1933	------	------	------
1934	9	943	3,943
1935	14	6,256	54,847
1936	13	14,417	86,567

Industry group and year	Number of strikes	Number of workers involved	Man-days idle during year
Other nonmanufacturing industries:			
1927–31	------	------	------
1932	1	40	40
1933	2	270	880
1934	1	55	2,200
1935	2	60	80
1936	7	292	1,460
Interindustry:			
1927–33	------	------	------
1934	1	26,000	26,000
1935–36	------	------	------

RHODE ISLAND

Industry group and year	Number of strikes	Number of workers involved	Man-days idle during year
Iron and steel and their products, not including machinery:			
1927	1	52	1,612
1928–32	------	------	------
1933	2	123	290
1934–36	------	------	------
Machinery, not including transportation equipment:			
1927–28	------	------	------
1929	1	22	66
1930–32	------	------	------
1933	1	57	228
1934–35	------	------	------
1936	1	285	1,425
Nonferrous metals and their products:			
1927	1	23	1,518
1928–29	------	------	------
1930	1	60	180
1931–32	------	------	------
1933	1	18	72
1934–36	------	------	------
Lumber and allied products:			
1927–32	------	------	------
1933	1	74	999
1934–36	------	------	------
Stone, clay, and glass products:			
1927	1	50	250
1928–31	------	------	------
1932	2	47	771
1933–36	------	------	------
Textiles and their products:			
1927	12	2,165	73,071
1928	7	818	13,579
1929	12	2,556	85,300
1930	4	240	1,361
1931	14	4,341	100,354
1932	8	1,290	25,435
1933	36	11,469	198,036
1934	8	29,695	333,615
1935	16	3,340	78,882
1936	19	3,049	69,029
Paper and printing:			
1927–29	------	------	------
1930	1	23	92
1931–32	------	------	------
1933	2	76	1,593
1934–36	------	------	------

Industry group and year	Number of strikes	Number of workers involved	Man-days idle during year
Rubber products:			
1927	1	320	3,520
1928–32	------	------	------
1933	1	116	348
1934–35	------	------	------
1936	2	942	4,629
Miscellaneous manufacturing:			
1927–32	------	------	------
1933	1	18	36
1934–36	------	------	------
Transportation and communication:			
1927–28	------	------	------
1929	1	75	450
1930	------	------	------
1931	1	200	9,600
1932–34	------	------	------
1935	1	80	160
1936	2	625	1,125
Trade:			
1927–33	------	------	------
1934	2	81	81
1935	------	------	------
1936	2	209	1,881
Professional service:			
1927–28	------	------	------
1929	1	7	210
1930–32	------	------	------
1933	2	58	58
1934	1	87	87
1935–36	------	------	------
Building and construction:			
1927	7	2,973	168,657
1928	2	550	15,500
1929	2	260	920
1930	4	210	1,790
1931	5	295	10,076
1932	1	65	455
1933	------	------	------
1934	1	20	20
1935	3	61	518
1936	------	------	------
Agriculture and fishing:			
1927–35	------	------	------
1936	1	700	4,200
Relief work and W. P. A.:			
1927–32	------	------	------
1933	2	500	1,500
1934	2	315	595
1935	1	31	62
1936	------	------	------

TABLE 35.—*Strikes beginning in 1927-36, in States having 25 or more strikes in any year, by industry group*—Continued

SOUTH CAROLINA

Industry group and year	Number of strikes	Number of workers involved	Man-days idle during year
Lumber and allied products:			
1927-32			
1933	3	610	1,620
1934			
1935	1	814	5,698
1936			
Stone, clay, and glass products:			
1927-30			
1931	1	8	8
1932-33			
1934	1	22	154
1935-36			
Textiles and their products:			
1927-28			
1929	14	11,907	302,034
1930-31			
1932	3	1,850	72,050
1933	26	14,441	109,255
1934	16	42,392	544,204
1935	10	4,236	178,062
1936	12	4,204	254,280
Food and kindred products:			
1927-32			
1933	2	216	416
1934-36			
Transportation and communication:			
1927-35			
1936	2	190	2,675
Domestic and personal service:			
1927-29			
1930	1	48	240
1931-32			
1933	1	9	36
1934-36			
Professional service:			
1927-31			
1932	1	7	847
1933-36			
Building and construction:			
1927-35			
1936	2	51	420

TENNESSEE

Industry group and year	Number of strikes	Number of workers involved	Man-days idle during year
Iron and steel and their products, not including machinery:			
1927			
1928	2	124	2,494
1929	1	15	285
1930-32			
1933	2	130	400
1934	1	299	8,671
1935			
1936	2	124	3,859
Machinery, not including transportation equipment:			
1927-33			
1934	1	550	13,200
1935-36			
Nonferrous metals and their products:			
1927	1	1,100	37,400
1928-33			
1934	2	2,177	42,622
1935	1	467	10,274
1936			
Lumber and allied products:			
1927-31			
1932	1	70	210
1933	4	489	932
1934	2	344	3,016
1935	8	1,022	26,285
1936	1	200	800
Stone, clay, and glass products:			
1927-34			
1935	1	38	84
1936	1	14	882
Textiles and their products:			
1927			
1928	1	300	4,800
1929	4	8,128	147,783
1930-31			
1932	1	151	755
1933	9	1,832	35,926
1934	6	7,174	76,756
1935	7	702	48,968
1936	4	1,180	14,950
Leather and its manufactures:			
1927-34			
1935	1	108	1,188
1936	1	70	1,820
Food and kindred products:			
1927	1	15	465
1928-33			
1934	1	44	88
1935	1	18	108
1936	2	112	926
Paper and printing:			
1927-28			
1929	1	53	[illegible]
1930-35			
1936	1	17	17
Chemicals and allied products:			
1927-33			
1934	1	119	476
1935	1	70	560
1936			
Extraction of minerals:			
1927-28			
1929	1	250	1,250
1930			
1931	3	680	7,750
1932	1	400	49,600
1933	2	1,050	15,900
1934	1	100	300
1935	1	1,530	36,720
1936	1	500	30,500
Transportation and communication:			
1927-30			
1931	1	88	264
1932-33			
1934	2	59	355
1935	1	75	450
1936			
Trade:			
1927-29			
1930	1	8	8
1931-34			
1935	1	35	70
1936	3	164	4,204

TABLE 35.—*Strikes beginning in 1927-36, in States having 25 or more strikes in any year, by industry group*—Continued

TENNESSEE—Continued

Industry group and year	Number of strikes	Number of workers involved	Man-days idle during year
Domestic and personal service:			
1927			
1928	1	20	20
1929-34			
1935	1	7	21
1936			
Professional service:			
1927	1	7	42
1928-30			
1931	1	34	238
1932	1	44	968
1933	1	11	319
1934-36			
Building and construction:			
1927	1	250	3,750
1928	2	18	60
Building and construction—Continued.			
1929	1	10	20
1930-31			
1932	1	40	400
1933	1	7	7
1934			
1935	2	67	1,081
1936	4	186	3,618
Relief work and W. P. A.:			
1927-34			
1935	1	6	6
1936	3	193	746
Other nonmanufacturing industries:			
1927-32			
1933	1	500	2,500
1934-36			

TEXAS

Industry group and year	Number of strikes	Number of workers involved	Man-days idle during year
Nonferrous metals and their products:			
1927-34			
1935	1	38	190
1936			
Lumber and allied products:			
1927-32			
1933	1	300	1,500
1934	1	59	708
1935			
1936	1	261	12,267
Textiles and their products:			
1927			
1928	1	110	550
1929			[1] 6,710
1930-32			
1933	1	475	1,425
1934	2	717	10,688
1935	3	606	8,669
1936	2	277	5,615
Food and kindred products:			
1927-30			
1931	1	9	18
1932	2	232	4,012
1933			
1934	5	418	8,829
1935	1	200	12,400
1936	3	30	78
Tobacco manufactures:			
1927-32			
1933	1	400	7,200
1934			
1935	1	215	16,985
1936			
Paper and printing:			
1927	1	7	427
1928	1	60	4,560
1929	1	40	40
1930	2	33	287
1931-33			
1934	1	11	132
1935-36			
Chemicals and allied products:			
1927	1	27	567
1928			
Chemicals and allied products—Continued.			
1929	1	69	69
1930-33			
1934	1	18	54
1935			
1936	1	42	252
Miscellaneous manufacturing:			
1927-34			
1935	2	38	206
1936	1	60	60
Extraction of minerals:			
1927-33			
1934	2	339	3,818
1935	2	955	5,667
1936			
Transportation and communication:			
1927-29			
1930	2	3,150	6,150
1931	2	2,520	45,060
1932-33			
1934	2	3,598	35,294
1935	4	3,074	103,295
1936	14	5,264	63,729
Trade:			
1927-32			
1933	1	15	30
1934	3	800	5,800
1935	5	176	335
1936	1	27	351
Domestic and personal service:			
1927-29			
1930	1	30	660
1931			
1932	1	60	180
1933-35			
1936	2	48	1,122
Professional service:			
1927	3	25	101
1928	1	35	1,260
1929			
1930	1	16	416
1931	1	75	750
1932	3	49	3,229
1933	1	12	360
1934-36			

[1] Man-days idle as a result of a strike which began in the preceding year and continued into this year.

TABLE 35.—*Strikes beginning in 1927–36, in States having 25 or more strikes in any year, by industry group*—Continued

TEXAS—Continued

Industry group and year	Number of strikes	Number of workers involved	Man-days idle during year
Building and construction:			
1927	3	72	6,768
1928	2	106	4,062
1929	4	392	2,153
1930	----	----	----
1931	9	530	6,832
1932	1	12	60
1933	2	1,900	3,860
1934	4	762	5,884
1935	2	40	140
1936	11	906	7,466
Agriculture and fishing:			
1927–33	----	----	----
Agriculture and fishing—Continued.			
1934	1	1,500	40,500
1935	1	2,000	8,000
1936	1	100	2,400
Relief work and W. P. A.:			
1927–34	----	----	----
1935	1	248	496
1936	1	43	301
Other nonmanufacturing industries:			
1927–34	----	----	----
1935	1	25	25
1936	----	----	----

WASHINGTON

Industry group and year	Number of strikes	Number of workers involved	Man-days idle during year
Iron and steel and their products, not including machinery:			
1927–32	----	----	----
1933	1	19	19
1934–35	----	----	----
1936	2	107	4,131
Machinery, not including transportation equipment:			
1927	----	----	----
1928	2	128	6,688
1929	1	36	3,200
1930–36	----	----	----
Transportation equipment:			
1927	1	15	105
1928	----	----	----
1929	1	300	57,000
1930–34	----	----	----
1935	2	61	1,756
1936	1	58	1,450
Lumber and allied products:			
1927	2	1,021	33,302
1928	4	215	4,137
1929	2	65	807
1930	3	469	27,651
1931	8	2,060	37,879
1932	----	----	----
1933	7	1,110	11,888
1934	5	2,285	15,538
1935	20	25,388	927,234
1936	35	12,092	286,991
Stone, clay, and glass products:			
1927–35	----	----	----
1936	1	68	816
Textiles and their products:			
1927–28	----	----	----
1929	1	18	72
1930–34	----	----	----
1935	4	153	10,092
1936	1	15	90
Food and kindred products:			
1927	----	----	----
1928	1	68	136
1929	1	15	120
1930–31	----	----	----
1932	1	19	19
1933	3	71	1,151
1934	4	78	386
1935	6	530	21,336
1936	4	788	14,778
Paper and printing:			
1927–30	----	----	----
1931	1	15	15
1932	----	----	----
1933	2	245	4,022
1934–35	----	----	----
1936	3	805	59,395
Miscellaneous manufacturing:			
1927–35	----	----	----
1936	1	15	420
Extraction of minerals:			
1927–32	----	----	----
1933	1	900	73,800
1934	2	862	14,710
1935	1	2,196	10,980
1936	----	----	----
Transportation and communication:			
1927	1	23	1,449
1928–30	----	----	----
1931	1	250	250
1932	----	----	----
1933	1	50	900
1934	10	4,136	233,517
1935	16	3,210	19,207
1936	7	9,665	416,383
Trade:			
1927	1	6	312
1928	1	7	35
1929–32	----	----	----
1933	2	222	299
1934	1	20	80
1935	4	114	5,973
1936	7	1,204	27,818
Domestic and personal service:			
1927	2	165	4,710
1928–29	----	----	----
1930	1	30	930
1931	1	26	390
1932	1	750	6,000
1933	1	26	52
1934	2	166	252
1935	1	62	310
1936	----	----	----
Professional service:			
1927	1	37	481
1928	1	9	9
1929	1	49	2,352
1930	2	43	295
1931	2	24	998
1932	----	----	----
1933	1	6	228
1934–36	----	----	----

TABLE 35.—*Strikes beginning in 1927–36, in States having 25 or more strikes in any year, by industry group*—Continued

WASHINGTON—Continued

Industry group and year	Number of strikes	Number of workers involved	Man-days idle during year
Building and construction:			
1927	1	25	3,825
1928	4	220	1,214
1929	3	99	434
1930	-	-	-
1931	1	10	80
1932	3	650	10,600
1933	3	174	3,475
1934	2	70	238
1935	6	316	2,978
1936	7	678	12,876
Agriculture and fishing:			
1927–30	-	-	-
1931	1	1,200	62,400
1932	2	315	2,490
1933	1	400	400
Agriculture and fishing—Continued.			
1934	-	-	-
1935	1	1,800	43,200
1936	6	1,657	17,054
Relief work and W. P. A.:			
1927–33	-	-	-
1934	1	20	40
1935	-	-	-
1936	6	846	4,548
Other nonmanufacturing industries:			
1927–33	-	-	-
1934	1	28	392
1935	-	-	-
1936	1	75	75

WEST VIRGINIA

Industry group and year	Number of strikes	Number of workers involved	Man-days idle during year
Iron and steel and their products, not including machinery:			
1927–31	-	-	-
1932	2	3,020	365,420
1933	3	11,398	199,596
1934	3	882	25,206
1935	3	845	12,200
1936	1	484	7,744
Nonferrous metals and their products:			
1927–33	-	-	-
1934	2	559	9,331
1935	1	460	7,820
1936	1	212	12,084
Lumber and allied products:			
1927	2	1,435	37,980
1928	-	-	[1] 3,230
1929–33	-	-	-
1934	1	2,053	93,628
1935	1	19	38
1936	-	-	-
Stone, clay, and glass products:			
1927	1	220	220
1928	-	-	-
1929	1	190	2,660
1930	-	-	-
1931	1	125	4,125
1932	-	-	-
1933	2	141	562
1934	4	1,172	10,860
1935	2	82	11,893
1936	5	2,768	70,404
Textiles and their products:			
1927–31	-	-	-
1932	1	200	3,000
1933	2	388	9,588
1934	3	2,335	67,650
1935	-	-	-
1936	3	527	37,720
Leather and its manufactures:			
1927–33	-	-	-
1934	1	442	11,050
1935–36	-	-	-
Food and kindred products:			
1927–34	-	-	-
1935	1	32	192
1936	2	72	156
Tobacco manufactures:			
1927–30	-	-	-
1931	1	665	6,650
1932	-	-	-
1933	1	260	3,640
1934–36	-	-	-
Paper and printing:			
1927–31	-	-	-
1932	1	17	17
1933–36	-	-	-
Miscellaneous manufacturing:			
1927–35	-	-	-
1936	1	400	5,600
Extraction of minerals:			
1927	2	1,300	171,900
1928	-	-	-
1929	1	175	350
1930	9	4,070	78,875
1931	5	7,822	377,720
1932	3	4,047	160,222
1933	5	13,279	166,535
1934	7	27,117	338,117
1935	6	102,946	537,832
1936	6	2,349	5,065
Transportation and communication:			
1927–34	-	-	-
1935	1	11	55
1936	-	-	-
Trade:			
1927–34	-	-	-
1935	1	12	372
1936	5	41	640
Domestic and personal service:			
1927–34	-	-	-
1935	1	24	24
1936	1	155	930
Building and construction:			
1927	1	8	888
1928–29	-	-	-

[1] Man-days idle as a result of a strike which began in the preceding year and continued into this year.

TABLE 35.—*Strikes beginning in 1927–36, in States having 25 or more strikes in any year, by industry group*—Continued

WEST VIRGINIA—Continued

Industry group and year	Number of strikes	Number of workers involved	Man-days idle during year
Building and construction—Continued.			
1930	1	35	280
1931	1	50	300
1932			[1] 50
1933	1	200	600
1934	1	35	175
1935			
1936	4	175	475
Relief work and W. P. A.:			
1927–32			
1933	1	100	100
1934	1	500	500
1935			
1936	1	150	150

WISCONSIN

Industry group and year	Number of strikes	Number of workers involved	Man-days idle during year
Iron and steel and their products, not including machinery:			
1927–30			
1931	2	47	222
1932	1	59	944
1933	1	277	1,385
1934	7	4,245	109,678
1935	4	2,000	41,300
1936	3	350	1,986
Machinery, not including transportation equipment:			
1927–28			
1929	1	55	825
1930–33			
1934	3	1,720	31,715
1935	4	2,321	123,720
1936	3	2,608	102,290
Transportation equipment:			
1927–32			
1933	2	3,236	25,588
1934	7	5,744	148,903
1935	3	1,566	41,782
1936	2	1,965	8,060
Nonferrous metals and their products:			
1927–33			
1934	2	1,134	63,306
1935	3	276	814
1936	1	1,575	9,450
Lumber and allied products:			
1927–32			
1933	3	207	586
1934	7	3,584	51,422
1935	4	673	12,121
1936	4	440	9,676
Stone, clay, and glass products:			
1927–33			
1934	1	20	240
1935–36			
Textiles and their products:			
1927			
1928	2	570	7,730
1929			
1930	1	93	1,860
1931	2	1,814	43,312
1932			
1933	2	187	7,524
1934	5	1,774	63,149
1935	3	219	1,601
1936	3	378	4,428
Leather and its manufactures:			
1927			
1928	1	436	3,052
1929			
1930	1	35	280
Leather and its manufactures—Continued.			
1931	1	103	103
1932	1	100	600
1933			
1934	7	3,329	83,299
1935	1	481	6,508
1936			
Food and kindred products:			
1927–30			
1931	1	30	210
1932–33			
1934	10	849	21,523
1935	1	128	3,968
1936	4	974	26,723
Tobacco manufactures:			
1927–29			
1930	1	14	350
1931	1	40	421
1932–36			
Paper and printing:			
1927–32			
1933	1	7	21
1934–35			
1936	1	21	2,604
Chemicals and allied products:			
1927–35			
1936	1	396	9,504
Rubber products:			
1927–33			
1934	3	2,922	75,324
1935			
1936	3	3,355	8,069
Miscellaneous manufacturing:			
1927–34			
1935	1	75	1,500
1936	1	28	84
Transportation and communication:			
1927–29			
1930	2	240	760
1931	1	400	6,000
1932–33			
1934	4	4,802	29,385
1935	3	325	500
1936	4	409	2,629
Trade:			
1927–28			
1929	1	20	2,020
1930–32			
1933	1	12	12
1934	9	939	21,268
1935	6	674	11,953
1936	8	493	3,643
Domestic and personal service:			
1927–29			
1930	1	115	920
1931–33			

[1] Man-days idle as a result of a strike which began in the preceding year and continued into this year.

TABLE 35. *Strikes beginning in 1927–36, in States having 25 or more strikes in any year, by industry group*—Continued

WISCONSIN—Continued

Industry group and year	Number of strikes	Number of workers involved	Man-days idle during year
Domestic and personal service—Continued			
1944	3	610	21,912
1935	3	54	735
1936	4	103	564
Professional service:			
1927–29	--	--	--
1930	1	172	2,236
1931	--	--	--
1932	1	46	1,150
1933	3	193	1,071
1934	--	--	--
1935	1	400	3,000
1936	--	--	--
Building and construction:			
1927	3	621	11,089
1928	5	239	1,523
1929	4	208	4,992
1930	2	90	1,440
Building and construction—Continued.			
1931	7	2,499	58,107
1932	4	308	4,552
1933	--	--	--
1934	8	1,113	65,753
1935	5	525	3,645
1936	5	246	2,924
Agriculture and fishing:			
1927–32	--	--	--
1933	1	50	50
1934–36	--	--	--
Relief work and W. P. A.:			
1927–31	--	--	--
1932	1	75	75
1933	3	501	6,075
1934	1	300	4,500
1935	4	558	14,556
1936	3	3,076	40,566

Major Causes of Strikes in Each Industry

In 10 of the 20 industry groups shown in table 36, the greatest number of strikes were chiefly due to questions of union organization. In seven, questions of wages and hours were the causes of most of the strikes and in two there were about an equal number of strikes due to wages and hours and union organization matters. While more of the strikes in the textile group, as a whole, were due to wages and hours, in the wearing-apparel industry the majority of strikes were due to union organization matters. The greatest number of strikes in mining are classified under "Miscellaneous." Many of these were strikes between rival unions which took place in the anthracite mines of Pennsylvania and in the bituminous-coal fields in Illinois.

In 12 of the industry groups the greatest number of workers were involved in union organization strikes, and in 8 the largest number of workers were involved in strikes over wages and hours matters. In both branches of the textile industry, fabrics and wearing apparel, more workers were involved in strikes in which the major issues were matters of union organization than in strikes concerned only with wages and hours. The relatively large number of workers involved in the miscellaneous classification in the building and construction industry was chiefly due to jurisdictional strikes; in textiles, to sympathetic strikes called by one branch or section of the industry when another was on strike over wages and hours or union organization matters; in mining, to disputes between rival unions. The comparatively large number of workers listed under miscellaneous causes in transportation and communication refer mostly to water transportation—longshoremen and seamen. While some of these strikes were disputes between rival unions or factions of unions, a good number were due to dissatisfaction over working conditions other than wages and hours.

In 14 industrial groups the greatest amount of time was lost because of strikes chiefly due to matters of union organization, and in 6 to strikes over wages and hours. Strikes primarily due to union organization in the textile-fabric industries caused almost 10 million man-days of idleness during the 10-year period, and over 7 million in the wearing apparel industries. Wages and hours strikes in textile fabrics resulted in almost 9 million man-days of idleness, and in the apparel industries over 4 million. Wages and hours strikes in mining caused over 40 million man-days of idleness, and in the building and construction industries almost 5½ million.

TABLE 36.—*Major issues involved in strikes in various industry groups for the 10-year period 1927–36*

Industry group	Number of strikes			
	Total	Major issues		
		Wages and hours	Union organization	Miscellaneous
Iron and steel and their products, not including machinery	358	153	169	36
Machinery, not including transportation equipment	295	127	149	19
Transportation equipment	205	91	98	16
Nonferrous metals and their products	169	60	90	19
Lumber and allied products	658	266	316	76
Stone, clay, and glass products	187	85	83	19
Textiles and their products	[1] 2,881	1,275	1,207	399
Fabrics	1,214	680	321	213
Wearing apparel	1,673	595	892	186
Leather and its manufactures	604	243	295	66
Food and kindred products	575	225	293	57
Tobacco manufactures	64	35	15	14
Paper and printing	297	129	140	28
Chemicals and allied products	76	34	31	11
Rubber products	99	48	41	10
Extraction of minerals	895	301	226	368
Transportation and communication	736	305	259	172
Trade	553	182	340	31
Domestic and personal service	549	215	291	43
Professional service	326	154	65	107
Building and construction	1,817	899	526	392
Agriculture and fishing	176	138	35	3

[1] See footnote 2, p. 137.

TABLE 36.—*Major issues involved in strikes in various industry groups for the 10-year period 1927–36*—Continued

Industry group	Number of workers			
	Total	Major issues		
		Wages and hours	Union organization	Miscellaneous
Iron and steel and their products, not including machinery	114,718	35,071	68,614	11,033
Machinery, not including transportation equipment	95,635	28,098	65,029	2,508
Transportation equipment	183,476	67,375	100,644	15,457
Nonferrous metals and their products	52,890	14,880	36,674	1,336
Lumber and allied products	167,562	54,678	102,031	10,853
Stone, clay, and glass products	62,372	24,634	33,688	4,050
Textiles and their products	**1,833,158**	**657,395**	**988,485**	**187,278**
Fabrics	867,258	279,180	508,437	79,641
Wearing apparel	965,900	378,215	480,048	107,637
Leather and its manufactures	238,202	94,830	124,378	18,994
Food and kindred products	125,617	56,047	65,985	3,585
Tobacco manufactures	32,532	18,460	3,600	10,472
Paper and printing	33,504	18,406	13,966	1,132
Chemicals and allied products	24,359	5,400	16,705	2,254
Rubber products	100,212	40,322	34,397	25,493
Extraction of minerals	1,673,625	873,850	304,320	495,455
Transportation and communication	333,580	112,228	169,437	51,915
Trade	125,133	56,939	49,622	18,572
Domestic and personal service	244,182	107,199	130,420	6,563
Professional service	28,206	16,227	5,359	6,620
Building and construction	359,189	236,843	70,172	52,174
Agriculture and fishing	123,258	89,446	33,112	700
	Number of man-days idle			
Iron and steel and their products, not including machinery	2,536,246	945,459	1,496,819	93,968
Machinery, not including transportation equipment	2,185,796	453,397	1,720,380	12,019
Transportation equipment	2,861,469	887,484	1,883,266	90,719
Nonferrous metals and their products	1,005,445	196,178	790,967	18,300
Lumber and allied products	4,349,062	1,015,064	3,184,027	149,971
Stone, clay, and glass products	1,461,339	323,990	1,063,283	74,066
Textiles and their products	**32,098,562**	**12,749,202**	**16,996,202**	**2,353,158**
Fabrics	20,167,694	8,693,684	9,949,515	1,524,495
Wearing apparel	11,930,868	4,055,518	7,046,687	828,663
Leather and its manufactures	4,833,127	1,947,167	2,548,192	337,768
Food and kindred products	2,319,457	736,337	1,507,528	75,592
Tobacco manufactures	486,642	227,795	97,919	160,928
Paper and printing	618,359	191,380	416,237	10,742
Chemicals and allied products	406,664	131,670	262,998	11,996
Rubber products	782,220	494,871	259,339	28,010
Extraction of minerals	51,299,723	40,330,882	6,375,902	4,592,939
Transportation and communication	6,252,912	1,285,912	4,188,278	778,722
Trade	1,339,190	364,059	819,663	155,468
Domestic and personal service	3,407,856	1,243,312	2,056,040	108,504
Professional service	650,207	232,533	162,109	255,565
Building and construction	7,573,081	5,409,328	1,273,364	890,389
Agriculture and fishing	1,816,971	1,353,413	455,718	7,840

Strikes beginning each year in each industry are given in table 37 according to major issues involved.

TABLE 37.—*Strikes beginning 1927-36, by industries and major issues involved* [a]

Industry and year	Number of strikes				Number of workers involved				Number of man-days idle during year			
	Total	Major issues			Total	Major issues			Total	Major issues		
		Wages and hours	Union organization	Miscellaneous		Wages and hours	Union organization	Miscellaneous		Wages and hours	Union organization	Miscellaneous
Iron and steel and their products, not including machinery:												
1927	13	7	3	3	1,996	1,214	460	322	11,835	6,276	2,137	3,422
1928	14	7	5	2	944	677	188	79	66,117	13,823	49,855	2,439
1929	20	6	9	5	4,131	2,225	601	1,305	171,142	125,705	21,132	24,305
1930	13	9	3	1	2,050	1,700	310	40	28,591	18,261	9,930	400
1931	17	12	4	1	3,321	2,801	472	48	24,927	13,800	11,031	96
1932	10	9	-	1	4,083	4,058	-	25	387,985	387,360	-	625
1933	70	35	28	7	33,948	7,213	25,489	1,246	413,738	87,321	320,360	6,057
1934	65	23	36	6	26,043	3,769	19,544	2,730	633,224	128,008	486,670	18,546
1935	67	28	32	7	16,592	6,982	6,042	3,568	314,597	125,118	162,701	26,778
1936	69	17	49	3	21,610	4,432	15,508	1,670	484,090	39,787	433,003	11,300
Blast furnaces, steel works, and rolling mills:												
1927	1	1	-	-	450	450	-	-	1,350	1,350	-	-
1928	3	1	2	-	366	300	66	-	5,298	5,100	198	-
1929	2	-	-	2	765	-	-	765	10,825	-	-	10,825
1930	3	3	-	-	1,019	1,019	-	-	11,303	11,303	-	-
1931	5	3	2	-	1,865	1,640	225	-	9,680	6,180	3,500	-
1932	5	5	-	-	3,619	3,619	-	-	378,616	378,616	-	-
1933	11	4	6	1	21,272	1,042	19,730	500	252,302	3,982	246,820	1,500
1934	8	1	4	3	11,534	40	9,844	1,650	286,710	160	278,660	7,890
1935	9	4	2	3	5,023	2,045	77	2,901	36,792	7,387	7,893	21,512
1936	11	3	8	-	9,412	848	8,564	-	298,445	6,895	291,550	-
Bolts, nuts, washers, and rivets:												
1927-32	-	-	-	-	-	-	-	-	-	-	-	-
1933	1	1	-	-	79	79	-	-	158	158	-	-
1934	-	-	-	-	-	-	-	-	-	-	-	-
1935	3	1	2	-	1,314	1,142	172	-	68,458	63,952	4,506	-
1936	-	-	-	-	-	-	-	-	-	-	-	-
Cast-iron pipe:												
1927-33	-	-	-	-	-	-	-	-	-	-	-	-
1934	2	-	2	-	1,600	-	1,600	-	18,250	-	18,250	-
1935	5	2	2	1	954	250	488	216	22,721	13,040	9,033	648
1936	1	-	1	-	160	-	160	-	2,820	[1] 1,700	1,120	-

[1] Man-days idle as a result of a strike which began in the preceding year and continued into this year.

[a] See p. 180 for index to this table.

TABLE 37.—*Strikes beginning 1927–36, by industries and major issues involved*—Continued

Industry and year	Number of strikes: Total	Number of strikes: Major issues: Wages and hours	Number of strikes: Major issues: Union organization	Number of strikes: Major issues: Miscellaneous	Number of workers involved: Total	Number of workers involved: Major issues: Wages and hours	Number of workers involved: Major issues: Union organization	Number of workers involved: Major issues: Miscellaneous	Number of man-days idle during year: Total	Number of man-days idle during year: Major issues: Wages and hours	Number of man-days idle during year: Major issues: Union organization	Number of man-days idle during year: Major issues: Miscellaneous
Iron and steel and their products, not including machinery—Con.												
Cutlery (not including silver and plated cutlery) and edge tools:												
1927–31												
1932	1	1			70	70			70	70		
1933	2	1	1		196	58	138		6,252	870	5,382	
1934	1		1		69		69		4,347		4,347	
1935	5	3	2		1,004	153	851		12,773	2,215	10,558	
1936	1		1		484		484		7,744		7,744	
Forgings, iron and steel:												
1927	1	1			405	405			1,215	1,215		
1928												
1929	1		1		130		130		650		650	
1930												
1931	1	1			40	40			40	40		
1932												
1933	4	4			871	871			13,078	13,078		
1934	10	3	7		2,253	995	1,258		28,953	13,390	15,563	
1935	2	2			647	647			18,776	18,776		
1936	3	1	1	1	428	35	300	93	3,098	1,505	1,500	93
Hardware:												
1927–28												
1929	2	1	1		32	21	11		285	252	33	
1930	1		1		60		60		180		180	
1931	1	1			600	600			1,200	1,200		
1932												
1933	7	6	1		1,918	918	1,000		25,403	4,403	21,000	
1934	6	4	2		863	438	425		9,992	6,832	3,160	
1935	1	1			120	120			1,020	1,020		
1936	5	2	3		2,390	1,828	562		14,040	7,084	6,956	
Plumbers' supplies and fixtures:												
1927												
1928	1	1			65	65			715	715		
1929	1	1			120	120			2,640	2,640		
1930–32												
1933	1			1	350			350	1,050			1,050
1934	6		6		3,528		3,528		99,060		99,060	

1935	5		4	1	276		248	28	3, 363		3, 251	112
1936	2		2		322		322		30, 469		30, 469	
Steam and hot-water heating apparatus and steam fittings:												
1927–28												
1929	1	1			42	42			42	42		
1930	1	1			500	500			4, 000	4, 000		
1931	3	3			232	232			1, 536	1, 536		
1932												
1933	9	3	4	2	3, 280	1, 186	2, 000	94	49, 426	37, 799	9, 508	2, 119
1934												
1935	3	2		1	618	595		23	2, 866	2, 360		506
1936	4	1	3		1, 044	400	644		11, 230	2, 800	8, 430	
Stoves:												
1927	7	2	3	2	805	43	460	302	5, 704	205	2, 137	3, 362
1928	8	4	2	2	455	262	114	79	59, 896	7, 808	49, 649	2, 439
1929	8	2	5	1	282	42	190	50	13, 005	771	9, 784	2, 450
1930	7	5	2		431	181	250		12, 708	2, 958	9, 750	
1931	1	1			143	143			3, 146	3, 146		
1932	1			1	25			25	625			625
1933	13	6	6	1	1, 690	804	849	37	11, 588	5, 650	5, 124	814
1934	18	11	5	2	3, 782	2, 058	684	1, 040	130, 723	104, 351	17, 276	9, 096
1935	14	4	9	1	3, 005	960	1, 645	400	61, 888	7, 740	50, 148	4, 000
1936	18	4	12	2	4, 061	697	1, 787	1, 577	62, 354	16, 416	34, 731	11, 207
Structural and ornamental metalwork:												
1927	1	1			250	250			3, 000	3, 000		
1928	1		1		8		8		8		8	
1929	1	1			2, 000	2, 000			122, 000	122, 000		
1930												
1931	2	1	1		194	14	180		6, 926	266	6, 660	
1932												
1933	4	3	1		1, 188	1, 063	125		15, 399	14, 399	1, 000	
1934	2		1	1	265		225	40	2, 235		675	1, 560
1935	3	1	2		509	98	411		17, 500	490	17, 010	
1936	3	2	1		395	379	16		1, 883	1, 467	416	
Tin cans and other tinware:												
1927												
1928	1	1			50	50			200	200		
1929	1		1		45		45		765		765	
1930–32												
1933	4	1	2	1	880	270	389	221	19, 460	270	18, 748	442
1934	2		2		202		202		3, 726		3, 726	
1935												
1936	3		3		294		294		8, 614		8, 614	

TABLE 37.—*Strikes beginning 1927–36, by industries and major issues involved*—Continued

Industry and year	Number of strikes				Number of workers involved				Number of man-days idle during year			
	Total	Major issues			Total	Major issues			Total	Major issues		
		Wages and hours	Union organization	Miscellaneous		Wages and hours	Union organization	Miscellaneous		Wages and hours	Union organization	Miscellaneous
Iron and steel and their products, not including machinery—Con.												
Tools (not including edge tools, machine tools, files, and saws) (hand tools):												
1927	1	1			26	26			26	26		
1928												
1929	3		1	2	715		225	490	20,930		9,900	11,030
1930	1			1	40			40	400			400
1931–32												
1933	1	1			63	63			126	126		
1934	4	2	2		1,311	108	1,203		33,834	1,335	32,499	
1935	1		1		66		66		1,054	[1] 328	726	
1936	2		2		238		238		4,807		4,807	
Wirework:												
1927	1	1			40	40			480	480		
1928–30												
1931	3	1	1	1	122	7	67	48	1,149	182	871	96
1932	2	2			139	139			2,464	2,464		
1933	5	1	3	1	503	50	409	44	9,184	300	8,752	132
1934	3	1	2		272	100	172		2,284	1,100	1,184	
1935	3	2	1		229	89	140		1,810	1,530	280	
1936	4	1	3		947	57	890		17,064	114	16,950	
Other:												
1927	1			1	20			20	60			60
1928–30												
1931	1	1			125	125			1,250	1,250		
1932	1	1			230	230			6,210	6,210		
1933	8	4	4		1,658	809	849		10,312	6,286	4,026	
1934	3	1	2		364	30	334		13,110	840	12,270	
1935	13	6	7		2,827	883	1,944		65,576	6,280	59,296	
1936	12	3	9		1,435	188	1,247		21,522	1,806	19,716	
Machinery, not including transportation equipment:												
1927	8	6	1	1	395	245	30	120	12,127	9,457	1,590	1,080
1928	9	2	4	3	329	128	141	60	8,472	6,688	1,314	470
1929	23	14	9		3,569	2,639	930		86,785	31,507	55,278	
1930	13	7	5	1	554	314	160	80	10,811	6,392	2,579	1,840
1931	10	6	3	1	281	150	61	70	1,956	1,211	535	210
1932	7	7			484	484			7,191	7,191		

Industry and year												
1933	45	22	18	5	16,053	6,486	8,365	1,202	159,611	45,546	109,119	4,946
1934	57	21	34	2	28,564	10,333	17,946	285	578,379	191,672	385,922	785
1935	50	17	31	2	16,159	3,796	11,891	472	375,744	97,064	277,546	1,134
1936	73	25	44	4	29,247	3,523	25,505	219	944,720	56,669	886,497	1,554
Agricultural implements:												
1927	1	1			33	33			33	33		
1928–32												
1933	1	1			104	104			1,248	1,248		
1934	3	1	2		2,125	95	2,030		37,020	3,610	33,410	
1935	4		4		3,302		3,302		143,274		143,274	
1936	2	1	1		2,316	166	2,150		108,022	6,972	101,050	
Cash registers, adding machines, and typewriters:												
1927–28												
1929	1	1			1,050	1,050			19,950	19,950		
1930												
1931	1	1			15	15			360	360		
1932												
1933	1	1			185	185			3,515	3,515		
1934	4	1	3		8,708	200	8,508		234,075	20,280	213,795	
1935									2,600	[1] 2,600		
1936	1		1		7,000		7,000		462,475		462,475	
Electrical machinery, apparatus, and supplies:												
1927	1	1			93	93			372	372		
1928												
1929	5	3	2		1,594	844	750		57,210	5,010	52,200	
1930												
1931	1		1		14		14		266		266	
1932	1	1			29	29			377	377		
1933	7	3	2	2	4,714	768	3,691	255	80,783	16,687	62,311	1,785
1934	14	7	6	1	5,043	2,846	2,037	160	66,937	27,104	39,673	160
1935	11	3	7	1	3,782	1,054	2,446	282	82,978	39,284	43,130	564
1936	15	7	7	1	2,286	811	1,385	90	66,671	11,236	54,535	900
Engines, turbines, tractors, and water wheels:												
1927												
1928	1		1		39		39		663		663	
1929–31												
1932	1	1			43	43			2,193	2,193		
1933	1		1		20		20		160		160	
1934	2	2			490	490			5,840	5,840		
1935												
1936	2	1	1		918	283	635		14,405	4,245	10,160	
Foundry and machine-shop products:												
1927	6	4	1	1	269	119	30	120	11,722	9,052	1,590	1,080
1928	8	2	3	3	290	128	102	60	7,809	6,688	651	470
1929	15	8	7		736	556	180		8,232	5,154	3,078	
1930	9	4	4	1	349	128	141	80	9,646	5,246	2,560	1,840
1931	7	4	2	1	192	75	47	70	1,210	731	269	210
1932	3	3			56	56			1,447	1,447		
1933	16	10	5	1	1,998	949	704	345	17,419	4,951	11,013	1,455
1934	17	5	11	1	6,322	2,531	3,666	125	102,417	14,887	86,905	625
1935	21	9	11	1	2,323	916	1,217	190	18,051	9,149	8,332	570
1936	36	14	19	3	6,099	2,028	3,942	129	106,551	30,446	75,451	654

[1] Man-days idle as a result of a strike which began in the preceding year and continued into this year.

Table 37.—*Strikes beginning 1927–36, by industries and major issues involved*—Continued

Industry and year	Number of strikes: Total	Number of strikes: Major issues: Wages and hours	Number of strikes: Major issues: Union organization	Number of strikes: Major issues: Miscellaneous	Number of workers involved: Total	Number of workers involved: Major issues: Wages and hours	Number of workers involved: Major issues: Union organization	Number of workers involved: Major issues: Miscellaneous	Number of man-days idle during year: Total	Number of man-days idle during year: Major issues: Wages and hours	Number of man-days idle during year: Major issues: Union organization	Number of man-days idle during year: Major issues: Miscellaneous
Machinery, not including transportation equipment—Con.												
Machine tools (power drivers):												
1927–29												
1930	1	1			52	52			104	104		
1931												
1932	1	1			70	70			2,030	2,030		
1933	2		2		746		746		7,881		7,881	
1934	3	2	1		3,856	3,606	250		123,446	118,446	5,000	
1935–36												
Radios and phonographs:												
1927–29												
1930	2	1	1		45	26	19		305	286	19	
1931–32												
1933	9	5	3	1	7,420	4,355	2,965	100	42,555	17,455	24,900	200
1934	7		7		1,125		1,125		5,079		5,079	
1935	8	2	6		4,207	792	3,415		72,994	19,752	53,242	
1936	8		8		8,165		8,165		170,916		170,916	
Textile machinery and parts:												
1927–32												
1933	1		1		25		25		50		50	
1934	1	1			80	80			560	560		
1935	1		1		62		62		930		930	
1936												
Other:												
1927–28												
1929	2	2			189	189			1,393	1,393		
1930	1	1			108	108			756	756		
1931	1	1			60	60			120	120		
1932	1	1			286	286			1,144	1,144		
1933	7	2	4	1	841	125	214	502	6,000	1,690	2,804	1,506
1934	6	2	4		815	485	330		3,005	945	2,060	
1935	5	3	2		2,483	1,034	1,449		54,917	26,279	28,638	
1936	9	2	7		2,463	235	2,228		15,680	3,770	11,910	
Transportation equipment: [2]												
1927	3	2	1		250	235	15		2,010	1,905	105	
1928	4	1	2	1	1,156	800	304	52	22,150	10,400	11,594	156
1929	16	11	4	1	5,182	3,294	1,588	300	85,565	67,477	15,688	2,400

1930	9	6	1	2	6,577	6,303	30	244	60,544	60,226	30	288
1931	2	2			2,035	2,035			28,775	28,775		
1932	3	3			545	545			4,990	4,990		
1933	31	19	10	2	29,294	14,425	14,766	103	573,565	191,873	381,154	538
1934	42	26	14	2	46,172	26,443	19,177	552	722,582	368,163	336,323	18,096
1935	42	10	28	4	38,216	8,226	18,805	11,185	642,700	93,620	497,485	51,595
1936	53	11	38	4	54,049	5,069	45,959	3,021	718,588	60,055	640,887	17,646
Aircraft:												
1927	1		1		15		15		105		105	
1928–29												
1930	1	1			600	600			9,600	9,600		
1931–32									6,600	[1] 6,600		
1933	2	2			538	538			2,660	2,660		
1934	4	2	1	1	3,207	1,983	1,212	12	111,048	78,048	32,724	276
1935	1		1		1,700		1,700		6,800		6,800	
1936												
Automobiles, bodies, and parts:												
1927	2	2			235	235			1,905	1,905		
1928	2		1	1	326		274	52	11,390		11,234	156
1929	13	8	4	1	3,062	1,174	1,588	300	22,245	4,157	15,688	2,400
1930	4	3		1	5,543	5,343		200	48,126	47,926		200
1931	2	2			2,035	2,035			22,175	22,175		
1932	1	1			45	45			90	90		
1933	21	12	8	1	24,038	13,172	10,850	16	432,434	186,344	246,074	16
1934	24	16	8		34,164	21,331	12,833		377,195	244,139	133,056	
1935	34	8	22	4	31,642	8,046	12,411	11,185	335,794	91,610	192,589	51,595
1936	36	6	27	3	40,797	1,971	36,605	2,221	390,459	30,509	343,104	16,846
Cars, electric- and steam-railroad:												
1927–28												
1929	1	1			1,500	1,500			6,000	6,000		
1930	3	2		1	404	360		44	2,788	2,700		88
1931–32												
1933	1		1		416		416		2,080		2,080	
1934	2	1	1		510	415	95		1,840	415	1,425	
1935	1	1			150	150			750	750		
1936	2	2			780	780			8,113	8,113		
Shipbuilding:												
1927												
1928	2	1	1		830	800	30		10,760	10,400	360	
1929	2	2			620	620			57,320	57,320		
1930	1		1		30		30		30		30	
1931												
1932	2	2			500	500			4,900	4,900		
1933	4	3	1		3,831	331	3,500		134,801	1,801	133,000	
1934	5	1	3	1	4,702	125	4,037	540	166,438	1,500	147,118	17,820
1935	4	1	3		4,099	30	4,069		295,906	1,260	294,646	
1936	15	3	11	1	12,472	2,318	9,354	800	320,016	21,433	297,783	800

[1] Man-days idle as a result of a strike which began in the preceding year and continued into this year.
[2] No strikes in locomotive manufacturing and railroad repair shops, 1927–36.

TABLE 37.—*Strikes beginning 1927–36, by industries and major issues involved*—Continued

Industry and year	Number of strikes: Total	Number of strikes: Major issues: Wages and hours	Number of strikes: Major issues: Union organization	Number of strikes: Major issues: Miscellaneous	Number of workers involved: Total	Number of workers involved: Major issues: Wages and hours	Number of workers involved: Major issues: Union organization	Number of workers involved: Major issues: Miscellaneous	Number of man-days idle during year: Total	Number of man-days idle during year: Major issues: Wages and hours	Number of man-days idle during year: Major issues: Union organization	Number of man-days idle during year: Major issues: Miscellaneous
Transportation equipment—Continued.												
Other:												
1927–32												
1933	3	2		1	471	384		87	1,590	1,068		522
1934	7	6	1		3,589	2,589	1,000		66,061	44,061	22,000	
1935	2		2		625		625		3,450		3,450	
1936												
Nonferrous metals and their products:												
1927	5	2	2	1	1,163	43	1,106	14	40,116	1,778	38,072	266
1928	5		2	3	270		140	130	8,502		6,640	1,862
1929	5	4	1		2,579	2,569	10		29,511	29,231	10	[1] 270
1930	6	4	1	1	563	541	14	8	2,601	2,425	168	8
1931	7	3	2	2	155	49	93	13	1,565	362	1,157	46
1932	7	4	2	1	1,207	704	478	25	4,340	2,302	1,888	150
1933	24	8	15	1	9,355	4,340	4,996	19	154,591	43,449	111,085	57
1934	35	13	19	3	20,587	2,520	17,528	539	424,377	73,042	345,485	5,850
1935	44	13	29	2	7,486	823	6,567	96	187,139	10,907	173,963	2,269
1936	31	9	17	5	9,525	3,291	5,742	492	152,703	32,682	112,499	7,522
Aluminum manufactures:												
1927												
1928	2		1	1	96		80	16	4,096		4,000	96
1929–30												
1931	1	1			26	26			26	26		
1932–33												
1934	5	2	3		13,286	270	13,016		219,194	8,760	210,434	
1935	3	1	1	1	232	68	135	29	7,099	2,856	4,185	58
1936	2	1	1		1,239	887	352		9,391	7,983	1,408	
Brass, bronze, and copper products:												
1927	2		1	1	20		6	14	938		672	266
1928									470		[1] 120	[1] 350
1929												
1930	1	1			60	60			180	180		
1931												
1932	2	1	1		22	14	8		120	112	8	
1933	3	1	2		673	143	530		23,747	572	23,175	
1934	8	4	4		2,053	447	1,606		37,082	5,304	31,778	
1935	8	4	4		729	168	561		18,214	1,355	16,859	

1936	4	2	2		3,550	1,675	1,875		30,625	10,075	20,550	
Clocks and watches and time-recording devices:												
1927	1	1			20	20			260	260		
1928-32												
1933	1	1			47	47			47	47		
1934-35												
1936	2	1		1	322	29		293	1,874	116		1,758
Jewelry:												
1927-30												
1931	5	1	2	2	118	12	93	13	1,275	72	1,157	46
1932												
1933	4	2	2		3,756	3,062	694		49,750	24,448	25,302	
1934									12,000		[1] 12,000	
1935	5	1	4		2,431	126	2,305		40,926	126	40,800	
1936	3	1	2		151	28	123		1,632	84	1,548	
Lighting equipment:												
1927												
1928	1			1	24			24	336			336
1929-34												
1935	6	2	4		397	137	260		1,519	765	754	
1936	1		1		556		556		2,780		2,780	
Silverware and plated ware:												
1927	1	1			23	23			1,518	1,518		
1928												
1929	4	3	1		79	69	10		1,741	1,731	10	
1930	4	2	1	1	68	46	14	8	1,116	940	168	8
1931	1	1			11	11			264	264		
1932	1			1	25			25	150			150
1933	6	1	4	1	1,661	18	1,624	19	30,207	72	30,078	57
1934	4		4		386		386		1,806		1,806	
1935	1		1		28		28		5,396		5,396	
1936	4		1	3	799		606	193	21,267		18,180	3,087
Smelting and refining—copper, lead, and zinc:												
1927-28												
1929	1	1			2,500	2,500			27,500	27,500		
1930	1	1			435	435			1,305	1,305		
1931-32												
1933	3	1	2		1,022	320	702		12,692	2,560	10,132	
1934	7	3	3	1	2,138	1,138	600	400	75,490	46,132	24,158	5,200
1935	6	1	5		1,179	105	1,074		20,888	4,725	16,163	
1936									2,625	[1] 2,625		
Stamped and enameled ware:												
1927	1		1		1,100		1,100		37,400		37,400	
1928	2		1	1	150		60	90	3,600		2,520	1,080
1929									[1] 270			[1] 270
1930-31												
1932	4	3	1		1,160	690	470		4,070	2,190	1,880	
1933	7	2	5		2,196	750	1,446		38,148	15,750	22,398	
1934	8	3	5		2,413	493	1,920		72,479	7,170	65,309	
1935	9	2	7		2,124	85	2,039		87,777	290	87,487	
1936	10	3	7		1,606	634	972		44,730	11,571	33,159	

[1] Man-days idle as a result of a strike which began in the preceding year and continued into this year

TABLE 37.—*Strikes beginning 1927–36, by industries and major issues involved*—Continued

Industry and year	Number of strikes				Number of workers involved				Number of man-days idle during year			
	Total	Major issues			Total	Major issues			Total	Major issues		
		Wages and hours	Union organization	Miscellaneous		Wages and hours	Union organization	Miscellaneous		Wages and hours	Union organization	Miscellaneous
Nonferrous metals and their products—Continued.												
Other:												
1927–33												
1934	3	1	-	2	311	172	-	139	6,326	5,676	-	650
1935	6	2	3	1	366	134	165	67	5,320	790	2,319	2,211
1936	5	1	3	1	1,302	38	1,258	6	37,779	228	34,874	2,677
Lumber and allied products:												
1927	46	11	27	8	5,834	2,757	1,421	1,656	167,520	67,896	54,415	45,209
1928	32	17	7	8	1,534	1,211	152	171	53,440	28,245	19,850	5,345
1929	38	9	21	8	3,642	1,011	1,874	757	79,654	18,875	56,708	4,071
1930	21	10	10	1	1,360	613	732	15	54,551	31,773	22,763	15
1931	26	19	-	7	3,254	2,977	-	277	46,565	38,501	-	8,064
1932	30	13	15	2	3,813	3,215	298	300	145,714	139,816	4,798	1,100
1933	91	56	28	7	27,348	13,274	13,409	665	569,671	210,235	356,097	3,339
1934	96	36	51	9	19,800	6,529	10,761	2,510	394,651	102,880	275,017	16,754
1935	135	59	68	8	62,707	15,235	46,185	1,287	1,818,012	172,810	1,621,736	23,466
1936	143	36	89	18	38,270	7,856	27,199	3,215	1,019,284	204,033	772,643	42,608
Furniture:												
1927	37	6	25	6	1,957	492	1,319	146	69,018	8,874	51,865	8,279
1928	25	11	6	8	611	338	102	171	37,673	15,908	16,420	5,345
1929	35	6	21	8	2,964	333	1,874	757	66,170	5,391	56,708	4,071
1930	18	7	10	1	891	144	732	15	26,900	4,122	22,763	15
1931	18	14	-	4	1,197	1,130	-	67	8,714	8,060	-	654
1932	27	11	14	2	2,767	2,176	291	300	37,629	31,738	4,791	1,100
1933	57	34	20	3	20,372	7,790	12,473	109	511,342	164,065	346,664	613
1934	58	21	33	4	9,501	4,086	5,134	281	159,645	54,662	99,215	5,768
1935	64	23	36	5	14,229	5,975	7,834	420	214,049	61,888	143,103	9,058
1936	60	17	41	2	7,744	1,925	5,650	169	261,389	17,735	241,747	1,907
Millwork and planing:												
1927	3	1	2	-	1,302	1,200	102	-	24,150	21,600	2,550	-
1928	2	2	-	-	308	308	-	-	9,230	6,000	[1] 3,230	-
1929	2	2	-	-	528	528	-	-	11,384	11,384	-	-
1930												
1931	3	1	-	2	295	125	-	170	6,665	375	-	6,290
1932	3	2	1	-	1,046	1,039	7	-	108,085	108,078	7	-
1933	6	6	-	-	841	841	-	-	11,386	11,386	-	-
1934	3	2	-	1	327	74	-	253	1,692	933	-	759

1935	15	9	5	1	3,928	3,145	636	147	60,510	38,229	21,693	588
1936	15	3	11	1	3,544	475	2,717	352	73,838	9,214	64,272	352
Sawmills and logging camps:												
1927	3	2		1	2,371	1,021		1,350	69,752	33,302		36,450
1928	5	4	1		615	565	50		6,537	6,337	200	
1929												
1930	3	3			469	469			27,651	27,651		
1931	3	3			1,402	1,402			18,866	18,866		
1932												
1933	8	6		2	4,373	3,873		500	31,126	29,026		2,100
1934	13	6	5	2	5,467	768	2,828	1,871	111,939	7,898	96,478	7,563
1935	39	15	22	2	42,689	4,453	37,516	720	1,515,730	46,158	1,455,752	13,820
1936	39	10	20	9	18,502	5,121	12,100	1,281	507,112	163,919	320,200	22,993
Turpentine and rosin:												
1927–32												
1933	1	1			6	6			6	6		
1934–36												
Other:												
1927	3	2		1	204	44		160	4,600	4,120		480
1928												
1929	1	1			150	150			2,100	2,100		
1930												
1931	2	1		1	360	320		40	12,320	11,200		1,120
1932												
1933	19	9	8	2	1,756	764	936	56	15,811	5,752	9,433	626
1934	22	7	13	2	4,505	1,601	2,799	105	121,375	39,387	79,324	2,664
1935	17	12	5		1,861	1,662	199		27,723	26,535	1,188	
1936	29	6	17	6	8,480	335	6,732	1,413	176,945	13,165	146,424	17,356
Stone, clay, and glass products:												
1927	10	6	2	2	3,289	2,577	185	527	45,592	38,878	2,725	3,989
1928	6	1	4	1	1,034	45	816	173	26,279	22,145	2,058	2,076
1929	6	3	1	2	1,153	823	60	270	11,048	3,688	4,140	3,220
1930	5	2	3		371	210	161		3,656	835	2,821	
1931	10	8	2		1,227	1,013	214		9,887	7,089	2,798	
1932	13	12		1	1,747	1,347		400	35,366	20,166		15,200
1933	29	20	8	1	6,946	5,842	1,009	95	59,439	53,336	5,628	475
1934	34	11	17	6	10,083	1,620	7,874	589	199,610	11,754	181,194	6,662
1935	35	12	20	3	11,833	6,172	5,086	575	346,940	63,717	272,185	11,038
1936	39	10	26	3	24,689	4,985	18,283	1,421	723,522	102,382	589,734	31,406
Brick, tile, and terra cotta:												
1927	2	2			187	187			7,648	7,648		
1928												
1929	3	2	1		283	223	60		6,628	2,488	4,140	
1930	2	2			210	210			835	835		
1931	1	1			226	226			760	760		
1932												
1933	10	6	3	1	2,108	1,703	310	95	26,400	23,414	2,511	475
1934	12	3	8	1	5,349	656	4,553	140	127,703	5,064	117,599	5,040
1935	14	3	11		3,691	239	3,452		187,927	11,328	173,239	[1] 3,360
1936	4	1	2	1	817	100	557	160	43,525	3,300	38,785	1,440

[1] Man-days idle as a result of a strike which began in the previous year and continued into this year.

TABLE 37.—*Strikes beginning 1927–36, by industries and major issues involved*—Continued

Industry and year	Number of strikes: Total	Number of strikes: Major issues: Wages and hours	Number of strikes: Major issues: Union organization	Number of strikes: Major issues: Miscellaneous	Number of workers involved: Total	Number of workers involved: Major issues: Wages and hours	Number of workers involved: Major issues: Union organization	Number of workers involved: Major issues: Miscellaneous	Number of man-days idle during year: Total	Number of man-days idle during year: Major issues: Wages and hours	Number of man-days idle during year: Major issues: Union organization	Number of man-days idle during year: Major issues: Miscellaneous
Stone, clay, and glass products—Continued.												
Cement:												
1927–31	-	-	-	-	-	-	-	-	-	-	-	-
1932	1	1	-	-	65	65	-	-	325	325	-	-
1933	-	-	-	-	-	-	-	-	-	-	-	-
1934	1	1	-	-	231	231	-	-	3,234	3,234	-	-
1935	-	-	-	-	-	-	-	-	-	-	-	-
1936	3	-	3	-	670	-	670	-	1,880	-	1,880	-
Glass:												
1927	7	4	2	1	2,952	2,390	185	377	36,594	31,230	2,725	2,639
1928	4	1	3	-	611	45	566	-	23,703	22,145	1,558	-
1929	1	-	-	1	80	-	-	80	560	-	-	560
1930	1	-	1	-	11	-	11	-	121	-	121	-
1931	5	5	-	-	772	772	-	-	6,314	6,314	-	-
1932	3	3	-	-	148	148	-	-	752	752	-	-
1933	11	10	1	-	4,177	3,912	265	-	28,712	28,182	530	-
1934	11	4	3	4	2,051	675	933	443	35,548	2,790	31,202	1,556
1935	7	4	1	2	5,400	4,983	17	400	58,753	40,189	11,936	6,628
1936	18	5	12	1	21,268	4,440	16,273	555	608,222	84,958	501,064	22,200
Marble, granite, slate, and other products:												
1927–29	-	-	-	-	-	-	-	-	-	-	-	-
1930	1	-	1	-	50	-	50	-	1,300	-	1,300	-
1931	4	2	2	-	229	15	214	-	1,713	15	1,698	-
1932	5	4	-	1	777	377	-	400	29,771	14,571	-	15,200
1933	1	-	1	-	9	-	9	-	9	-	9	-
1934	3	2	-	1	44	38	-	6	492	426	-	66
1935	2	1	-	1	255	80	-	175	2,890	1,840	-	1,050
1936	3	1	2	-	151	6	145	-	2,151	6	2,145	-
Pottery:												
1927	1	-	-	1	150	-	-	150	1,350	-	-	1,350
1928	2	-	1	1	423	-	250	173	2,576	-	500	2,076
1929	1	-	-	1	190	-	-	190	2,660	-	-	2,660
1930	1	-	1	-	100	-	100	-	1,400	-	1,400	-
1931	-	-	-	-	-	-	-	-	1,100	-	[1] 1,100	-
1932	2	2	-	-	150	150	-	-	2,620	2,620	-	-
1933	1	1	-	-	55	55	-	-	770	770	-	-
1934	4	-	4	-	1,650	-	1,650	-	17,750	-	17,750	-

1935	7	4	3		2,149	870	1,279		94,541	10,360	84,181	
1936	1			1	706			706	47,186		[1] 39,420	7,766
Other:												
1927–28												
1929	1	1			600	600			1,200	1,200		
1930–31												
1932	2	2			607	607			1,898	1,898		
1933	6	3	3		597	172	425		3,548	970	2,578	
1934	3	1	2		758	20	738		14,883	240	14,643	
1935	5		5		338		338		2,829		2,829	
1936	10	3	7		1,077	439	638		20,558	14,118	6,440	
Textiles and their products:												
1927	165	58	69	38	20,548	8,108	7,639	4,801	404,269	168,967	138,555	96,747
1928	137	50	56	31	72,148	48,506	19,621	4,021	4,357,882	3,927,405	368,131	62,346
1929	237	79	119	39	75,694	13,703	45,663	16,328	1,379,367	249,191	701,699	428,477
1930	137	71	44	22	67,892	13,007	47,329	7,556	1,261,792	391,439	816,226	54,127
1931	197	99	69	29	126,555	57,200	52,273	17,082	3,174,428	1,929,708	1,037,568	207,152
1932	187	124	34	29	103,001	51,590	49,071	2,340	1,184,869	503,656	663,681	17,532
1933	506	301	156	49	461,063	273,233	170,783	17,047	6,652,446	2,584,219	3,756,001	312,226
1934	[2] 363	107	193	63	577,043	47,496	444,147	85,400	7,271,023	604,463	6,050,521	616,039
1935	497	213	232	52	200,636	107,196	69,695	23,745	3,634,988	1,466,482	1,900,498	268,008
1936	455	173	235	47	128,578	37,366	82,264	8,958	2,777,498	923,672	1,563,322	290,504
Fabrics:												
1927	69	39	10	20	9,678	4,856	1,377	3,445	224,313	121,749	27,044	75,520
1928	54	32	10	12	36,447	29,380	5,649	1,418	4,025,697	3,737,567	269,408	18,722
1929	116	62	27	27	34,653	9,383	10,351	14,919	837,729	183,883	241,425	412,421
1930	51	36	7	8	8,901	4,285	4,306	310	395,959	71,566	317,357	7,036
1931	62	41	7	14	62,050	45,097	2,658	14,295	2,092,005	1,720,961	228,453	142,591
1932	61	49	2	10	15,142	12,997	867	1,278	245,744	196,047	44,606	5,091
1933	247	179	34	34	146,400	80,446	53,459	12,495	3,204,186	843,916	2,131,298	228,972
1934	184	59	92	33	434,928	25,508	393,549	15,871	5,894,390	247,406	5,363,774	283,210
1935	202	103	65	34	75,180	46,507	18,077	10,596	1,815,717	996,151	645,998	173,568
1936	168	80	67	21	43,879	20,721	18,144	5,014	1,431,954	574,438	680,152	177,364
Carpets and rugs:												
1927												
1928	2		1	1	267		142	125	1,971		1,846	125
1929	4	3		1	654	324		330	9,472	8,812		660
1930	2	2			95	95			4,332	4,332		
1931	4	4			690	690			16,120	16,120		
1932	1	1			100	100			100	100		
1933	2		1	1	290		90	200	12,360		360	12,000
1934	4	1	3		2,957	1,200	1,757		19,867	8,400	11,467	
1935	4	2	1	1	3,956	3,606	75	275	23,316	18,866	3,075	1,375
1936	7	6	1		1,209	835	374		38,925	38,551	374	

[1] Man-days idle as a result of a strike which began in the preceding year and continued into this year.

[2] The general textile strike of September 1934, involving 309,500 workers, extended into 7 industries, i. e., carpets and rugs, cotton goods, cotton small wares, dyeing and finishing textiles, silk and rayon goods, woolen and worsted goods, and knit goods. In the totals for the industry group "Textiles and their products" this is included as 1 strike, but in the figures for each of the 7 industries affected it is broken down and included as a separate strike in each industry with the proper distribution of "Workers involved" and "Man-days idle." The sympathetic strikes called in connection with the textile strike are included as separate strikes in their respective industries.

TABLE 37.—*Strikes beginning 1927–36, by industries and major issues involved*—Continued

Industry and year	Number of strikes				Number of workers involved				Number of man-days idle during year			
	Total	Major issues			Total	Major issues			Total	Major issues		
		Wages and hours	Union organization	Miscellaneous		Wages and hours	Union organization	Miscellaneous		Wages and hours	Union organization	Miscellaneous
Textiles and their products—Continued.												
Fabrics—Continued.												
Cotton goods:												
1927	24	13	2	9	4, 721	2, 321	327	2, 073	133, 531	65, 948	8, 154	59, 429
1928	17	8	5	4	28, 674	26, 949	1, 040	685	3, 750, 193	3, 696, 111	41, 797	12, 285
1929	35	9	11	15	18, 982	3, 781	6, 503	8, 698	488, 062	94, 102	97, 615	296, 345
1930	10	6	2	2	5, 910	1, 716	4, 108	86	329, 786	12, 699	316, 540	547
1931	6	4		2	3, 709	3, 164		545	315, 723	206, 788	[1] 96, 000	12, 935
1932	26	21	1	4	6, 800	5, 390	800	610	163, 080	117, 740	43, 200	2, 140
1933	77	53	6	18	51, 462	35, 765	5, 565	10, 132	514, 878	268, 577	64, 637	181, 664
1934	66	9	33	24	274, 380	13, 026	247, 002	14, 352	3, 462, 596	77, 059	3, 134, 019	251, 518
1935	44	14	23	7	25, 105	8, 902	10, 540	5, 663	946, 190	339, 439	494, 340	112, 411
1936	29	15	6	8	17, 029	10, 203	3, 506	3, 320	554, 952	189, 127	217, 639	148, 186
Cotton small wares:												
1927	1		1		30		30		720		720	
1928	1	1			34	34			136	136		
1929	1	1			70	70			770	770		
1930–32												
1933	9	6	2	1	2, 421	1, 657	370	394	27, 335	20, 077	2, 530	4, 728
1934	9	2	7		2, 068	546	1, 522		39, 774	11, 910	27, 864	
1935									4, 950		[1] 4, 950	
1936	4	1	3		120	15	105		1, 809	165	1, 644	
Dyeing and finishing textiles:												
1927	1	1			14	14			14	14		
1928	4	2	1	1	1, 240	231	995	14	7, 807	786	6, 965	56
1929	1		1		362		362		3, 620		3, 620	
1930												
1931	1	1			20	20			80	80		
1932												
1933	11	8	3		20, 874	5, 390	15, 484		585, 185	28, 135	557, 050	
1934	9	2	6	1	34, 973	1, 602	32, 528	843	784, 060	5, 301	755, 998	22, 761
1935	15	4	8	3	2, 664	531	1, 464	669	31, 780	15, 292	7, 541	8, 947
1936	18	3	14	1	5, 351	108	5, 154	89	179, 511	641	178, 603	267
Silk and rayon goods:												
1927	33	23	3	7	3, 519	2, 369	395	755	57, 952	47, 975	1, 775	8, 202
1928	25	17	2	6	5, 312	1, 566	3, 152	594	249, 196	26, 060	216, 880	6, 256
1929	65	44	12	9	13, 557	5, 011	2, 941	5, 605	322, 004	78, 912	128, 820	114, 272
1930	34	24	5	5	2, 624	2, 292	198	134	58, 489	52, 803	817	4, 869

[illegible]	[illegible]	[illegible]	[illegible]	[illegible]	17,207	13,509	2,658	1,040	917,636	763,920	132,453	21,263
1932	24	19	1	4	5,949	5,351	67	531	59,530	55,507	1,406	2,617
1933	88	67	16	5	58,187	28,559	29,089	539	1,923,444	440,153	1,477,313	5,978
1934	50	26	17	7	38,941	4,185	34,255	501	643,856	90,985	544,290	8,581
1935	97	62	18	17	29,416	23,414	3,157	2,845	549,193	421,584	89,603	38,006
1936	65	44	15	6	11,047	7,937	2,708	402	411,767	317,724	84,095	9,948
Woolen and worsted goods:												
1927	5		1	4	707		90	617	8,249		360	7,889
1928	4	4			600	600			14,474	14,474		
1929	9	5	3	1	760	197	545	18	12,729	1,287	11,370	72
1930	3	2		1	250	160		90	3,180	1,560		1,620
1931	18	10		8	40,328	27,618		12,710	840,394	732,001		108,393
1932	9	7		2	2,217	2,080		137	20,554	20,220		334
1933	45	36	3	6	10,214	7,089	2,514	611	102,180	70,382	23,652	8,146
1934	27	10	16	1	75,876	2,811	72,890	175	867,945	40,552	827,043	350
1935	30	14	10	6	11,446	8,395	1,907	1,144	222,969	185,595	24,545	12,829
1936	27	8	13	6	6,940	1,329	4,408	1,203	157,066	12,079	126,024	18,963
Other:												
1927	5	2	3		687	152	535		23,847	7,812	16,035	
1928	1		1		320		320		1,920		1,920	
1929	1			1	268			268	1,072			1,072
1930	2	2			22	22			172	172		
1931	2	2			36	36			2,052	2,052		
1932	1	1			76	76			2,480	2,480		
1933	15	9	3	3	2,952	1,986	347	619	38,804	16,592	5,756	16,456
1934	19	9	10		5,733	2,138	3,595		76,292	13,199	63,093	
1935	12	7	5		2,593	1,659	934		37,319	15,375	21,944	
1936	18	3	15		2,183	294	1,889		87,924	16,151	71,773	
Wearing apparel:												
1927	96	19	59	18	10,870	3,252	6,262	1,356	179,956	47,218	111,511	21,227
1928	83	18	46	19	35,701	19,126	13,972	2,603	332,185	189,838	98,723	43,624
1929	121	17	92	12	41,041	4,320	35,312	1,409	541,638	65,308	460,274	16,056
1930	86	35	37	14	58,991	8,722	43,023	7,246	865,833	319,873	498,869	47,091
1931	135	58	62	15	64,505	12,103	49,615	2,787	1,082,423	208,747	809,115	64,561
1932	126	75	32	19	87,859	38,593	48,204	1,062	939,125	307,609	619,075	12,441
1933	259	122	122	15	314,663	192,787	117,324	4,552	3,448,260	1,740,303	1,624,703	83,254
1934	185	48	107	30	142,115	21,988	50,598	69,529	1,376,633	357,057	686,747	332,829
1935	295	110	167	18	125,456	60,689	51,618	13,149	1,819,271	470,331	1,254,500	94,440
1936	287	93	168	26	84,699	16,635	64,120	3,944	1,345,544	349,234	883,170	113,140
Clothing, men's:												
1927	18		16	2	2,909		2,774	135	30,714		30,534	180
1928	26	5	18	3	26,742	15,883	10,504	355	207,992	160,431	46,041	1,520
1929	50	3	44	3	10,951	2,344	8,037	570	108,942	13,780	93,742	1,420
1930	13	6	4	3	2,824	589	369	1,866	32,223	5,536	15,175	11,512
1931	31	12	11	8	40,545	1,079	37,140	2,326	501,907	6,765	433,262	61,880
1932	27	17	6	4	28,521	6,563	21,524	434	326,394	49,910	268,622	7,862
1933	73	29	36	8	71,849	10,191	59,271	2,387	711,627	102,472	561,135	48,020
1934	37	11	22	4	9,239	2,347	6,342	550	94,879	29,820	56,864	8,195
1935	59	28	27	4	14,127	10,590	2,399	1,138	114,124	64,114	46,003	4,007
1936	31	12	15	4	3,685	1,153	1,694	838	29,852	5,823	18,518	5,511

[1] Man-days idle as a result of a strike which began in the preceding year and continued into this year.

TABLE 37.—*Strikes beginning 1927–36, by industries and major issues involved*—Continued

Industry and year	Number of strikes				Number of workers involved				Number of man-days idle during year			
	Total	Major issues			Total	Major issues			Total	Major issues		
		Wages and hours	Union organization	Miscellaneous		Wages and hours	Union organization	Miscellaneous		Wages and hours	Union organization	Miscellaneous
Textiles and their products—Continued.												
Wearing apparel—Continued.												
Clothing, women's:												
1927	22	3	12	7	1,273	423	479	371	24,925	10,998	7,417	6,510
1928	21	2	14	5	3,534	712	2,325	497	47,121	3,946	30,037	13,138
1929	21	1	17	3	23,637	750	22,657	230	266,352	7,500	251,557	7,295
1930	24	5	17	2	48,086	3,772	41,089	3,225	584,212	123,481	439,806	20,925
1931	36	15	20	1	6,714	1,107	5,277	330	56,510	25,992	29,528	990
1932	31	18	9	4	36,503	11,025	25,269	209	464,228	133,793	328,393	2,042
1933	43	23	20		118,800	99,556	19,244		928,641	707,330	221,311	
1934	30	8	20	2	32,803	4,585	3,163	25,055	182,715	42,829	39,556	100,330
1935	81	21	53	7	68,232	22,341	34,606	11,285	944,079	147,563	723,363	73,153
1936	126	33	86	7	19,889	2,843	16,421	625	263,167	63,953	190,098	9,116
Corsets and allied garments:												
1927												
1928	1	1			700	700			3,500	3,500		
1929–32												
1933	6	2	4		2,810	1,623	1,187		38,648	23,607	15,041	
1934	2	1	1		556	540	16		1,160	1,080	80	
1935	1		1		271		271		1,355		1,355	
1936	2		2		65		65		1,660		1,660	
Men's furnishings:												
1927	6		3	3	500		193	307	16,163		4,472	11,691
1928	2		2		212		212		1,240		1,240	
1929	5	1	3	1	426	6	120	300	3,854	24	230	3,600
1930	1			1	500			500	4,500			4,500
1931	5	2	3		1,043	545	498		10,293	4,755	5,538	
1932	2		2		80		80		1,920		1,920	
1933	7	2	3	2	12,942	10,026	2,850	66	81,614	60,182	20,850	582
1934	7	1	3	3	1,136	55	656	425	15,336	165	9,016	6,155
1935	9	6	3		1,407	1,267	140		14,344	10,204	4,140	
1936	10	4	5	1	2,665	1,971	687	7	33,497	30,342	3,029	126
Hats, caps, and millinery:												
1927	23	6	16	1	2,588	370	2,204	14	70,583	18,441	51,876	266
1928	10	2	5	3	923	75	101	747	20,529	6,300	6,361	7,868
1929	13	3	8	2	2,472	70	2,362	40	67,500	360	66,960	180
1930	6	2	2	2	260	86	78	96	20,277	1,552	17,789	936
1931	16	5	10	1	486	181	280	25	10,851	3,402	6,224	1,225

1932	16	4	7	5	10,492	10,116	129	247	16,388	12,441	2,992	955
1933	20	10	9	1	15,073	10,769	4,181	123	228,922	162,192	66,238	492
1934	26	14	11	1	12,551	12,132	408	11	271,432	255,343	16,023	66
1935	21	5	15	1	3,651	605	2,941	105	87,664	25,020	61,699	945
1936	23	2	20	1	25,963	91	25,725	147	162,775	551	142,967	19,257
Shirts and collars:												
1927	9	2	5	2	630	33	176	421	7,259	1,148	4,438	1,673
1928	11	5	3	3	1,457	1,320	48	89	11,737	7,710	2,804	1,223
1929	8	3	3	2	1,518	161	1,122	235	13,303	1,468	9,600	2,235
1930	15	8	4	3	1,750	1,418	151	181	47,981	46,261	996	724
1931	11	8	3		1,673	800	873		20,850	10,416	10,434	
1932	10	8	1	1	665	494	159	12	4,023	3,852	159	12
1933	28	14	13	1	18,449	6,526	10,823	1,100	288,496	96,647	164,349	27,500
1934	28	5	14	9	6,869	1,272	3,083	2,514	86,369	17,223	55,535	13,611
1935	39	27	10	2	22,562	19,799	2,438	325	256,008	172,910	80,553	2,545
1936	16	7	5	4	3,344	1,511	769	1,064	112,237	18,734	18,519	74,984
Hosiery:												
1927	8	4	4		674	319	355		19,698	7,761	11,937	
1928	7	2		5	1,334	419		915	32,122	7,747	[1] 4,500	19,875
1929	12	5	6	1	1,435	839	562	34	72,387	41,576	29,485	1,326
1930	16	7	7	2	3,565	2,260	1,227	78	147,113	123,738	22,681	694
1931	16	8	8		11,588	7,681	3,907		454,498	141,034	313,464	
1932	18	14	4		8,505	8,054	451		101,377	91,821	9,556	
1933	31	14	16	1	21,274	6,702	14,461	111	564,712	112,689	451,468	555
1934	23	4	14	5	49,386	875	7,967	40,544	344,371	10,133	134,580	199,658
1935	31	7	21	3	6,635	615	5,746	274	271,145	13,032	244,455	13,658
1936	32	19	9	4	14,148	5,814	7,209	1,125	480,091	147,810	329,756	2,525
Knit goods:												
1927	3	1	1	1	78	32	9	37	810	320	9	481
1928												
1929	2	1	1		156	150	6		618	600	18	
1930	1	1			18	18			252	252		
1931	4	2	1	1	185	65	70	50	1,550	400	1,050	106
1932	14	11		3	905	779		126	9,658	8,776		882
1933	22	14	8		31,752	30,564	1,188		344,890	332,233	12,657	
1934	20	2	14	4	28,358	141	28,022	195	349,047	323	345,490	3,234
1935	20	3	16	1	1,254	96	1,136	22	20,227	688	19,407	132
1936	28	9	15	4	11,610	2,301	9,221	88	217,874	49,978	167,575	321
Other:												
1927	7	3	2	2	2,218	2,075	72	71	9,804	8,550	828	426
1928	5	1	4		799	17	782		7,944	204	7,740	
1929	10		10		446		446		8,682		8,682	
1930	10	6	3	1	1,988	579	109	1,300	29,275	19,053	2,422	7,800
1931	16	6	6	4	2,271	645	1,570	56	25,964	15,983	9,615	366
1932	8	3	3	2	2,188	1,562	592	34	15,137	7,016	7,433	688
1933	29	14	13	2	21,714	16,830	4,119	765	260,710	142,951	111,654	6,105
1934	12	2	8	2	1,217	41	941	235	31,324	141	29,603	1,580
1935	34	13	21		7,317	5,376	1,941		110,325	36,800	73,525	
1936	19	7	11	1	3,330	951	2,329	50	44,391	32,043	11,048	1,300

[1] Man-days idle as a result of a strike which began in the preceding year and continued into this year.

TABLE 37.—Strikes beginning [illegible] major issues involved—Continued

Industry and year	Number of strikes: Total	Major issues: Wages and hours	Union organization	Miscellaneous	Number of workers involved: Total	Major issues: Wages and hours	Union organization	Miscellaneous	Number of man-days idle during year: Total	Major issues: Wages and hours	Union organization	Miscellaneous
Leather and its manufactures:												
1927	20	4	14	2	4,960	3,092	1,751	117	86,594	40,385	44,489	1,720
1928	34	13	17	4	11,252	9,471	1,603	178	115,822	91,614	21,840	2,368
1929	54	16	33	5	27,475	9,765	16,974	736	1,069,144	679,515	358,389	31,240
1930	25	5	13	7	2,209	429	1,528	252	83,238	3,920	75,153	4,165
1931	42	26	13	3	8,230	7,090	977	163	113,681	98,479	12,833	2,369
1932	49	26	19	4	8,152	3,545	2,496	2,111	107,020	25,233	41,051	40,736
1933	142	55	69	18	90,273	26,059	55,292	8,922	1,939,022	444,233	1,293,899	200,890
1934	88	36	45	7	48,872	20,478	27,700	694	840,681	385,731	449,618	5,332
1935	78	32	39	7	16,307	5,354	6,588	4,365	258,929	92,506	144,130	22,293
1936	72	30	33	9	20,472	9,547	9,469	1,456	218,996	85,551	106,790	26,655
Boots and shoes:												
1927	12	2	9	1	3,789	3,014	665	110	54,154	36,266	16,238	1,650
1928	29	10	16	3	10,648	8,969	1,532	147	94,846	72,730	20,988	1,128
1929	44	14	25	5	23,561	9,700	13,125	736	969,977	679,170	259,567	31,240
1930	19	4	10	5	1,904	388	1,316	200	76,893	3,059	69,935	3,899
1931	27	18	8	1	1,779	1,184	540	55	16,729	11,575	4,969	185
1932	45	23	18	4	7,747	3,265	2,371	2,111	100,250	22,213	37,301	40,736
1933	104	39	49	16	69,553	17,638	43,078	8,837	1,402,043	251,371	950,892	199,780
1934	65	24	36	5	30,463	11,213	18,648	602	560,013	188,195	366,924	4,894
1935	57	24	29	4	11,099	3,363	4,420	3,316	174,369	37,891	115,773	20,705
1936	44	23	17	4	11,885	7,908	3,733	244	83,994	65,396	18,077	521
Leather:												
1927	5	1	3	1	444	33	404	7	6,343	429	5,844	70
1928	4	3	1		573	502	71		14,786	13,934	852	
1929	4	2	2		176	65	111		2,589	345	2,244	
1930	3	1	1	1	201	41	135	25	3,071	861	2,160	50
1931	4	3		1	456	408		48	6,882	6,258		624
1932	2	2			95	95			915	915		
1933	12	5	6	1	10,004	1,154	8,775	75	305,106	16,802	287,254	1,050
1934	8	5	3		8,554	779	7,775		46,800	12,750	34,050	
1935	7	2	3	2	2,571	1,131	501	939	13,151	7,165	4,618	1,368
1936	10	1	7	2	5,965	182	4,952	831	62,980	1,638	49,618	11,724
Other leather goods:												
1927	3	1	2		727	45	682		26,097	3,690	22,407	
1928	1			1	31			31	6,190	[1] 4,950		1,240
1929	6		6		3,738		3,738		96,578		96,578	

1930	3		2	1	104		77	27	3, 274		3, 058	216
1931	11	5	5	1	5, 995	5, 498	437	60	90, 070	80, 646	7, 864	1, 560
1932	2	1	1		310	185	125		5, 855	2, 105	3, 750	
1933	26	11	14	1	10, 716	7, 267	3, 439	10	231, 873	176, 060	55, 753	60
1934	15	7	6	2	9, 855	8, 486	1, 277	92	233, 868	184, 786	48, 644	438
1935	14	6	7	1	2, 637	860	1, 667	110	71, 409	47, 450	23, 739	220
1936	18	6	9	3	2, 622	1, 457	784	381	72, 022	18, 517	39, 095	14, 410
Food and kindred products:												
1927	24	12	8	4	2, 651	1, 957	429	265	45, 026	30, 910	7, 538	6, 578
1928	17	5	8	4	708	288	341	79	6, 195	3, 023	1, 781	1, 391
1929	17	4	9	4	2, 262	666	277	1, 319	10, 218	2, 759	2, 949	4, 510
1930	14	6	6	2	1, 165	932	175	58	10, 520	5, 197	4, 999	324
1931	29	22	4	3	7, 933	7, 075	835	23	36, 510	26, 932	9, 483	95
1932	44	30	9	5	3, 925	3, 602	265	58	101, 239	87, 554	12, 872	813
1933	83	40	36	7	33, 339	23, 974	9, 208	157	566, 350	456, 941	106, 539	2, 870
1934	138	41	88	9	33, 092	10, 021	22, 498	573	456, 572	73, 922	379, 533	3, 117
1935	103	42	54	7	26, 683	5, 649	20, 495	539	842, 109	35, 703	753, 063	53, 343
1936	106	23	71	12	13, 859	1, 883	11, 462	514	244, 718	13, 396	228, 771	2, 551
Baking:												
1927	11	4	5	2	619	455	58	106	27, 540	24, 064	2, 161	1, 315
1928	11	4	6	1	489	213	257	19	4, 740	2, 948	1, 697	95
1929	10	2	4	4	1, 930	496	115	1, 319	7, 012	1, 549	953	4, 510
1930	8	3	3	2	367	178	131	58	7, 091	2, 043	4, 724	324
1931	15	10	3	2	238	186	35	17	4, 336	3, 630	683	23
1932	33	21	8	4	1, 881	1, 577	256	48	25, 615	12, 209	12, 863	543
1933	37	15	20	2	11, 000	8, 795	2, 176	29	303, 598	258, 071	45, 480	47
1934	58	18	38	2	4, 460	1, 278	3, 153	29	93, 762	9, 545	83, 893	324
1935	38	18	19	1	12, 998	3, 566	9, 418	14	565, 546	9, 669	555, 835	42
1936	43	10	29	4	2, 786	586	2, 115	85	82, 782	4, 104	77, 948	730
Beverages:												
1927	2	1	1		95	80	15		1, 025	560	465	
1928	2		2		84		84		84		84	
1929–30												
1931	3	2		1	32	26		6	178	106		72
1932	3	2		1	97	87		10	514	244		270
1933	7	2	2	3	229	36	130	63	4, 588	540	2, 110	1, 938
1934	11	3	4	4	2, 120	181	1, 810	129	11, 631	4, 221	6, 727	683
1935	7	1	1	5	448	25	23	400	52, 172	1, 000	621	50, 551
1936	10	3	3	4	891	36	743	112	8, 498	353	7, 801	344
Butter:												
1927–35												
1936	1		1		11		11		176		176	
Canning and preserving:												
1927	2	2			73	73			222	222		
1928	1	1			75	75			75	75		
1929												
1930	1	1			600	600			3, 000	3, 000		
1931	5	5			5, 559	5, 559			20, 334	20, 334		
1932	2	2			1, 700	1, 700			72, 400	72, 400		
1933	5	4		1	6, 275	6, 250		25	142, 775	142, 650		125
1934	6	1	5		6, 831	4, 150	2, 681		61, 797	8, 300	53, 497	

[1] Man-days idle as a result of a strike which began in the preceding year and continued into this year.

Table 37.—*Strikes beginning 1927–36, by industries and major issues involved*—Continued

Industry and year	Number of strikes: Total	Number of strikes: Major issues: Wages and hours	Number of strikes: Major issues: Union organization	Number of strikes: Major issues: Miscellaneous	Number of workers involved: Total	Number of workers involved: Major issues: Wages and hours	Number of workers involved: Major issues: Union organization	Number of workers involved: Major issues: Miscellaneous	Number of man-days idle during year: Total	Number of man-days idle during year: Major issues: Wages and hours	Number of man-days idle during year: Major issues: Union organization	Number of man-days idle during year: Major issues: Miscellaneous
Food and kindred products—Continued.												
Canning and preserving—Continued.												
1935	14	7	6	1	1,373	550	698	125	24,020	1,322	19,948	2,750
1936	11	4	7		3,437	571	2,866		17,200	2,539	14,661	
Confectionery:												
1927–28												
1929	1		1		15		15		75		75	
1930												
1931	2	2			1,150	1,150			2,450	2,450		
1932												
1933	8	5	2	1	1,502	1,236	226	40	10,492	7,240	2,492	760
1934	2		2		115		115		2,265		2,265	
1935	9	5	4		2,088	675	1,413		27,206	6,728	20,478	
1936	8	2	5	1	589	23	556	10	8,650	36	8,584	30
Flour and grain mills:												
1927–29												
1930	1	1			50	50			50	50		
1931–32												
1933	1		1		60		60		3,120		3,120	
1934	3		3		319		319		2,340		2,340	
1935	7	2	5		739	75	664		23,991	759	23,232	
1936	8	2	5	1	2,421	559	1,717	145	48,269	4,280	42,974	1,015
Ice cream:												
1927	1	1			500	500			500	500		
1928												
1929	3		3		111		111		1,165		1,165	
1930												
1931	1	1			8	8			16	16		
1932												
1933	1		1		16		16		224		224	
1934	4	2	2		384	94	290		2,650	524	2,126	
1935	1	1			22	22			22	22		
1936	2	1	1		28	20	8		268	60	208	
Slaughtering and meat packing:												
1927	6	3	1	2	970	805	6	159	10,795	5,520	12	5,263
1928	2			2	42			42	378			378
1929	1	1			50	50			250	250		

1930	3		3		44		44		275		275	
1931	1	1			21	21			21	21		
1932	5	4	1		239	230	9		2,574	2,565	9	
1933	15	6	9		9,127	4,527	4,600		78,522	29,409	49,113	
1934	45	11	31	3	16,995	3,371	13,209	415	256,180	32,135	221,935	2,110
1935	15	5	10		4,564	376	4,188		111,727	2,388	109,339	
1936	18	1	15	2	2,905	88	2,655	162	73,059	2,024	70,603	432
Sugar beet:												
1927–33												
1934	1	1			417	417			8,757	8,757		
1935	1		1		48		48		871	[1] 775	96	
1936												
Sugar refining, cane:												
1927–32												
1933	1	1			967	967			4,835	4,835		
1934	2		2		286		286		400		400	
1935	2		2		3,000		3,000		10,500		10,500	
1936	1		1		702		702		5,610		5,610	
Other:												
1927	2	1	1		394	44	350		4,944	44	4,900	
1928	1			1	18			18	918			918
1929	2	1	1		156	120	36		1,716	960	756	
1930	1	1			104	104			104	104		
1931	2	1	1		925	125	800		9,175	375	8,800	
1932	1	1			8	8			136	136		
1933	8	7	1		4,163	2,163	2,000		18,196	14,196	4,000	
1934	6	5	1		1,165	530	635		16,790	10,440	6,350	
1935	9	3	6		1,403	360	1,043		26,054	13,040	13,014	
1936	4		4		89		89		206		206	
Tobacco manufactures: [3]												
1927	2	1		1	887	97		790	12,112	7,372		4,740
1928	2	1	1		46	24	22		1,098	1,032	66	
1929	5	4	1		891	666	225		37,591	19,366	18,225	
1930	2			2	114			114	550			550
1931	10	4	2	4	9,785	917	999	7,869	121,621	10,195	3,021	108,405
1932	2	1	1		36	14	22		364	210	154	
1933	21	11	5	5	14,515	11,467	1,579	1,469	132,647	76,003	26,681	29,963
1934	9	8	1		4,266	3,942	324		132,086	98,648	33,438	
1935	5	2	2	1	902	465	222	215	36,000	6,695	12,320	16,985
1936	6	3	2	1	1,090	868	207	15	12,573	8,274	4,014	285
Chewing and smoking tobacco and snuff:												
1927–34												
1935	1	1			325	325			2,755	2,755		
1936												
Cigars:												
1927	2	1		1	887	97		790	12,112	7,372		4,740
1928	2	1	1		46	24	22		1,098	1,032	66	
1929	5	4	1		891	666	225		37,591	19,366	18,225	
1930	2			2	114			114	550			550
1931	10	4	2	4	9,785	917	999	7,869	121,621	10,195	3,021	108,405

[1] Man-days idle as a result of a strike which began in the preceding year and continued into this year.
[3] There were no strikes in the cigarette industry.

TABLE 37.—*Strikes beginning 1927–36, by industries and major issues involved*—Continued

Industry and year	Number of strikes				Number of workers involved				Number of man-days idle during year			
	Total	Major issues			Total	Major issues			Total	Major issues		
		Wages and hours	Union organization	Miscellaneous		Wages and hours	Union organization	Miscellaneous		Wages and hours	Union organization	Miscellaneous
Tobacco manufactures—Continued.												
Cigars—Continued.												
1932	2	1	1		36	14	22		364	210	154	
1933	21	11	5	5	14,515	11,467	1,579	1,469	132,647	76,003	26,681	29,963
1934	9	8	1		4,266	3,942	324		132,086	98,648	33,438	
1935	4	1	2	1	577	140	222	215	33,245	3,940	12,320	16,985
1936	6	3	2	1	1,090	868	207	15	12,573	8,274	4,014	285
Paper and printing:												
1927	22	13	4	5	1,262	929	225	108	53,973	23,796	26,905	3,272
1928	14	3	9	2	2,022	93	1,779	150	24,916	737	23,729	450
1929	15	6	7	2	1,775	548	1,165	62	42,603	8,632	31,649	2,322
1930	14	5	4	5	258	109	35	114	2,641	1,423	704	514
1931	17	12	4	1	599	428	121	50	10,407	7,428	1,679	1,300
1932	33	27	3	3	3,279	3,201	43	35	40,390	38,470	818	1,102
1933	35	21	12	2	7,533	6,687	556	290	52,351	42,867	9,154	330
1934	48	22	26		6,548	4,224	2,324		65,467	34,811	30,656	
1935	52	14	34	4	5,025	1,621	3,273	131	134,543	18,716	115,487	340
1936	47	6	37	4	5,203	566	4,445	192	191,068	14,500	175,456	1,112
Boxes, paper:												
1927												
1928	1		1		1,200		1,200		13,200		13,200	
1929	3	1	2		115	78	37		631	234	397	
1930	1	1			30	30			480	480		
1931												
1932	2	2			618	618			4,818	4,818		
1933	7	5	2		4,644	4,591	53		20,947	19,133	1,814	
1934	6	2	4		381	147	234		1,246	294	952	
1935	7	2	5		1,221	1,024	197		13,407	11,488	1,919	
1936	13	2	11		2,932	432	2,500		91,575	12,760	78,815	
Paper and pulp:												
1927	1			1	15			15	90			90
1928	2	1		1	129	28		101	975	672		303
1929	1			1	12			12	72			72
1930	2			2	58			58	162			162
1931	1		1		14		14		140		140	
1932	3	2		1	789	783		6	13,104	13,098		6
1933	4	3	1		423	383	40		5,325	4,085	1,240	

1934	7	2	5	-----	2,168	622	1,546	-----	29,294	6,044	23,250	-----
1935	8	2	5	1	2,373	194	2,125	54	85,978	5,474	80,342	162
1936	7	-----	4	3	671	-----	491	180	12,840	-----	12,040	800
Printing and publishing:												
Book and job:												
1927	3	2	1	-----	263	71	192	-----	25,131	555	24,576	-----
1928	3	1	2	-----	158	48	110	-----	7,608	48	7,560	-----
1929	2	1	1	-----	1,006	6	1,000	-----	28,258	258	28,000	-----
1930	7	3	1	3	131	69	6	56	1,221	863	6	352
1931	3	3	-----	-----	73	73	-----	-----	345	345	-----	-----
1932	11	9	1	1	1,054	1,025	18	11	6,060	4,514	468	1,078
1933	4	4	-----	-----	50	50	-----	-----	129	129	-----	-----
1934	14	6	8	-----	1,283	1,087	196	-----	12,706	10,886	1,820	-----
1935	9	2	7	-----	406	19	387	-----	22,188	249	21,939	-----
1936	8	1	7	-----	270	58	212	-----	4,687	464	4,223	-----
Newspapers and periodicals:												
1927	7	4	1	2	209	149	7	53	1,926	953	427	546
1928	6	1	5	-----	441	17	424	-----	2,941	17	2,924	-----
1929	7	3	4	-----	339	211	128	-----	6,079	2,827	3,252	-----
1930	2	1	1	-----	16	10	6	-----	86	80	6	-----
1931	11	7	3	1	394	237	107	50	9,158	6,319	1,539	1,300
1932	13	11	1	1	557	526	13	18	5,004	4,648	338	18
1933	15	6	7	2	1,086	385	411	290	7,048	982	5,736	330
1934	18	11	7	-----	2,654	2,356	298	-----	20,355	17,551	2,804	-----
1935	19	4	12	3	608	145	386	77	8,560	691	7,691	178
1936	10	1	8	1	808	28	768	12	62,919	224	62,383	312
Other:												
1927	11	7	2	2	775	709	26	40	26,826	22,288	1,902	2,636
1928	2	-----	1	1	94	-----	45	49	192	-----	45	147
1929	2	1	-----	1	303	253	-----	50	7,563	5,313	-----	2,250
1930	2	-----	2	-----	23	-----	23	-----	692	-----	692	-----
1931	2	2	-----	-----	118	118	-----	-----	764	764	-----	-----
1932	4	3	1	-----	261	249	12	-----	11,404	11,392	12	-----
1933	5	3	2	-----	1,330	1,278	52	-----	18,902	18,538	364	-----
1934	3	1	2	-----	62	12	50	-----	1,866	36	1,830	-----
1935	9	4	5	-----	417	239	178	-----	4,410	814	3,596	-----
1936	9	2	7	-----	522	48	474	-----	19,047	1,052	17,995	-----
Chemicals and allied products:												
1927	4	3	-----	1	295	247	-----	48	2,115	1,587	-----	528
1928	1	-----	-----	1	1,479	-----	-----	1,479	8,874	-----	-----	8,874
1929	8	5	1	2	437	185	13	239	3,205	2,561	65	579
1930	1	1	-----	-----	44	44	-----	-----	44	44	-----	-----
1931	-----	-----	-----	-----	-----	-----	-----	-----	-----	-----	-----	-----
1932	2	1	-----	1	70	30	-----	40	220	180	-----	40
1933	10	5	4	1	1,824	964	760	100	13,042	1,522	11,420	100
1934	22	12	10	-----	5,388	2,485	2,903	-----	142,736	93,422	49,314	-----
1935	8	2	5	1	832	370	440	22	5,662	1,760	3,748	154
1936	20	5	11	4	13,990	1,075	12,589	326	230,766	30,594	198,451	1,721

[1] Man-days idle as a result of a strike which began in the preceding year and continued into this year.

TABLE 37.—*Strikes beginning 1927–36, by industries and major issues involved*—Continued

Industry and year	Number of strikes: Total	Number of strikes: Major issues: Wages and hours	Number of strikes: Major issues: Union organization	Number of strikes: Major issues: Miscellaneous	Number of workers involved: Total	Number of workers involved: Major issues: Wages and hours	Number of workers involved: Major issues: Union organization	Number of workers involved: Major issues: Miscellaneous	Number of man-days idle during year: Total	Number of man-days idle during year: Major issues: Wages and hours	Number of man-days idle during year: Major issues: Union organization	Number of man-days idle during year: Major issues: Miscellaneous
Chemicals and allied products—Continued.												
Chemicals:												
1927–28												
1929	1	1			10	10			10	10		
1930–32												
1933	2	1	1		270	150	120		1,380	300	1,080	
1934	5	2	3		2,071	171	1,900		44,657	1,557	43,100	
1935	2	1	1		634	300	334		4,206	1,200	3,006	
1936	4	2	1	1	1,378	897	341	140	31,144	28,617	2,387	140
Cottonseed—oil, cake, and meal:												
1927	1			1	48			48	528			528
1928–31												
1932	1			1	40			40	40			40
1933	1	1			600	600			600	600		
1934	1	1			52	52			104	104		
1935–36												
Explosives:												
1927–35												
1936	1		1		30		30		870		870	
Fertilizers:												
1927–29												
1930	1	1			44	44			44	44		
1931–32												
1933	3	3			214	214			622	622		
1934	3	3			415	415			2,686	2,686		
1935	1		1		16		16		256		256	
1936	1		1		38		38		342		342	
Paints and varnishes:												
1927	2	2			220	220			1,020	1,020		
1928–32												
1933	3		2	1	570		470	100	9,930		9,830	100
1934	3	2	1		644	633	11		3,220	3,165	55	
1935	3		3		90		90		486		486	
1936	3		2	1	615		576	39	13,398		12,384	1,014
Petroleum refining:												
1927	1	1			27	27			567	567		
1928	1			1	1,479			1,479	8,874			8,874

1929	3	2		1	176	107		69	1,483	1,414		69
1930–32												
1933	1		1		170		170		510		510	
1934	7	2	5		1,654	714	940		76,601	71,690	4,911	
1935												
1936	4	1	3		2,521	50	2,471		61,935	100	61,835	
Rayon and allied products:												
1927–35												
1936	2		1	1	8,905		8,800	105	114,715		114,400	315
Soap:												
1927–28												
1929	2	1		1	219	49		170	1,343	833		510
1930–33												
1934	1	1			470	470			14,100	14,100		
1935–36												
Other:												
1927–28												
1929	2	1	1		32	19	13		369	304	65	
1930–31												
1932	1	1			30	30			180	180		
1933												
1934	2	1	1		82	30	52		1,368	120	1,248	
1935	2	1		1	92	70		22	714	560		154
1936	5	2	2	1	503	128	333	42	8,362	1,877	6,233	252
Rubber products:												
1927	2	2			384	384			4,096	4,096		
1928	2	2			1,700	1,700			11,000	11,000		
1929	4	3		1	659	254		405	2,349	1,134		1,215
1930–31												
1932	2	1	1		1,328	60	1,268		5,492	420	5,072	
1933	19	13	6		7,236	4,192	3,044		43,849	25,265	18,584	
1934	20	7	13		10,898	5,095	5,803		219,166	68,297	150,869	
1935	7	3	4		1,308	271	1,037		18,982	772	18,210	
1936	43	17	17	9	76,699	28,366	23,245	25,088	477,286	383,887	66,604	26,795
Rubber boots and shoes:												
1927	2	2			384	384			4,096	4,096		
1928	1	1			900	900			5,400	5,400		
1929–31												
1932	1		1		1,268		1,268		5,072		5,072	
1933	3	2	1		2,158	622	1,536		11,464	3,784	7,680	
1934	2		2		2,750		2,750		68,100		68,100	
1935	2	2			210	210			650	650		
1936												
Rubber tires and inner tubes:												
1927												
1928	1	1			800	800			5,600	5,600		
1929	3	2		1	619	214		405	2,229	1,014		1,215
1930–31												
1932	1	1			60	60			420	420		
1933	5	5			2,745	2,745			18,140	18,140		
1934	7	5	2		5,927	5,036	891		70,552	66,802	3,750	

[1] Man-days idle as a result of a strike which began in the preceding year and continued into this year.

TABLE 37.—*Strikes beginning 1927–36, by industries and major issues involved*—Continued

Industry and year	Number of strikes: Total	Number of strikes: Major issues: Wages and hours	Number of strikes: Major issues: Union organization	Number of strikes: Major issues: Miscellaneous	Number of workers involved: Total	Number of workers involved: Major issues: Wages and hours	Number of workers involved: Major issues: Union organization	Number of workers involved: Major issues: Miscellaneous	Number of man-days idle during year: Total	Number of man-days idle during year: Major issues: Wages and hours	Number of man-days idle during year: Major issues: Union organization	Number of man-days idle during year: Major issues: Miscellaneous
Rubber products—Continued.												
Rubber tires and inner tubes—Continued.												
1935	1		1		190		190		2,090		2,090	
1936	22	6	10	6	70,571	24,217	21,594	24,760	443,700	366,417	52,023	25,260
Other rubber goods:												
1927–28												
1929	1	1			40	40			120	120		
1930–32												
1933	11	6	5		2,333	825	1,508		14,245	3,341	10,904	
1934	11	2	9		2,221	59	2,162		80,514	1,495	79,019	
1935	4	1	3		908	61	847		16,242	122	16,120	
1936	21	11	7	3	6,128	4,149	1,651	328	33,586	17,470	14,581	1,535
Miscellaneous manufacturing:												
1927	15	6	7	2	1,655	284	1,261	110	21,099	3,904	16,985	210
1928	9	3	5	1	1,297	273	1,012	12	56,285	9,305	46,956	24
1929	11	5	5	1	819	207	567	45	13,836	2,518	11,183	135
1930	11	5	4	2	2,000	1,221	704	75	20,469	14,055	5,589	825
1931	21	12	6	3	3,349	2,441	732	176	45,152	34,826	8,426	1,900
1932	20	13	5	2	5,372	1,636	3,596	140	72,792	22,416	47,536	2,840
1933	49	25	21	3	13,987	5,942	7,706	339	187,512	47,918	134,592	5,002
1934	42	12	26	4	8,755	2,685	5,608	462	110,467	34,370	69,169	6,928
1935	67	18	45	4	9,249	2,696	5,803	750	222,789	55,776	159,335	7,678
1936	76	31	38	7	9,536	3,671	5,162	703	211,069	63,359	139,169	8,541
Electric light and power and manufactured gas:												
1927	1	1			25	25			3,125	3,125		
1928									3,750	[1] 3,750		
1929	1		1		300		300		1,200		1,200	
1930												
1931	1		1		300		300		900		900	
1932–33												
1934	3		3		78		78		408		408	
1935	10	2	8		2,287	959	1,328		59,817	2,618	57,199	
1936	9	3	5	1	904	242	649	13	11,142	5,940	5,189	13
Broom and brush:												
1927												
1928	1		1		100		100		800		800	
1929	1		1		170		170		5,270		5,270	

1930	1	1			30	30			300	300		
1931	2	2			142	142			6, 844	6, 844		
1932	2	2			142	142			1, 443	1, 443		
1933	3	3			327	327			9, 218	9, 218		
1934	5	1	3	1	177	60	88	29	1, 561	640	602	319
1935	2	1		1	124	48		76	2, 832	96		2, 736
1936	3	3			157	157			2, 047	1, 135		[1] 912
Furriers and fur factories:												
1927	7	1	4	2	1, 118	94	914	110	10, 478	94	10, 174	210
1928	5	2	3		362	266	96		10, 088	5, 548	4, 540	
1929	5	3	2		248	160	88		6, 960	2, 256	4, 704	
1930	5		3	2	179		104	75	3, 414		2, 589	825
1931	10	5	2	3	2, 113	1, 910	27	176	27, 067	24, 643	524	1, 900
1932	11	6	4	1	458	262	96	100	12, 691	9, 055	1, 036	2, 600
1933	14	3	10	1	837	109	720	8	5, 224	661	4, 547	16
1934	10	5	4	1	3, 859	1, 071	2, 690	98	34, 991	19, 757	14, 940	294
1935	20	4	14	2	1, 620	386	1, 160	74	38, 177	9, 394	26, 161	2, 622
1936	19	5	13	1	2, 529	203	2, 287	39	70, 212	1, 368	68, 649	195
Other:												
1927	7	4	3		512	165	347		7, 496	685	6, 811	
1928	3	1	1	1	835	7	816	12	41, 647	7	41, 616	24
1929	4	2	1	1	101	47	9	45	406	262	9	135
1930	5	4	1		1, 791	1, 191	600		16, 755	13, 755	3, 000	
1931	8	5	3		794	389	405		10, 341	3, 339	7, 002	
1932	7	5	1	1	4, 772	1, 232	3, 500	40	58, 658	11, 918	46, 500	240
1933	32	19	11	2	12, 823	5, 506	6, 986	331	173, 070	38, 039	130, 045	4, 986
1934	24	6	16	2	4, 641	1, 554	2, 752	335	73, 507	13, 973	53, 219	6, 315
1935	35	11	23	1	5, 218	1, 303	3, 315	600	121, 963	43, 668	75, 975	2, 320
1936	45	20	20	5	5, 946	3, 069	2, 226	651	127, 668	54, 916	65, 331	7, 421
Extraction of minerals:												
1927	60	15	24	21	202, 989	174, 549	14, 509	13, 931	23, 187, 356	23, 010, 917	76, 638	99, 801
1928	78	19	13	46	143, 796	55, 758	14, 540	73, 498	6, 528, 264	5, 885, 271	103, 036	539, 957
1929	93	37	20	36	75, 794	13, 766	11, 185	50, 843	428, 437	141, 995	42, 981	243, 461
1930	74	35	16	23	47, 204	16, 642	14, 048	16, 514	1, 002, 716	419, 612	415, 342	167, 762
1931	75	33	24	18	114, 158	29, 869	39, 356	44, 933	2, 203, 299	354, 129	1, 306, 316	542, 854
1932	64	32	10	22	83, 456	68, 288	9, 175	5, 993	6, 084, 357	5, 134, 230	884, 172	65, 955
1933	135	51	34	50	240, 687	28, 051	114, 857	97, 779	3, 328, 638	679, 051	1, 687, 733	961, 854
1934	143	35	43	65	229, 964	57, 720	58, 026	114, 218	3, 279, 853	1, 127, 143	1, 231, 148	921, 562
1935	90	22	22	46	479, 514	416, 544	9, 386	53, 584	4, 019, 333	2, 991, 466	262, 034	765, 833
1936	83	22	20	41	56, 063	12, 663	19, 238	24, 162	1, 237, 470	587, 068	366, 502	283, 900
Coal mining, anthracite:												
1927	32	7	12	13	26, 052	3, 856	10, 162	12, 034	157, 857	35, 645	40, 210	82, 002
1928	41	4	10	27	78, 424	4, 059	12, 581	61, 784	573, 404	18, 426	93, 039	461, 939
1929	32	2	8	22	57, 276	1, 022	8, 757	47, 497	239, 206	3, 685	14, 685	220, 836
1930	18	1	8	9	20, 036	1, 580	6, 848	11, 608	117, 338	3, 160	29, 505	84, 673
1931	14	4	4	6	61, 416	21, 675	2, 151	37, 590	655, 203	250, 633	17, 610	386, 960
1932	18	6	2	10	19, 592	16, 105	333	3, 154	167, 036	125, 175	9, 570	32, 291
1933	27	9	2	16	96, 297	8, 559	3, 300	84, 438	1, 012, 787	103, 026	42, 100	867, 66[illegible]
1934	38	10	1	27	105, 296	11, 130	313	93, 853	948, 767	136, 009	939	811, 819
1935	33	7	1	25	50, 191	9, 517	1, 100	39, 574	788, 724	75, 604	41, 800	671, 320
1936	26	5	6	15	23, 073	3, 596	13, 005	6, 472	264, 545	43, 043	53, 083	68, 419

[1] Man-days idle as a result of a strike which began in the preceding year and continued into this year.

TABLE 37.—*Strikes beginning 1927–36, by industries and major issues involved*—Continued

Industry and year	Number of strikes				Number of workers involved				Number of man-days idle during year			
	Total	Major issues			Total	Major issues			Total	Major issues		
		Wages and hours	Union organization	Miscellaneous		Wages and hours	Union organization	Miscellaneous		Wages and hours	Union organization	Miscellaneous
Extraction of minerals—Continued.												
Coal mining, bituminous:												
1927	22	5	10	7	176, 022	169, 857	4, 310	1, 855	23, 024, 211	22, 970, 872	36, 254	17, 085
1928	30	10	2	18	63, 279	51, 154	459	11, 666	5, 940, 992	5, 862, 745	997	77, 250
1929	58	34	11	13	18, 093	12, 594	2, 253	3, 246	181, 631	138, 010	21, 296	22, 325
1930	52	32	7	13	26, 841	14, 786	7, 189	4, 866	882, 599	414, 044	385, 826	82, 729
1931	57	27	18	12	52, 392	7, 944	37, 105	7, 343	1, 542, 506	98, 546	1, 288, 066	155, 894
1932	43	25	7	11	63, 619	52, 123	8, 792	2, 704	5, 913, 886	5, 007, 375	873, 252	33, 259
1933	102	38	30	34	142, 242	17, 488	111, 413	13, 341	2, 211, 375	472, 521	1, 644, 661	94, 193
1934	78	21	23	34	109, 827	46, 309	43, 741	19, 777	1, 562, 358	981, 282	473, 735	107, 341
1935	42	10	12	20	420, 574	403, 790	3, 174	13, 610	2, 971, 449	2, 860, 358	24, 178	86, 913
1936	38	5	9	24	19, 648	1, 378	2, 934	15, 336	533, 314	356, 058	43, 431	133, 825
Metalliferous mining:												
1927–33												
1934	11	4	7		11, 719	281	11, 438		725, 230	9, 852	715, 378	
1935	5	2	2	1	6, 660	3, 110	3, 150	400	191, 733	52, 535	131, 598	7, 600
1936	9	4	3	2	6, 959	3, 330	1, 275	2, 354	247, 528	136, 852	29, 020	81, 656
Quarrying and nonmetallic mining:												
1927	4	2	1	1	886	814	30	42	5, 160	4, 356	90	714
1928	7	5	1	1	2, 093	545	1, 500	48	13, 868	4, 100	9, 000	768
1929	3	1	1	1	425	150	175	100	7, 600	300	7, 000	300
1930	4	2	1	1	327	276	11	40	2, 779	2, 408	11	360
1931	4	2	2		350	250	100		5, 590	4, 950	640	
1932	3	1	1	1	245	60	50	135	3, 435	1, 680	1, 350	405
1933	5	3	2		2, 078	1, 934	144		104, 336	103, 364	972	
1934	13		9	4	1, 638		1, 050	588	30, 620		28, 218	2, 402
1935	6	2	4		1, 809	119	1, 690		64, 202	2, 897	61, 305	
1936	7	5	2		6, 274	4, 250	2, 024		191, 043	50, 075	140, 968	
Crude-petroleum producing:												
1927	1		1		7		7		84		84	
1928–32												
1933	1	1			70	70			140	140		
1934	3		3		1, 484		1, 484		12, 878		12, 878	
1935	4	1	3		280	8	272		3, 225	72	3, 153	
1936												

Other:												
1927	1	1			22	22			44	44		
1928–35												
1936	3	3			109	109			1,040	1,040		
Transportation and communication:												
1927	16	11	4	1	9,816	9,562	239	15	52,617	43,616	8,986	15
1928	11	2	4	5	8,737	31	7,663	1,043	52,538	134	18,743	33,661
1929	41	21	15	5	9,384	4,261	4,532	591	224,007	22,445	195,494	6,068
1930	30	12	13	5	8,073	3,636	3,817	620	236,086	11,734	220,322	4,030
1931	41	21	13	7	13,339	8,288	4,569	482	283,513	66,068	213,419	4,026
1932	26	24	1	1	8,575	8,348	27	200	173,315	172,581	534	200
1933	52	25	21	6	22,586	5,328	16,652	606	188,752	81,365	103,342	4,045
1934	156	68	55	33	105,614	47,375	45,327	12,912	1,986,699	411,716	1,122,689	452,294
1935	198	54	75	69	64,225	11,713	40,745	11,767	959,950	293,790	569,604	96,556
1936	165	67	58	40	83,231	13,686	45,866	23,679	2,095,435	182,463	1,735,145	177,827
Water transportation:												
1927	2	2			675	675			3,325	3,225		
1928												
1929	5	3		2	577	344		233	6,220	3,264		2,956
1930	7	3	3	1	3,978	3,240	538	200	13,982	6,760	5,822	1,400
1931	10	6	3	1	8,711	5,071	3,360	280	250,844	53,354	195,530	1,960
1932	7	6		1	3,018	2,818		200	57,198	56,998		200
1933	14	10	2	2	3,071	2,561	325	185	32,752	29,867	2,375	510
1934	76	28	25	23	28,590	5,846	12,844	9,900	1,068,867	134,260	501,193	433,414
1935	122	23	41	58	29,490	7,188	14,571	7,731	749,534	202,283	462,525	84,726
1936	79	26	19	34	68,761	5,157	40,136	23,468	1,961,267	138,259	1,647,599	175,409
Motortruck transportation:												
1927	2	2			8,000	8,000			28,000	28,000		
1928	1			1	400			400	400			400
1929	16	7	7	2	4,745	2,651	1,776	318	18,274	10,138	5,064	3,072
1930	7	2	4	1	386	148	198	40	4,401	2,217	2,024	160
1931	17	7	7	3	2,445	1,532	881	32	11,040	2,859	7,825	356
1932	7	6	1		2,033	2,006	27		79,110	78,576	534	
1933	26	8	15	3	17,627	1,907	15,305	415	87,025	10,271	73,231	3,523
1934	46	25	15	6	23,260	8,455	12,596	2,209	301,968	38,475	251,548	11,945
1935	36	15	18	3	27,760	3,695	23,862	203	153,806	83,436	67,600	2,770
1936	55	24	28	3	9,235	6,152	2,989	94	75,953	26,150	48,369	1,434
Motorbus transportation:												
1927	4	2	2		445	365	80		5,850	5,300	550	
1928	3	2	1		124	31	93		227	134	93	
1929	4	1	3		83	29	54		345	29	316	
1930	5	3	1	1	880	115	645	120	14,794	2,179	12,255	360
1931	1	1			75	75			225	225		
1932	2	2			118	118			1,437	1,437		
1933	3	1	2		263	153	110		1,315	459	856	
1934	10	4	5	1	681	316	284	81	25,973	2,986	20,719	2,268
1935	5	2	3		293	187	106		5,140	958	1,023	[1] 3,159
1936	12	7	4	1	920	549	357	14	10,144	7,737	2,309	98

[1] Man-days idle as a result of a strike which began in the preceding year and continued into this year.

TABLE 37.—*Strikes beginning 1927–36, by industries and major issues involved*—Continued

Industry and year	Number of strikes				Number of workers involved				Number of man-days idle during year			
	Total	Major issues			Total	Major issues			Total	Major issues		
		Wages and hours	Union organization	Miscellaneous		Wages and hours	Union organization	Miscellaneous		Wages and hours	Union organization	Miscellaneous
Transportation and communication—Continued.												
Taxicabs and miscellaneous:												
1927	6	3	2	1	623	449	159	15	13,143	4,692	8,436	15
1928	4		2	2	942		570	372	6,772		4,650	2,122
1929	9	5	3	1	1,685	593	1,052	40	9,774	4,270	5,464	40
1930	7	3	3	1	2,666	93	2,323	250	200,641	418	198,723	1,500
1931	11	6	2	3	2,038	1,580	288	170	21,144	9,570	9,864	1,710
1932	8	8			3,176	3,176			35,179	35,179		
1933	7	4	2	1	1,556	638	912	6	67,225	40,333	26,880	12
1934	11	4	5	2	43,982	31,062	12,823	97	531,716	213,386	316,163	2,167
1935	23	8	7	8	5,797	564	1,400	3,833	43,447	6,440	31,106	5,901
1936	13	8	4	1	3,460	1,596	1,848	16	23,561	9,733	13,812	16
Electric railroads:												
1927	1	1			50	50			950	950		
1928	2			2	271			271	31,139			31,139
1929	3	1	2		1,878	228	1,650		185,106	456	184,650	
1930	1	1			40	40			160	160		
1931												
1932	1	1			207	207			207	207		
1933	1	1			48	48			288	288		
1934	10	4	5	1	8,751	1,346	6,780	625	57,709	22,143	33,066	2,500
1935	4		4		611		611		5,596	[1]487	5,109	
1936	1	1			60	60			240	240		
Steam railroads:												
1927												
1928	1		1		7,000		7,000		14,000		14,000	
1929	3	3			396	396			4,048	4,048		
1930	1		1		106		106		1,484		1,484	
1931–34												
1935	1	1			28	28			56	56		
1936	2		1	1	587		500	87	22,870		22,000	870
Telephone and telegraph:												
1927	1	1			23	23			1,449	1,449		
1928–29												
1930	1		1		7		7		14		14	
1931	2	1	1		70	30	40		260	60	200	
1932–33												
1934	3	3			350	350			466	466		

1935	3	3			39	39			94	94		
1936												
Air transportation:												
1927–31												
1932	1	1			23	23			184	184		
1933	1	1			21	21			147	147		
1934												
1935	1		1		69		69		1,863		1,863	
1936												
Radio broadcasting and transmitting:												
1927–28												
1929	1	1			20	20			240	240		
1930	1			1	10			10	610			610
1931–34												
1935	3	2	1		138	12	126		414	36	378	
1936	1		1		12		12		912		912	
Other:												
1927–35												
1936	2	1	1		196	172	24		488	344	144	
Trade:												
1927	20	5	9	6	7,876	3,675	2,600	1,601	158,027	18,530	67,840	71,657
1928	10	5	4	1	2,118	116	1,988	14	30,445	1,573	28,606	266
1929	25	6	18	1	8,345	4,775	3,561	9	158,634	59,925	98,682	27
1930	21	8	9	4	3,032	1,154	759	1,119	34,790	18,858	9,904	6,028
1931	12	5	5	2	1,177	978	168	31	16,980	9,933	6,916	131
1932	24	19	5		4,543	3,983	560		22,564	18,288	4,276	
1933	39	19	17	3	29,089	11,962	2,867	14,260	141,477	61,134	17,203	63,140
1934	100	33	63	4	22,744	9,472	12,745	527	230,372	39,733	182,058	8,581
1935	138	37	94	7	15,677	6,020	9,363	294	219,152	64,078	153,669	1,405
1936	164	45	116	3	30,532	14,804	15,011	717	326,749	72,007	250,509	4,233
Wholesale:												
1927	4	2	1	1	4,920	3,200	920	800	32,080	6,000	22,080	4,000
1928	2	2			65	65			1,165	1,165		
1929	7	4	3		5,900	3,550	2,350		108,550	43,750	64,800	
1930	6	1	5		589	150	439		5,933	300	5,633	
1931												
1932	4	3	1		81	58	23		744	514	230	
1933	7	6		1	1,430	1,290		140	3,050	2,770		280
1934	21	9	11	1	1,641	650	981	10	13,835	5,304	8,281	250
1935	23	7	16		2,979	1,064	1,915		43,884	14,754	29,060	[1]70
1936	51	16	35		6,637	1,151	5,486		115,798	6,455	109,343	
Retail:												
1927	16	3	8	5	2,956	475	1,680	801	125,947	12,530	45,760	67,657
1928	8	3	4	1	2,053	51	1,988	14	29,280	408	28,606	266
1929	18	2	15	1	2,445	1,225	1,211	9	50,084	16,175	33,882	27
1930	15	7	4	4	2,443	1,004	320	1,119	28,857	18,558	4,271	6,028
1931	12	5	5	2	1,177	978	168	31	16,980	9,933	6,916	131
1932	20	16	4		4,462	3,925	537		21,820	17,774	4,046	
1933	32	13	17	2	27,659	10,672	2,867	14,120	138,427	58,364	17,203	62,860
1934	79	24	52	3	21,103	8,822	11,764	517	216,537	34,429	173,777	8,331
1935	115	30	78	7	12,698	4,956	7,448	294	175,268	49,324	124,609	1,335
1936	113	29	81	3	23,895	13,653	9,525	717	210,951	65,552	141,166	4,233

[1] Man-days idle as a result of a strike which began in the preceding year and continued into this year.

TABLE 37.—Strikes beginning 1927–36, by industries and major issues involved—Continued

Industry and year	Number of strikes: Total	Number of strikes: Major issues: Wages and hours	Number of strikes: Major issues: Union organization	Number of strikes: Major issues: Miscellaneous	Number of workers involved: Total	Number of workers involved: Major issues: Wages and hours	Number of workers involved: Major issues: Union organization	Number of workers involved: Major issues: Miscellaneous	Number of man-days idle during year: Total	Number of man-days idle during year: Major issues: Wages and hours	Number of man-days idle during year: Major issues: Union organization	Number of man-days idle during year: Major issues: Miscellaneous
Domestic and personal service:												
1927	34	13	18	3	9,095	2,256	6,783	56	182,631	62,242	119,946	443
1928	29	7	16	6	30,692	1,048	29,050	594	498,764	13,006	477,778	17,980
1929	22	8	12	2	11,025	5,674	2,811	2,540	319,465	71,998	164,007	83,460
1930	20	6	11	3	5,042	2,857	1,630	555	32,336	9,396	17,930	5,010
1931	26	15	10	1	6,165	3,886	2,267	12	49,324	21,982	27,306	36
1932	34	17	14	3	13,581	10,028	3,403	150	180,236	143,189	35,507	1,540
1933	64	24	37	3	22,507	9,156	13,284	67	488,042	165,708	322,152	182
1934	111	54	47	10	44,764	22,327	20,244	2,193	514,468	283,874	227,926	2,668
1935	93	36	53	4	29,065	7,925	20,922	218	281,476	64,505	215,863	1,108
1936	116	35	73	8	72,246	42,042	30,026	178	861,114	407,412	447,625	6,077
Hotels, restaurants, and boarding houses:												
1927	4		3	1	1,552		1,532	20	33,783		33,703	80
1928	5	2	2	1	124	52	64	8	2,996	908	2,064	24
1929	6	1	5		1,798	21	1,777		159,309	42	159,267	
1930	9	1	5	3	1,158	30	573	555	12,406	930	6,466	5,010
1931	8	7	1		2,120	2,074	46		14,644	14,368	276	
1932	4	3	1		132	126	6		626	620	6	
1933	17	9	8		853	370	483		18,542	3,316	15,226	
1934	44	22	18	4	11,107	1,393	9,633	81	175,652	22,144	153,415	93
1935	47	12	33	2	1,954	549	1,348	57	32,961	8,028	24,191	742
1936	49	13	33	3	2,141	379	1,735	27	36,283	3,960	28,292	4,031
Personal service, barbers, beauty parlors:												
1927	12	8	3	1	4,837	1,316	3,500	21	65,881	9,318	56,500	63
1928	10	4	4	2	5,054	987	3,601	466	43,302	12,080	25,886	5,336
1929	4	3	1		861	855	6		1,044	978	66	
1930	7	5	2		3,543	2,827	716		12,986	8,466	4,520	
1931	10	6	4		2,765	1,233	1,532		15,665	4,235	11,430	
1932	10	7	2	1	8,041	5,455	2,536	50	122,700	97,480	25,020	200
1933	4	4			1,574	1,574			10,732	8,140	2,592	
1934	9	7	1	1	3,048	2,992	6	50	21,784	21,678	6	100
1935	5	2	2	1	1,400	650	600	150	10,850	9,950	600	300
1936	8	5	3		24,805	2,525	22,280		289,960	5,440	284,520	
Laundries:												
1927	5	2	3		380	172	208		13,810	5,050	8,760	
1928	5	1	3	1	223	9	194	20	10,016	18	9,978	20
1929	3	2	1		3,199	3,173	26		22,880	21,228	1,652	

1930	1		1		42		42		3, 486		3, 486	
1931	3		2	1	520		508	12	13, 728		13, 692	36
1932	9	1	8		930	750	180		9, 003	6, 000	3, 003	
1933	13	3	9	1	4, 990	237	4, 726	27	141, 231	1, 002	140, 202	27
1934	21	9	10	2	5, 318	2, 029	1, 278	2, 011	69, 325	36, 612	30, 702	2, 011
1935	16	6	10		3, 330	1, 428	1, 902		59, 406	6, 624	52, 782	
1936	26	6	16	4	1, 519	249	1, 154	116	63, 538	4, 026	57, 501	2, 011
Dyeing, cleaning, and pressing:												
1927	9		8	1	1, 478		1, 463	15	20, 243		19, 943	300
1928	2		1	1	25, 040		25, 000	40	425, 480		425, 040	440
1929	7	1	4	2	3, 652	125	987	2, 540	86, 277	250	2, 567	83, 460
1930	1		1		36		36		72		72	
1931	4	2	2		730	579	151		4, 207	3, 379	828	
1932	7	4	2	1	4, 232	3, 522	670	40	45, 614	37, 064	7, 390	1, 160
1933	20	6	14		11, 843	4, 575	7, 268		260, 406	110, 850	149, 556	
1934	23	9	12	2	17, 440	15, 350	2, 049	41	223, 891	197, 036	26, 461	394
1935	13	9	3	1	12, 453	4, 676	7, 766	11	116, 870	34, 634	82, 170	66
1936	18	4	13	1	4, 469	623	3, 811	35	52, 516	3, 150	49, 331	35
Domestics:												
1927–36												
Elevator and maintenance workers (when not attached to specific industry):												
1927	4	3	1		848	768	80		48, 914	47, 874	1, 040	
1928	7		6	1	251		191	60	16, 970		14, 810	2, 160
1929	2	1	1		1, 515	1, 500	15		49, 955	49, 500	455	
1930	1		1		113		113		2, 486		2, 486	
1931–33												
1934	10	6	3	1	7, 628	555	7, 063	10	20, 957	6, 396	14, 491	70
1935	5	2	3		8, 413	13	8, 400		37, 229	1, 029	36, 200	
1936	12	5	7		39, 081	38, 167	914		417, 094	390, 301	26, 793	
Other:												
1927–29												
1930	1		1		150		150		900		900	
1931	1		1		30		30		1, 080		1, 080	
1932	4	2	1	1	246	175	11	60	2, 293	2, 025	88	180
1933	10	2	6	2	3, 247	2, 400	807	40	57, 131	42, 400	14, 576	155
1934	4	1	3		223	8	215		2, 859	8	2, 851	
1935	7	5	2		1, 515	609	906		24, 160	4, 240	19, 920	
1936	3	2	1		231	99	132		1, 723	535	1, 188	
Professional service:												
1927	34	9	12	13	2, 734	264	783	1, 687	93, 279	6, 831	14, 070	72, 378
1928	27	5	5	17	2, 540	268	1, 275	997	108, 963	1, 274	68, 395	39, 294
1929	39	13	11	15	2, 131	888	435	808	45, 134	3, 645	7, 364	34, 125
1930	25	7	1	17	1, 591	671	15	905	45, 865	13, 408	390	32, 067
1931	25	15		10	1, 196	435		761	66, 526	8, 755		57, 771
1932	54	40	3	11	3, 486	3, 011	47	428	26, 131	19, 036	953	6, 142
1933	45	27	6	12	8, 693	7, 359	815	519	203, 475	161, 902	34, 926	6, 647
1934	30	16	10	4	2, 861	1, 096	1, 564	201	30, 814	3, 914	23, 744	3, 156
1935	23	11	9	3	1, 922	1, 446	305	171	15, 626	6, 490	6, 156	2, 980
1936	24	11	8	5	1, 052	789	120	143	14, 394	7, 278	6, 111	1, 005

TABLE 37.—*Strikes beginning 1927–36, by industries and major issues involved*—Continued

Industry and year	Number of strikes: Total	Number of strikes: Major issues: Wages and hours	Number of strikes: Major issues: Union organization	Number of strikes: Major issues: Miscellaneous	Number of workers involved: Total	Number of workers involved: Major issues: Wages and hours	Number of workers involved: Major issues: Union organization	Number of workers involved: Major issues: Miscellaneous	Number of man-days idle during year: Total	Number of man-days idle during year: Major issues: Wages and hours	Number of man-days idle during year: Major issues: Union organization	Number of man-days idle during year: Major issues: Miscellaneous
Professional service—Continued.												
Recreation and amusement:												
1927	33	9	12	12	2, 720	264	783	1, 673	93, 223	6, 831	14, 070	72, 322
1928	26	5	5	16	2, 529	268	1, 275	986	108, 842	1, 274	68, 395	39, 173
1929	36	12	10	14	1, 376	288	420	668	43, 019	2, 445	7, 289	33, 285
1930	24	7	1	16	1, 567	671	15	881	45, 721	13, 408	390	31, 923
1931	25	15		10	1, 196	435		761	66, 526	8, 755		57, 771
1932	53	39	3	11	3, 445	2, 970	47	428	26, 090	18, 995	953	6, 142
1933	36	27	4	5	7, 617	7, 359	140	118	164, 314	161, 902	1, 776	636
1934	21	12	8	1	1, 182	898	277	7	4, 768	2, 278	2, 483	7
1935	18	11	6	1	1, 660	1, 446	184	30	7, 399	6, 490	549	360
1936	13	7	3	3	766	678	22	66	6, 115	5, 931	22	162
Professional:												
1927												
1928	1			1	11			11	121			121
1929	2	1		1	740	600		140	2, 040	1, 200		840
1930–31												
1932	1	1			41	41			41	41		
1933	7			7	401			401	6, 011			6, 011
1934	9	4	2	3	1, 679	198	1, 287	194	8, 646	1, 636	3, 861	3, 149
1935	3		1	2	156		15	141	2, 815		195	2, 620
1936	3	1		2	86	9		77	879	36		843
Semiprofessional, attendants, and helpers:												
1927	1			1	14			14	56			56
1928												
1929	1		1		15		15		75		75	
1930	1			1	24			24	144			144
1931–32												
1933	2		2		675		675		33, 150		33, 150	
1934									17, 400		[1] 17, 400	
1935	2		2		106		106		5, 412		5, 412	
1936	8	3	5		200	102	98		7, 400	1, 311	6, 089	
Building and construction:												
1927	194	97	53	44	50, 731	25, 864	7, 745	17, 122	1, 632, 112	924, 629	298, 246	409, 237
1928	154	64	56	34	25, 058	12, 177	7, 854	5, 027	585, 922	290, 603	211, 105	84, 214
1929	228	109	80	39	47, 689	32, 558	11, 466	3, 665	1, 124, 660	756, 678	234, 123	133, 859
1930	186	74	55	57	29, 241	20, 411	5, 152	3, 678	394, 229	271, 755	70, 091	52, 383

1931	227	133	58	36	30, 871	23, 138	5, 342	2, 391	545, 900	445, 365	71, 626	28, 909
1932	199	126	33	40	64, 044	60, 475	1, 519	2, 050	1, 839, 977	1, 792, 927	23, 063	23, 987
1933	125	88	13	24	27, 440	23, 907	1, 184	2, 349	338, 125	274, 140	19, 222	44, 763
1934	135	62	43	30	33, 075	20, 846	3, 751	8, 478	585, 173	473, 552	66, 842	44, 779
1935	139	48	56	35	17, 815	8, 191	6, 459	3, 165	181, 632	66, 824	92, 697	22, 111
1936	230	98	79	53	33, 225	9, 276	19, 700	4, 249	345, 351	112, 855	186, 349	46, 147
Buildings, exclusive of P. W. A.:												
1927	189	93	52	44	50, 376	25, 569	7, 685	17, 122	1, 626, 130	920, 627	296, 266	409, 237
1928	141	55	54	32	24, 421	11, 653	7, 811	4, 957	581, 879	287, 262	210, 518	84, 099
1929	198	97	66	35	42, 062	29, 438	9, 202	3, 422	1, 011, 173	691, 809	194, 119	125, 245
1930	163	65	46	52	26, 814	19, 054	4, 667	3, 093	376, 123	267, 880	66, 732	41, 511
1931	193	106	53	34	25, 183	18, 730	4, 164	2, 289	477, 338	397, 318	52, 185	27, 835
1932	182	112	31	39	62, 834	59, 407	1, 437	1, 990	1, 823, 025	1, 779, 555	20, 023	23, 447
1933	99	67	12	20	24, 298	21, 214	1, 108	1, 976	294, 508	231, 738	19, 070	43, 700
1934	87	44	21	22	26, 993	17, 904	1, 786	7, 303	463, 411	419, 661	24, 749	19, 001
1935	76	31	29	16	10, 576	5, 963	3, 400	1, 213	78, 941	47, 218	22, 765	8, 958
1936	111	49	39	23	22, 355	4, 959	15, 726	1, 670	180, 208	47, 333	113, 559	19, 316
All other construction (bridges, docks, etc., and P. W. A. buildings):												
1927	5	4	1		355	295	60		5, 982	4, 002	1, 980	
1928	13	9	2	2	637	524	43	70	4, 043	3, 341	587	115
1929	30	12	14	4	5, 627	3, 120	2, 264	243	113, 487	64, 869	40, 004	8, 614
1930	23	9	9	5	2, 427	1, 357	485	585	18, 106	3, 875	3, 359	10, 872
1931	34	27	5	2	5, 688	4, 408	1, 178	102	68, 562	48, 047	19, 441	1, 074
1932	17	14	2	1	1, 210	1, 068	82	60	16, 952	13, 372	3, 040	540
1933	26	21	1	4	3, 142	2, 693	76	373	43, 617	42, 402	152	1, 063
1934	48	18	22	8	6, 082	2, 942	1, 965	1, 175	121, 762	53, 891	42, 093	25, 778
1935	63	17	27	19	7, 239	2, 228	3, 059	1, 952	102, 691	19, 606	69, 932	13, 153
1936	119	49	40	30	10, 870	4, 317	3, 974	2, 579	165, 143	65, 522	72, 790	26, 831
Agriculture and fishing:												
1927	3	2		1	352	302		50	904	754		150
1928	6	4	1	1	635	455	70	110	3, 445	905	1, 330	1, 210
1929	1	1			1, 000	1, 000			5, 000	5, 000		
1930	6	5	1		2, 935	2, 830	105		26, 720	21, 260	5, 460	
1931	7	7			3, 570	3, 570			95, 825	95, 825		
1932	12	11	1		2, 028	1, 928	100		31, 825	31, 125	700	
1933	36	32	4		34, 072	31, 144	2, 928		517, 440	499, 132	18, 308	
1934	34	26	8		33, 409	18, 644	14, 765		312, 640	198, 512	114, 128	
1935	29	22	7		24, 211	20, 681	3, 530		474, 368	448, 508	25, 860	
1936	42	28	13	1	21, 046	8, 892	11, 614	540	348, 804	52, 392	289, 932	6, 480
Agriculture:												
1927	2	1		1	322	272		50	694	544		150
1928	4	2	1	1	410	230	70	110	2, 770	230	1, 330	1, 210
1929												
1930	5	4	1		2, 905	2, 800	105		26, 060	20, 600	5, 460	
1931	5	5			2, 020	2, 020			15, 225	15, 225		
1932	10	9	1		1, 762	1, 662	100		28, 687	27, 987	700	
1933	35	31	4		34, 012	31, 084	2, 928		516, 900	498, 592	18, 308	
1934	27	22	5		25, 943	13, 519	12, 424		244, 753	171, 787	72, 966	
1935	19	14	5		14, 888	11, 723	3, 165		139, 494	115, 399	24, 095	
1936	28	17	11		15, 369	5, 355	10, 014		259, 120	12, 588	246, 532	

[1] Man-days idle as a result of a strike which began in the preceding year and continued into this year.

TABLE 37.—*Strikes beginning 1927–36, by industries and major issues involved*—Continued

Industry and year	Number of strikes				Number of workers involved				Number of man-days idle during year			
	Total	Major issues			Total	Major issues			Total	Major issues		
		Wages and hours	Union organization	Miscellaneous		Wages and hours	Union organization	Miscellaneous		Wages and hours	Union organization	Miscellaneous
Agriculture and fishing—Continued.												
Fishing:												
1927	1	1			30	30			210	210		
1928	2	2			225	225			675	675		
1929	1	1			1, 000	1, 000			5, 000	5, 000		
1930	1	1			30	30			660	660		
1931	2	2			1, 550	1, 550			80, 600	80, 600		
1932	2	2			266	266			3, 138	3, 138		
1933	1	1			60	60			540	540		
1934	7	4	3		7, 466	5, 125	2, 341		67, 887	26, 725	41, 162	
1935	10	8	2		9, 323	8, 958	365		334, 874	333, 109	1, 765	
1936	14	11	2	1	5, 677	3, 537	1, 600	540	89, 684	39, 804	43, 400	6, 480
Relief work:												
1927–31												
1932	7	4	1	2	3, 128	2, 444	80	604	5, 792	2, 444	2, 640	708
1933	30	24		6	25, 967	24, 339		1, 628	113, 691	104, 608		9, 083
1934	76	55	6	15	26, 652	22, 101	825	3, 726	151, 208	106, 371	6, 122	38, 715
1935	95	68	4	23	41, 153	34, 922	60	6, 171	402, 340	362, 959	1, 875	37, 506
1936	80	37	10	33	40, 016	24, 808	3, 251	11, 957	232, 216	154, 099	40, 254	37, 863
Other nonmanufacturing industries:												
1927	7	3	2	2	777	683	14	80	3, 218	2, 569	189	460
1928	3	2	1		4, 715	65	4, 650		56, 490	690	55, 800	
1929	13	9	3	1	2, 936	2, 528	358	50	24, 185	22, 787	1, 348	50
1930	4	2	1	1	700	325	225	150	4, 058	2, 483	675	900
1931	9	3	5	1	4, 617	654	3, 951	12	16, 403	6, 752	9, 639	12
1932	12	8	1	3	4, 327	1, 027	60	3, 240	39, 864	16, 284	1, 740	21, 840
1933	14	10	3	1	4, 517	1, 596	2, 421	500	34, 654	14, 562	17, 592	2, 500
1934	8	3	5		301	78	223		8, 501	2, 746	5, 755	
1935	17	6	9	2	696	213	263	220	8, 326	970	6, 311	1, 045
1936	34	13	19	2	2, 920	1, 283	1, 287	350	29, 042	16, 041	12, 201	800
Interindustry:												
1927–33												
1934	3			3	31, 200			31, 200	31, 200			31, 200
1935	1			1	3, 000			3, 000	3, 000			3, 000
1936												
General strikes:[4]												
1927–33												
1934	1			1	90, 000			90, 000	270, 000			270, 000
1935	1			1	26, 000			26, 000	52, 000			52, 000
1936	1			1	1, 500			1, 500	4, 500			4, 500

[4] Involves all organized trades within the community. See table 33.

Appendix I

Strikes Involving 10,000 or More Workers, 1927–36

A list of all strikes occurring between 1927 and 1936, inclusive, involving 10,000 or more employees, is given in table 38.

TABLE 38.—*Strikes involving 10,000 or more workers, 1927–36*

Location and kind of strike	Date of strike	Approximate number of workers involved
	1927	
Bituminous coal, interstate	April–December	165,000
	1928	
Cleaning and dyeing, New York City	February–March	25,000
Bituminous coal, interstate	April–December	45,000
Cotton textile manufacturers, New Bedford, Mass	April–October	25,000
Children's clothing, New York City	June–July	10,000
Anthracite, Pittston and Avoca, Pa	November	32,300
	1929	
Cloak, suit, and skirt makers, New York City	July	15,000
	1930	
Dressmakers, New York City	February	30,000
	1931	
American Woolen Co., Lawrence, Mass	February	10,575
Glen Alden Coal Co., Pennsylvania	March–April	22,000
Bituminous coal, Pittsburgh district	June–August	15,000
Men's clothing, Greater New York	July–August	30,000
Glen Alden Coal Co., Pennsylvania	September–October	20,000
Wool and cotton textile, Lawrence, Mass	October–November	24,626
	1932	
Dressmakers, New York City	February–March	25,000
Millinery, New York City	March	10,000
Anthracite, Pennsylvania	do	15,000
Bituminous coal, Illinois	April–August	30,000
Building contractors, New York City	May–June	30,000
Painters, New York City	July–September	10,000
Men's clothing, New York and New Jersey	August	20,000
	1933	
Hosiery, Reading, Pa., and vicinity	June–August	10,000
Cloak, suit, and skirt makers, New York City	June–July	30,000
Bituminous coal, western and southern Pennsylvania	July–August	20,000
Men's clothing manufacturers, Pennsylvania, Maryland, New York, New Jersey.	July	50,000
Ladies' garments, Connecticut, New York, New Jersey	August	60,000
Anthracite, Pennsylvania	do	18,000
Do	August–November	14,406
Building contractors, New York City	September	12,000
Embroidery workers, New York City	do	12,000
Neckwear manufacturers, New York City	do	10,000
Underwear manufacturers, New York City	do	25,000
Weirton Steel Co., West Virginia	September–October	12,000
Bituminous coal, Pennsylvania, West Virginia, Ohio	September–November	75,000
Silk dyers, Paterson, N. J	September–October	15,000
Silk manufacturers, Scranton and Philadelphia, Pa	September–November	12,000
Anthracite, Pennsylvania	November	40,000
Trucking, retail trade, Philadelphia, Pa	December–January	14,000

TABLE 38.—*Strikes involving 10,000 or more workers, 1927–36*—Continued

Location and kind of strike	Date of strike	Approximate number of workers involved
	1934	
Anthracite, Pennsylvania	January–February	48,000
Bituminous coal, Alabama	February–March	10,000
Taxicab companies, New York City	February	30,000
Do	March	12,000
Dress manufacturers, New York City	April	25,000
Bituminous coal, West Virginia	do	20,000
Bituminous coal, Alabama	April–May	21,000
Bituminous coal, Kentucky	do	10,000
Cotton textile, Alabama	July–August	22,000
General, all unions, San Francisco Bay area	July	90,000
Paint contractors, Brooklyn, N. Y	July–August	10,000
Knit goods, New York and New Jersey	August	14,000
General, all unions, Hazleton, Pa	September	26,000
Hosiery, Philadelphia, Pa	do	15,000
Hosiery, interstate	do	25,000
Textile, interstate	do	309,500
Silk dyes and finishing, interstate	October–December	25,000
Glen Alden Coal Co., Pennsylvania	December	12,000
	1935	
Truck drivers, New York City	January	20,000
Shirt workers, interstate	do	15,000
Cotton goods, Chicago, Ill	February–April	10,000
Dressmakers, interstate	April	17,200
Lumber, Washington and Oregon	May–August	32,000
General, all unions, Terre Haute, Ind	July	26,000
Dressmakers, New York City	September	10,000
Bituminous coal, interstate	do	366,000
Bituminous coal, Alabama	September–November	20,000
	1936	
Millinery workers, New York City	February	19,600
Goodyear Tire & Rubber Co., Akron, Ohio	February–March	14,000
Building service employees, New York City	March	36,000
Barber shops, Brooklyn and New York City	April–July	20,200
Goodyear Tire & Rubber Co., Akron, Ohio	June	12,000
Painters, New York City	August–September	10,000
Maritime, Pacific Coast	October–February	37,000
Maritime, Atlantic and Gulf Coasts	November–January	20,000

Appendix II

Methods Used in Analyzing Strikes

Items Included in the Statistical Analysis

The basic measures in strike statistics as now compiled by the Bureau are the number of strikes, the number of persons involved, and the man-days idle.[1] It is from these data that analyses of frequency and severity of strikes are made. But if such data are to be compiled, certain correlated information is required, and if they are to be of value for fundamental analysis, they must be classified.

For such measurements and classifications, certain specific data on each strike are necessary. The following is a brief description of the data obtained by the Bureau at the present time and their use in statistical tabulation.[2]

Beginning date.—The fundamental basis of classification is the time when strikes occurred. The data are summarized by years, but currently they are compiled monthly. For this purpose the beginning date of a strike must be known, as it must also for computing man-days idle.

In the majority of cases, there is little difficulty in deciding the date a strike begins. With some strikes, however, the situation is more or less confused. Sometimes a union calls a strike for a certain day, but only a small portion of the workers respond, the remainder joining at later dates. Sometimes the union calls a general-industry strike but "pulls" the strike gradually, plant by plant. In any of these cases the beginning date used in the statistical tables is the first day any portion or group of the workers start the strike. Adjustment for the gradual development of the dispute is made in computing the man-days idle.

Ending date.—There is no question about the termination date of strikes which result in definite terms of settlement or agreement. A good many strikes, however, are never settled. There are strikes which, according to the union calling the strike, have lasted many years although the public has long forgotten them. Sometimes strikers, discouraged with the prospect of success, gradually return with no settlement; sometimes the employer moves out of town; sometimes the plant is opened with a new crew of workers, while the strikers maintain their picket line and receive strike benefits from their union; sometimes a strike appears to be lost and ended but, due

[1] See Introduction, p. 7.

[2] Some of these data were not obtained in earlier years. For example, the number of workers involved was not obtained in all cases until in 1927, and information regarding the method of settlement was not known previous to 1935. For other items there is only partial or incomplete information in some cases, resulting in a varying degree of satisfactory statistical presentation.

to the persistence of the union or the help of some outside agency, the case is reopened months later and definite terms of settlement gained.

In situations such as these, the rule of reason must be applied. The principal criterion for the termination of a strike for statistical purposes is the date of resumption of work. This can be considered from two viewpoints: When the employer resumes work by filling the vacancies, or when the strikers resume work either with their former employer or with new employers. In practice it is impossible to learn when all the strikers regain employment. Moreover, it is logical to consider a strike in relation to the employer or establishment against which the strike was called. For these reasons, a strike is considered ended when all or a majority of the vacancies caused by the strike have been filled either by returning strikers or new employees, or when vacancies disappear through the closing of the plant or moving it to another city. Thus, for statistical purposes, a strike may be considered ended although some strikers are picketing and the union paying strike benefits, but such cases are comparatively infrequent.

Duration.—Unlike the calculation of man-days idle, the duration of strikes is measured in terms of calendar weeks or months, thus including Sundays and holidays. While this is done largely for the purpose of simplicity, it is not unreasonable to include holidays, since it can be assumed that negotiations toward settlement can be carried on the same as on workdays.

Number of establishments.—The number of establishments involved in strikes might well be one of the basic measures in strike statistics. Unfortunately, it is often impossible to obtain the exact number of establishments involved in large strikes which spread throughout a city or several cities and States. Valid statistical tables, therefore, cannot be compiled to give total establishments. The number of establishments becomes merely one basis for classifying strike data, and frequency distributions are compiled showing the number of strikes involving specified numbers of establishments.

The term "establishment" as used in strike statistics has the same connotation as that used in the Census of Manufactures, namely, "a single plant or factory." In other industries than manufacturing, different units are considered as equivalent to establishments—a building project, a mine or colliery, a ship, a dock, a logging camp, etc.

Industry classification.—The industry classification used in strike statistics follows along the same lines as that used by the census and the Bureau of Labor Statistics' employment and pay-roll reports. This makes possible the correlation of strike data with other data known about an industry, such as the total number employed, total value of products, etc.

An industry classification in any field of statistics presents certain difficulties, due to the complexity, overlapping, and changing character of industrial organization and processes. For instance, there is the question of whether a productive activity should be classified according to the basic commodity or processes—e. g., chemical—or by the commodity produced—rayon or textiles; also, as to what classification should a business establishment be assigned which manufactures a number of different commodities or performs various functions; for example, should a garage be classified under "retail trade", "auto service and repair", or "transportation."

To these perplexities which are common to all statistics pertaining to industry classification, strike statistics involve an additional difficulty by reason of the fact that labor unions are not always coterminous with the industry as defined by the census. Thus a strike called by the Upholsterers, Carpet and Linoleum Mechanics' International Union of America may affect furniture factories,[3] mattress factories,[4] and linoleum departments in retail stores. In such situations, the Bureau classifies strikes within the industry most seriously affected. Thus, a strike of bakery deliverymen is classified under the baking industry, since it is initiated by a particular local or group of local unions and is directed against one class of employers. But a city-wide strike of all deliverymen or truck drivers is classified under "transportation." Since the census attaches these various types of deliverymen to their respective industries, there is some variation between the classification of strikes and the census industry classification. These cases, however, are relatively infrequent and, on the whole, the industry classification of strikes conforms to that of the census and the Bureau's statistics of employment and pay rolls.

Geographical location.—The classification of strikes by location is a simple matter except for strikes which extend across State or city lines. There are at least three distinct kinds of situations characterized as interstate (or intercity) strikes: (1) A large general-industry strike involving numbers of companies in two or more States; (2) a local strike which extends into contiguous areas which happen to lie in other States, as, for example, New York City and adjacent communities in Pennsylvania, New Jersey, and Connecticut; (3) a strike against one company which has branch plants in two or more States.

It is desirable that the incidence of all such strikes be revealed as accurately as possible; otherwise figures on strikes within a given State may exclude industrial disturbances which are of greater magnitude than those confined to that State alone. Whenever possible, therefore, the number of workers and man-days idle due to

[3] Classified by census under "Lumber and its products."

[4] Classified under "Miscellaneous" by the census.

interstate strikes are allocated as accurately as possible to the States concerned. Unfortunately, this cannot be done with intercity strikes, since it is impossible to get specific data by city. The best that can be done is to group the intercity strikes, listing all the cities involved.

Sex of workers.—All strikes are classified by the sex of persons engaged in the strike, that is, male, female, or both. In addition, the total number of men and the total number of women involved in strikes are tabulated. In certain cases where only one or two office women are involved in a strike called by craftsmen, such as at a foundry or streetcar company, the strike is classified under "male only."

Labor organization involved.—In former years, strikes were classified according to those ordered by labor organizations and those not so ordered. The latter not only included strikes by employees who were not members of an organization, but also strikes by union members which were not authorized by the proper union official—that is, so-called "illegal" or "outlaw" strikes.[5] This fine distinction has been dropped in recent years and strikes are now classified according to which labor organization the strikers belong to, or according to which organization was instrumental in calling the strike or allied itself with the strike after it was started or took part in the negotiations for settlement.

Even with this broadening of the term, the situation does not always lend itself to easy classification. Sometimes unorganized workers go out on strike and then request a union to come in to help them. Sometimes the reverse takes place: A group of organized workers go on strike with the sanction of their union but, because they fail to follow instructions or for some other reason, the union withdraws. Sometimes the strike starts under the auspices of one union and a rival union steps in and becomes the dominant force. In jurisdictional disputes, at least two unions are involved. Necessarily, some degree of arbitrary judgment must be used in the classification of such strikes. In general, the classification is based on whether most of those actively responsible for the strike were members of a union and whether they acted as an organized group when the strike was called or settled.

Major issues or causes.—Any statistical presentation of the causes of strikes is likely to appear more plausible than the actual situations analyzed really warrant. The causes reported by the various parties concerned are frequently at variance, and even if they agree the stated reasons are sometimes superficial and only partial. Due to the emotional factor connected with many strikes, the immediate issue which brought on the strike may have been of much less importance than other matters which had caused a cumulative dissatisfaction

[5] Twenty-first Annual Report of the Commissioner of Labor, Washington, 1907, p. 21.

extending over many months or years. Again, a strike may be called because of certain grievances but during the progress of the strike the situation or leadership may change sufficiently to bring about a shift in demands or statement of grievances.

Very few strikes are due to only one or two causes: In most cases the issues are many and complex. In an earlier period of strike statistics (1881–1905) this multiplicity of issues and demands was recognized by itemizing as many as 60 to 65 causes or groups of causes.[6] Obviously, this is more a listing than a statistical classification and precludes ready assimilation by the reader. At present, an effort is made to determine the major cause or dominant issue in each strike situation and to classify it under one of 18 headings. For greater convenience, these 18 classifications are divided into three groups: (1) Wages and hours, (2) union organization, (3) miscellaneous.

This neat classification of such complex situations as industrial disputes is necessarily based upon many arbitrary determinations and should therefore be considered only proximate. This is especially true in the numerous cases involving union recognition, wages, and hours. In some situations, these three issues are of almost equal importance; in others, one is more dominant even though the other two are present. Evaluation of the relative importance of each is a matter of judgment after studying all aspects of the situation. Some marginal cases could, no doubt, just as accurately be grouped under "wages and hours" as under "union organization," and vice versa

Results.—It seems logical to measure the terms of settlement in relation to the change in status which the strike has brought to the workers. It is just as logical to evaluate the results in relation to the causes for the strike, or the demands set forth by those calling the strike. The difficulty in accurately assaying causes of strikes has been mentioned above; the measurement of results is even more elusive. In only a portion of the strikes are the terms of settlement put down in writing. Even where the terms of settlement are apparently defined, the results cannot be measured automatically. A group of workers may strike for recognition but may return to work without recognition when the employer offers them a wage increase or makes other concessions. Each of the opposing parties may, at the beginning or sometime during the progress of the dispute, demand much more than it intends or hopes to obtain. For instance, the workers may call a strike for a wage increase in order to ward off an expected decrease. If the strike is settled with a continuation of existing rates, was the strike a success or failure?

Sometimes the actual results of a strike may not be known for a considerable time after the dispute has ended and may be quite differ-

[6] Twenty-first Annual Report of the Commissioner of Labor, Washington, 1907, pp. 600–612.

ent from the apparent results at the close of the strike. Workers may return to work after a strike, appearing to have won none of the demands they set out to gain, yet the experience and loss of production might influence the employer to give his employees better working conditions in order to avoid interruptions in the future. On the other hand, workers may go back after a strike, having apparently won a complete victory, but the strike might have caused the employer to decide to clean up a few odds and ends and then go out of business or move to a new locality. These far-reaching results cannot be measured or known, and any statistical measurement of the results of a strike must necessarily be based on the apparent results or the terms of agreement at the close of the dispute. In some cases, it is absolutely impossible to evaluate the results even though the immediate facts are known. These are therefore classified as "indeterminate."

Because of the many intangible features inherent in the nature of labor disputes, the Bureau does not categorically define results as successful or unsuccessful. Rather, an attempt is made to measure the results in such relative terms as (1) substantial gains to workers, (2) partial gains or compromises, (3) little or no gains to workers. Obviously there could just as well be five or even more classifications as the three used. In some particular cases the results would be portrayed more accurately if there were a greater refinement of classification. This is especially true with respect to the middle group, "partial gains or compromises", which includes strikes which might almost be rated as successful as well as those which verge on failure. However, when a large number of variables is included within a classification, it can be assumed that the extremes tend to offset each other and that the number within the classification represents an average.

It should be noted that the results classified under "substantial gains to workers" might include a strike where the terms of settlement merely provide for a retention of the status existing before the strike was called. In other words, a defensive strike, such as one against a wage decrease or against a renunciation of union recognition which had existed, would be included in this classification if the strike resulted in no change from the previous status. This should be especially borne in mind when reviewing the long-time trend of strikes. The total number of strikes in this classification does not represent a cumulative improvement in worker status but includes some strikes which merely won a retention of already existing conditions.

Results of strikes involving a number of establishments are measured quantitatively as well as qualitatively. In other words, in general-industry strikes where each establishment makes its own settlement with its employees, the workers in some plants may gain more favorable terms than in others. The results of such a general-industry strike must, necessarily, take into account the proportion of establishments or workers obtaining the varying terms of settlement. The results of sympathetic strikes are judged according to the terms of settlement of the strike for which the sympathetic strike was called.

Methods of settlement.—During one earlier period of strike statistics (1901–05), a count was kept of the number of strikes "settled by joint agreement" and the number "settled by arbitration." [7] Aside from this, no consistent record was kept of the method used in settlement of strikes until 1935.

Beginning with the year 1935, data are available to show the following classifications of the method of settlement of strikes:

(1) The number of strikes which are settled directly by the employer and the strikers. In such cases the workers are either unorganized or, if there had been a union present when the strike started, by the time it was terminated the union had withdrawn to such an extent that it took no part in the settlement negotiations.

(2) Those settled directly through negotiations between the employer and union representatives.

(3) Those settled with the assistance of Government conciliators or labor boards, and

(4) Those settled with the assistance of private conciliators and labor boards. In most of the strikes in the latter two classifications union representatives are usually also present.

(5) Those terminated with no formal settlement. In practically all of these the strikes are usually lost by the workers. In some instances they gradually return with no change in the working conditions; sometimes the employer fills the vacancies with new employees; in other cases the business is liquidated or moved to another locality.

The strikes in which outsiders assisted, either Government or private, in negotiating toward settlement are classified according to whether settlement was obtained by means of conciliation or arbitration.

It must be noted that this general classification is termed "negotiations toward settlement carried on by." It does not necessarily mean that a conciliator was actually present at the final conference or was solely responsible for the strike settlement. Because of the very nature of the procedure used by conciliators—working quietly behind the scenes, sometimes withdrawing for a time and then returning—it is impossible to evaluate the exact effectiveness of his activities. Also, several different conciliators may have assisted, together or separately, at different intervals. All strikes in which one or more outsiders took an active part at any time during the progress of the strike in trying to get the parties together, are included in this classification.

[7] Twenty-first Annual Report of the Commissioner of Labor, Washington, 1907, pp. 84–88. By far the largest proportion of strikes was terminated without either of these methods having been used. During the 5-year period, less than 6 percent of the total strikes were settled by joint agreement and less than 2 percent by arbitration.

Appendix III

Method of Collecting Strike Data

Notices or leads regarding strikes are obtained from daily papers, labor and trade journals, as well as reports from Government labor boards. At the present time the Bureau receives clippings from newspapers in all cities in the country with over 50,000 population, and from some industrial cities of less than 50,000. The Bureau either subscribes for or has access to every known labor or trade paper published in the country. From the information obtained in these 700 daily, weekly, and monthly papers and journals, it is believed that few, if any, strikes escape the Bureau's attention.

On the basis of these newspaper and other notices, schedules are sent to representatives of all parties engaged in the dispute, to get detailed and authentic information. In a few cases, when no replies are received by mail, agents of the Bureau call on the parties. From the answers to these questionnaires, the Bureau is able to analyze the disputes in the manner described above.

The questionnaire reads as follows:

U. S. DEPARTMENT OF LABOR
BUREAU OF LABOR STATISTICS
WASHINGTON

DEAR SIR: The Bureau of Labor Statistics has recently received information ....

As the designated Federal agency for keeping records of all industrial disputes, we shall greatly appreciate your courtesy in furnishing the information requested. If the dispute is still in progress, please answer as many questions as possible. If the dispute is ended, please answer all the questions on both sides of this form. A franked, addressed envelope is provided for your convenience. Your cooperation is greatly appreciated.

Very truly yours,

ISADOR LUBIN,
Commissioner of Labor Statistics.

---

1. Name of company ....
2. Address of central office ....
3. Principal products and services of plant(s) involved in dispute. List in order of their importance: ....
4. Number of establishments (or work places) involved in dispute ....
5. Location .... (City or town) (State) (Give similar address for each establishment involved)
6. Date on which employees involved in dispute stopped work ....
7. Number of days per week majority of employees worked preceding dispute ....
8. Number on pay roll immediately preceding dispute: Men ...... Women ...... Total ......
9. Number of employees involved on first day of dispute: Men ...... Women ...... Total ......
(Include all persons who stopped work in establishments reported under question 5; that is, those who were thrown out of work as well as those who walked out)
10. Date greatest number of employees were out ...... Number: Men ...... Women ...... Total ......
11. Did dispute originate among any specific group of workers? ...... If so, what occupation? .... How many? ......
12. What caused dispute? .... (What demands were made?) ....
13. Workers' organization(s) involved .... Local address ....
14. Is dispute ended? ...... (Yes or no) Date ended ....
15. If dispute is not settled, have any employees who were involved returned to work? ...... (Yes or no) Number ...... Have any vacancies been filled with new employees? ...... (Yes or no) Number ...... Date by which 50 percent of total positions were filled by old or new employees ....
16. If dispute is settled, give number of employees: (*a*) Still out day before termination ......; (*b*) taken back immediately after termination ......; (*c*) that will be taken back in next few weeks ......

13894°—38——12

17. Terms of settlement: ____________________
(Refer to the issues or demands listed in question 12)
____
____

Before dispute	Wage rate________ Hours per week ____ Was there a union agreement? ______	*After dispute*	Wage rate ________ Hours per week ______ Is there a union agreement? ______

(If dispute was terminated by signed agreement, please enclose copy)

18. Number of employees affected by terms of settlement ________________

19. Which one of the following methods was used in negotiating settlement?
(*a*) By employer and employees directly ____________________
(*b*) By employer and representatives of organized workers directly ______
____
(*c*) By conciliation ____________________
(Name of person or Government board)
(*d*) By arbitration ____________________
(Name of person or Government board)

20. Violence in connection with dispute:
(*a*) Any deaths?____________
Number______________
(*b*) Any injuries?____________
Number______________
(Necessitating medical attention)
(*c*) Any property damage?_____
______ Amount $_______
(*d*) Any damage suits?_______
Number ______
(*e*) Any arrests?______________
Number ________________
(*f*) Any criminal suits?___________
Number________________
(*g*) Was National Guard called in?
____
(*h*) Was martial law declared? _______

21. Were any injunctions issued during the dispute? __________ Principal
(Yes or no)
provisions ____________________
____

22. If dispute is still in progress, please explain briefly its present status ______
____
____

23. What is your opinion concerning the net result (gain or loss to workers) of this dispute? ____________________
____

24. Remarks: ____________________
____
____

____________________ (Signature of person making report)

____________________ (Date)

____________________ (Position or office)

____________________ (Address)

____________________ (Company or organization)

Appendix IV

Labor Disputes in Foreign Countries, 1927–36 [1]

TABLE 39.—*Labor disputes in foreign countries, 1927–36*

Period	Disputes	Workers involved	Working days lost
Argentina:			
1927	56	26,888	363,492
1928	137	73,989	251,054
1929	116	53,101	543,939
1930	127	38,299	853,219
1931	42	8,442	58,493
1932	122	165,376	1,357,790
1933	52	3,321	39,896
1934	42	25,940	742,256
1935	69	52,143	2,642,576
1936	109	85,438	1,344,461
Australia:			
1927	441	200,757	1,713,581
1928	287	96,422	777,278
1929	259	104,604	4,461,478
1930	183	54,222	1,511,241
1931	134	37,667	245,991
1932	127	32,917	212,318
1933	90	30,113	111,956
1934	155	50,858	370,386
1935	183	47,322	495,124
1936	235	60,586	494,319
Austria:			
1927	216	35,300	686,560
1928	266	38,290	658,024
1929	226	30,446	388,336
1930	88	7,173	49,373
1931	68	10,264	132,757
1932	33	6,646	190,163
1933	27	5,657	79,061
1934	4	137	220
1935	3	89	414
1936	3	123	269
Belgium:			
1927	186	45,071	1,658,836
1928	192	77,785	2,254,424
1929	168	60,557	799,117
1930	93	64,718	781,646
1931	74	23,010	399,037
1932	63	162,693	580,670
1933	87	39,136	664,044
1934	79	36,525	2,441,335
1935	150	104,013	623,002
1936	999	564,831	----------
Bulgaria:			
1927	23	2,919	57,196
1928	21	493	2,382
1929	36	22,339	378,236
1930	15	1,588	2,545
1931	34	6,891	74,094
1932	19	1,214	11,149
1933	[2] 85	[3] 3,395	26,132
1934	[2] 48	[2] [3] 5,942	47,116
Canada:			
1927	74	22,299	152,570
1928	98	17,581	224,212
1929	90	12,946	152,080
1930	67	13,768	91,797
1931	88	10,738	204,238
1932	116	23,390	255,000
1933	125	26,558	317,547
1934	191	45,800	574,519
1935	120	33,269	284,028
1936	155	34,812	276,997

Period	Disputes	Workers involved	Working days lost
China:			
1927	117	881,289	7,622,029
1928	118	204,563	2,049,826
1929	108	65,557	711,921
1930	87	64,130	801,531
1931	122	74,188	685,941
1932	82	71,395	710,605
1933	88	74,937	461,619
1934	73	31,473	501,245
1935	95	96,684	517,663
1936	128	78,992	666,931
Czechoslovakia:			
1927	208	172,043	1,466,045
1928	282	101,517	1,728,419
1929	230	63,564	753,205
1930	159	30,808	423,126
1931	254	49,508	498,891
1932	317	103,219	1,255,576
1933	209	36,636	289,409
1934	213	38,477	264,538
1935	[5] 219	39,903	490,417
1936	[5] 263	[5] 53,912	[5] 603,061
Denmark:			
1927	17	2,851	119,000
1928	11	469	11,000
1929	22	1,040	41,283
1930	37	5,349	144,000
1931	16	3,692	246,000
1932	17	5,760	87,000
1933	26	492	18,000
1934	38	11,546	146,000
1935	14	827	14,000
1936	12	96,862	2,946,000
Estonia:			
1927	5	218	3,067
1928	5	1,098	49,336
1929	16	1,915	6,395
1930	7	154	338
1931	3	[4] 700	[4] 20,000
1932	4	888	2,149
1933	8	162	339
1934	10	1,369	2,207
1935	27	5,043	45,000
1936	16	2,539	14,822
Finland:			
1927	79	13,368	1,528,182
1928	71	27,226	502,236
1929	26	2,443	74,887
1930	11	1,673	12,120
1931	1	53	106
1932	3	284	2,301
1933	4	1,274	9,536
1934	46	5,883	89,727
1935	23	2,274	60,843
1936	29	2,935	35,360
France:			
1927	404	112,634	1,046,019
1928	823	210,488	6,376,675
1929	1,217	241,040	2,764,606
1930	1,097	584,579	7,209,342
1931	[5] 261	35,723	----------
1932	[5] 330	[5] 54,088	----------
1933	[5] 331	[5] 84,391	----------
1934	[5] 374	[5] 61,445	----------
1935	[5] 425	[5] 89,726	----------

[1] International Labour Office, 1937 Year Book of Labour Statistics, Geneva, pp. 212–214.
[2] Strikes only. [3] Workers directly involved only. [4] Approximate figures. [5] Provisional figures.

TABLE 39.—*Labor disputes in foreign countries, 1927–36*—Continued

Period	Disputes	Workers involved	Working days lost
Germany			
1927	871	503, 217	6, 043, 698
1928	763	780, 396	20, 288, 211
1929	441	234, 543	4, 489, 870
1930	366	224, 983	3, 935, 977
1931	504	178, 223	2, 001, 978
1932	[5] 642	[5] 127, 587	[5] 1, 112, 056
1933	(6)	(6)	(6)
1934	(6)	(6)	(6)
1935	(6)	(6)	(6)
1936	(6)	(6)	(6)
Great Britain and Northern Ireland:			
1927	308	108, 000	1, 170, 000
1928	302	124, 000	1, 390, 000
1929	431	533, 000	8, 290, 000
1930	422	307, 000	4, 400, 000
1931	420	490, 000	6, 980, 000
1932	389	379, 000	6, 490, 000
1933	357	136, 000	1, 070, 000
1934	471	134, 000	960, 000
1935	553	271, 000	1, 960, 000
1936	808	315, 000	1, 830, 000
Hungary			
1927	84	24, 803	294, 941
1928	31	10, 289	131, 174
1929	63	15, 065	149, 204
1930	35	5, 770	79, 596
1931	38	11, 195	189, 781
1932	20	4, 925	32, 914
1933	31	10, 367	125, 178
1934	49	12, 762	92, 156
1935	50	16, 674	110, 967
1936	122	20, 747	232, 622
India			
1927	129	131, 655	2, 019, 970
1928	203	506, 851	31, 647, 404
1929	141	532, 016	12, 165, 691
1930	148	196, 301	2, 261, 731
1931	166	203, 008	2, 408, 123
1932	118	128, 099	1, 922, 437
1933	146	164, 938	2, 168, 961
1934	159	220, 808	4, 775, 559
1935	145	114, 217	973, 457
1936	157	169, 029	2, 358, 062
Irish Free State:			
1927	53	2, 312	64, 020
1928	52	2, 190	54, 292
1929	53	4, 533	101, 397
1930	83	3, 410	77, 417
1931	60	5, 431	310, 199
1932	70	4, 222	42, 152
1933	88	9, 059	200, 126
1934	99	9, 288	180, 080
1935	99	9, 513	288, 077
1936	107	9, 443	185, 623
Italy: [7]			
1927	169	18, 660	(6)
1928	77	2, 999	(6)
1929	83	3, 252	(6)
1930	82	2, 863	(6)
1931	67	4, 141	(6)
1932	23	598	(6)
1933	34	841	(6)
1934	38	576	(6)
1935	43	605	(6)
Japan			
1927	383	46, 672	1, 177, 352
1928	397	46, 252	583, 595
1929	576	77, 444	571, 860
1930	906	81, 362	1, 085, 074
1931	998	64, 536	980, 054
1932	893	54, 783	618, 614
1933	610	49, 423	384, 565
1934	626	49, 536	446, 176
1935	589	37, 614	297, 724
Latvia:			
1927	95	5, 273	60, 267
1928	179	13, 431	62, 254
1929	362	26, 462	45, 838
1930	38	1, 547	12, 077
1931	42	2, 903	14, 261
1932	139	4, 400	23, 003
1933	246	4, 323	22, 960
1934	35	3, 854	24, 543
1935	3	---------	---------
Mexico:			
1927	(6)	(6)	(6)
1928	(6)	(6)	(6)
1929	(6)	(6)	(6)
1930	(6)	(6)	(6)
1931	(6)	(6)	(6)
1932	(6)	(6)	(6)
1933	(6)	(6)	(6)
1934	(6)	(6)	(6)
1935	[5] 410	[5] 132, 651	(6)
1936	[5] 317	[5] 100, 791	(6)
Netherlands:			
1927	230	13, 500	220, 500
1928	205	16, 930	647, 700
1929	226	21, 310	990, 800
1930	212	10, 970	273, 000
1931	215	28, 210	856, 100
1932	216	32, 000	1, 772, 600
1933	184	14, 810	533, 800
1934	152	6, 200	114, 200
1935	152	12, 940	262, 400
1936	96	10, 420	99, 800
New Zealand:			
1927	38	4, 476	12, 485
1928	39	9, 258	21, 997
1929	47	7, 151	25, 889
1930	38	5, 467	31, 669
1931	24	6, 356	48, 486
1932	23	9, 355	108, 605
1933	15	3, 558	65, 099
1934	24	3, 773	10, 393
1935	12	2, 323	18, 565
1936	43	7, 354	16, 980
Norway:			
1927	96	22, 456	1, 374, 089
1928	63	8, 042	363, 844
1929	73	4, 796	196, 704
1930	94	4, 652	240, 454
1931	82	59, 524	7, 585, 832
1932	91	6, 360	394, 002
1933	93	6, 306	364, 240
1934	85	6, 364	235, 075
1935	103	3, 548	[5] 168, 000
Palestine:			
1927	20	562	13, 469
1928	22	886	4, 379
1929	45	679	8, 773
1930	22	393	9, 234
1931	50	1, 946	6, 704
1932	61	1, 409	10, 689
1933	57	2, 049	19, 354
1934	49	2, 051	17, 273
1935	60	3, 648	28, 415
1936	20	956	11, 625
Philippines:			
1927	[3] 53	8, 567	(6)
1928	38	4, 729	(6)
1929	26	4, 939	(6)
1930	36	6, 069	(6)
1931	45	6, 976	(6)
1932	31	4, 396	(6)
1933	59	8, 066	(6)
Poland:			
1927	625	236, 552	2, 483, 165
1928	776	354, 498	2, 787, 775
1929	510	221, 673	1, 071, 816

[3] Strikes only (for all years).
[5] Provisional figures.
[6] No figures exist.
[7] Since 1926 strikes and lock-outs have been forbidden by law. The figures denote the number of offenses and persons reported with a view to prosecution.

TABLE 39.—*Labor disputes in foreign countries, 1927–36*—Continued

Period	Disputes	Workers involved	Working days lost
Poland—Continued.			
1930	330	53,136	427,127
1931	363	109,074	636,921
1932	517	315,146	2,134,150
1933	649	347,460	3,843,631
1934	957	373,022	2,413,533
1935	1,187	452,550	2,025,554
1936	[5] 2,058	664,593	[5] 4,006,556
Rumania:			
1927	51	6,933	58,291
1928	57	10,801	109,666
1929	127	31,456	411,572
1930	101	17,337	184,002
1931	71	17,473	184,593
1932	102	[5] 19,154	103,673
1933	58	16,066	57,093
1934	72	11,059	156,086
1935	84	16,174	360,867
1936	[5] 90	[5] 15,231	[5] 195,606
Spain:			
1927	107	70,616	1,311,891
1928	87	70,024	771,293
1929	96	55,576	313,065
1930	402	247,460	3,745,360
1931	734	236,177	3,843,260
1932	681	269,104	3,589,473
1933	1,127	843,303	14,440,629
1934	594	741,878	11,103,493
Sweden:			
1927	189	9,477	400,000
1928	201	71,461	4,835,000
1929	180	12,676	667,000
1930	261	20,751	1,021,000
1931	193	40,899	2,627,000
1932	182	50,147	3,095,000
1933	140	31,980	3,434,000
1934	103	13,588	760,200
1935	98	17,189	888,000
Switzerland:			
1927	26	2,058	34,160
1928	45	5,474	98,015
Switzerland—Contd.			
1929	39	4,661	99,608
1930	31	6,397	265,695
1931	25	4,746	73,975
1932	38	5,083	159,154
1933	35	2,705	69,065
1934	20	2,763	33,309
1935	17	874	15,143
1936	41	3,612	38,789
Union of South Africa:			
1927	12	5,158	9,126
1928	10	5,746	10,535
1929	10	2,962	([6])
1930	12	5,050	2,600
1931	19	6,284	54,575
1932	12	4,011	26,034
1933	10	1,585	16,081
1934	12	2,379	52,132
1935	17	2,367	19,564
1936	20	2,198	5,009
Uruguay:			
1927	13	4,737	53,350
1928	3	289	[5] 420,600
1929	31	2,011	[5] 90,600
1930	8	1,361	[5] 11,100
1931	56	1,933	[5] 102,600
1932	6	2,262	—
1933	6	2,117	[5] 86,797
1934	17	862	[5] 70,782
1935	2	699	[5] 3,495
Yugoslavia:			
1927	78	7,588	239,183
1928	44	5,618	117,471
1929	14	2,246	12,897
1930	16	4,879	48,528
1931	5	1,253	14,204
1932	7	1,370	4,074
1933	8	2,451	13,937
1934	35	6,775	40,523
1935	141	25,486	221,239

[5] Provisional figures.
[6] No figures exist.

GENERAL INDEX[1]

[1] Index makes no reference to statistical tables. *See* Table of Contents, p. III.

INDEX TO TABLE 37

Page

O